"Be Not Deceived"

"Be Not Deceived"

The Sacred and Sexual Struggles of Gay and Ex-gay Christian Men

MICHELLE WOLKOMIR

RUTGERS UNIVERSITY PRESS
New Brunswick, New Jersey, and London

Library of Congress Cataloging-in-Publication Data

Wolkomir, Michelle, 1966–
    Be not deceived : the sacred and sexual struggle of gay and ex-gay
Christian men / Michelle Wolkomir
        p.   cm.
    Includes bibliographical references and index.
    ISBN-13: 978-0-8135-3821-1 (hardcover : alk. paper)
    ISBN-13: 978-0-8135-3822-8 pbk. : alk. paper)
1. Gay men—Religious life. 2. Gay men—Sexual behavior. 3. Christian
men—Sexual behavior. I. Title.
    BV4596.G38W65   2006
    261.8'357662—dc22

                                                                        2005019851

British Cataloguing-in-Publication information is available from the British
Library.

Manufactured in the United States of America

In loving memory of my Grandpa,
Herman Wolkomir, and all of his stories

Contents

Acknowledgments

When I was a child and worried or complained about something—or even when I achieved something at school—my father was in the habit of remarking, "Yeah, just don't feel too special. Look around you." It was his way of reminding me that there is little about the human experience unique to me or unconnected to other people. In looking around me, I saw that individual successes (or failures) often hinged on the kinds of opportunities and care others offered. This book, too, is the result of the guidance, efforts, and kindnesses extended to me by many people.

I am deeply grateful to the men and women who participated in this study. They accepted me as a participant in their groups and shared their lives with me. During lengthy interview sessions, they patiently and honestly answered difficult questions. Their experiences, reflections, and courage taught and inspired me. Without their openness and support, I simply could not have written this book.

Many friends and colleagues supported my efforts and helped me think through this material by taking time out of very busy schedules to read and comment on chapters or the whole book, to talk with me about my analysis as it developed, or to give me a pep talk when I got discouraged. These people include Ken Aizawa, Kim Vanhoosier-Carey, Karin Breuer, Kent Sandstrom, Sherryl Kleinman, Kristi Long, Ilene Kalish, Jodi Campbell, Scott Thumma, Christy M. Ponticelli,

Susan Brayford, and Harmony Newman. Thanks, to all of you, for your wisdom and effort.

My parents, Judie and Sig, allowed me great opportunity and never wavered in their belief or support. Thanks, Mom and Dad, for just about everything. I also owe thanks to my sisters, Margie and Shara, for their patience and interest as they listened to me talk about this material for years.

Several years ago, Centenary College awarded me the Mattie Allen Broyles Inaugural Year Research Chair. The additional time and resources afforded by this chair were a great benefit to this research, allowing me to collect most of the data on the women in this study. My thanks to Centenary and to the Broyles family for their support.

It is to my mentor and friend, Michael Schwalbe, that I owe the deepest thanks. Much of the analysis in this book was developed during our conversations over coffee or from his incredibly insightful and thorough comments on drafts. Our work together not only has shaped how I think as a sociologist, but also has given me something to aspire to as a teacher and a human being. Your time, your lessons, and your belief in me mean so much.

Finally, for the life support that I have received through years of research and writing, I am grateful to my husband, Michael Futreal. His great intellect, kindness, humor, and capacity to give were invaluable in the hours it took to craft this manuscript, prompting me to think, to laugh at my mistakes, and to keep faith and perspective. The life we have built together and the love we share are tremendous gifts. I could not make this journey without you.

Prologue

*Know ye not that the unrighteous shall not
inherit the kingdom of God? Be not deceived:
neither fornicators, nor idolaters, nor adulterers,
nor effeminate, nor abusers of themselves with
mankind, Nor thieves, nor covetous, nor drunkards, nor revilers, nor extortioners, shall inherit
the kingdom of God.*
1 Corinthians 6: 9–10, King James Bible

When the door opened, I saw a man of medium height and build, with dark brown hair and eyes, who just seemed used to smiling. He held the screen door open and said, "Come on in." After I made it through the door frame, he reached over and hugged me, telling me how glad he was that I had come. I responded awkwardly, unaccustomed to hugging people I did not know well—something that I soon discovered I would have to get over pretty quickly. I followed him down a short hallway into the living room, where about fifteen people were eating and talking. He asked for their attention and introduced me as "the researcher who was going to attend their Bible study to learn how they experienced being gay and Christian." Someone called out, "The truth will set you free," and others murmured, "Amen to that." One by one, the group members came over to introduce themselves and hugged me in welcome.

Soon, the group leader announced it was time to start the Bible study, and people began to find their way to the chairs and sofas that were arranged in a circle. I took a seat next to an empty chair. Everyone joined hands. The person sitting next to me leaned over and whispered that I should put my hand on the empty chair next to me, explaining that it was a symbolic chair, put in the circle to wait for the next gay person yet to find his or her way to the group. By touching it, I was symbolically reaching out to that person. I followed his directions, and then we bowed our heads and the leader began to pray:

> Dear Heavenly Parent, thank you for bringing us together and for this time together. As we move into your presence tonight, we pray that you will open our hearts and minds to your Word. Let your wisdom guide us in our study so that we may learn truth. Thank you for the new members among us and remember those who are not with us. Keep them safe and bring them back to us. Thank you for the great healing you have brought and guide others to us to fill the empty chair so that they too can be healed. In Jesus' name we pray. Amen. (Fieldnote excerpt from gay Christian Bible study)

When we looked up, I removed my hand from the empty chair, and someone handed me a Bible. I was beginning the process of learning how and why this group believed that homosexuality and Christianity were compatible.

———

The ex-gay ministry leader told me to use a side entrance that was well out of sight of the church's main doors. I entered a long hallway with lots of doors. I was wandering around, trying to find the right room, when the leader spotted me and said, "Good to have you here. We're in this room." The room could have held at least forty people, but only five were there, standing and talking. The leader introduced me as "that researcher who is interested in how we, as Christians, learn to overcome homosexuality." They welcomed me and began to ask questions: What was I studying? Why? Was I a Christian? As we talked, more people arrived, and the leader announced it was time to begin.

We moved to chairs (but did not sit down) that were arranged in a semicircle around a table with a TV/VCR and CD player on it. A man, who was apparently in charge of the group's music, told us that he brought a favorite CD for the worship segment of the meeting—something by Dennis Jernigan. He popped it into the CD player, and the group began to sing, some with great volume and fervor and some more quietly, swaying, eyes closed and palms turned heavenward. I never sing in public, for good reason, and stood with my head very bowed. After three songs, we joined hands and bowed our heads. The leader began to pray:

> Dear Heavenly Father, thank you for bringing the group here together, for giving us this space. Father, we know that you are a holy, holy God and we thank you for your many blessings. We know that it is only through your power that we can

do anything. Thank you, Jesus. We love you, Lord, and know
that you are truly an awesome God, and we ask you to fill us
with the Holy Spirit and bring healing. We praise you for the
healing that has taken place (murmurs of "Thank you, Jesus"
from the group) and pray that the Holy Spirit will work powerfully in people's lives during the meeting and throughout
the week. We pray that you will open our hearts and minds
to the truth of your Word as we learn tonight and that you
will guide us to do your will. In Jesus' name. Amen. (Fieldnote
excerpt from ex-gay Christian ministry meeting)

After the group repeated "Amen," we lifted our heads and sat. It was
time to begin the lesson. We were to watch a video made by a man
who would tell us how he had been healed of his homosexuality, transformed from gay to straight, and was now living in accord with God's
will.

———

These two groups of Christians, one gay and the other ex-gay, met just
a few miles apart in a southern city located in the Bible Belt. The above
prayers were typical openings to their Bible studies and ministry meetings. The first time I heard these prayers, I was stunned by the strikingly similarity in spite of being uttered by groups with such different
ideas about homosexuality. Both prayers expressed real gratitude for
God's blessings, an awe of God's power, and a reverent desire to know
and obey God's Word. The prayers also earnestly asked for God's help
in healing group members' wounds. There was a reason for this similarity; both groups emerged from the larger conservative Christian community to confront the mutual problem of how to handle homosexuality
within the context of Christianity. These groups not only addressed
the same problem, but they also used similar core beliefs to understand and resolve it. Put briefly, these core beliefs were that the Bible
is the true Word of God, that God's plan for each person's life can be
discovered through prayer, that God sacrificed Jesus to save the world,
and that God loves all people and will work positively in their lives
if they allow it.

Yet these groups embraced dramatically different views of homosexuality, views that offered opposing explanations and remedies for
group members' problems. In their prayers, the men in the gay Christian group asked God to heal the wounds inflicted by people who mis-
construed God's Word as condemning homosexuals. They also prayed

that God would help group members accept their homosexuality as God's will for their lives. By contrast, the ex-gay Christian men prayed for God to heal the spiritual and emotional wounds that caused homosexuality, thereby allowing them to expel homosexuality from their lives. In doing so, ex-gay group members hoped that they, too, could follow God's will for their lives, that is, to be heterosexual. Members of both groups were thus praying for the same things—God's healing, help, and strength—to enable them to cope with the shared problem of being gay and Christian. The resolutions they prayed for, however, were entirely contradictory.

This book is the story of how these men came to offer such prayers and how they perceived them to be answered—one way or the other.

PART I

The Cultural Origins and Biographical Paths of the Dilemma

1 The Problem with Being Gay and Christian

In the spring of 1995, the Reverend Jimmy Creech was a guest speaker at a meeting of gay and lesbian students on a university campus. Creech, a former Methodist minister defrocked because of his gay-affirmative ministry and activism (cf. Hartman 1996, 1–24), talked about the ridicule and harassment he had suffered because of his work and about the damage caused by his church's tenacious assertion of heterosexist doctrine. When he finished, he invited comments and questions from the audience. Among the many speakers was a young woman, a newcomer to the group, who told a story of the confusion and betrayal she felt as she sought salvation in a church that condemned her.

She was a first-year student at the university who had experienced homosexual attractions since puberty. She despised these desires, she said, because she felt "they were against God." Hoping to find a way to rid herself of these desires, she had recently confided in her pastor, who told her to pray and then quickly dismissed her. The next Sunday, the pastor preached a hellfire sermon against homosexuality, declaring that one of the "demonic" was among the congregation. His sermon so clearly revealed the identity of this "demon" that the woman left the church, humiliated. When she returned home several hours later, her belongings were in the driveway, the doors were locked, and no one answered her knock. She gathered her things and returned to school. "No one in my family has spoken to me since then," she said, adding, "I don't know what to do. I have never felt so dirty or so alone. I think I might be going to hell."

The young woman's story gripped me. I wondered why she felt badly about herself, rather than angry at being betrayed by her pastor and family. As a nonreligious heterosexual, I had had the luxury, until attending that meeting, of never thinking much about such issues. Now that I was confronted with them, I was puzzled and irritated. How could avowed Christians act with so little compassion? Why did this woman care about that lousy pastor? It was not until later, when I had heard similar stories from others, that I began to understand the woman's story, her predicament, and the depth of her feeling. In a faith that demands heterosexuality, people who feel homosexual desire can experience themselves as sinners, frauds, and failed Christians. This young woman felt that her homosexual desires went "against God" and disqualified her from being the kind of person she had always hoped to be, a situation that felt dire because of its potential consequences and because she had yet to figure out how she, as a Christian, might cope with these desires.

This woman's story, this kind of struggle, while troubling, is not unique. At present, there are thousands of Christians who experience homosexual desires and who must come to terms with what those desires mean in the context of their faith and in their lives. For some, predominately those from liberal or mainline denominations (cf. Roof and McKinney 1987, 155–157), such deliberations may pose little problem either because diversity is better tolerated within these groups and/or because adherents feel assured of God's love and see no significant contradiction between their religious beliefs and their sexuality. Some also choose to handle the situation by leaving the church and its teachings behind. For many others, particularly those affiliated with conservative denominations, these deliberations are enormously difficult and consequential. Unable to alter either their religious beliefs or their sexuality, these Christians feel that what is at stake in this struggle is much of what they hold most valuable: relationships with friends, family, and a faith community; their sense of themselves as good and moral; and, most critically, their spiritual journeys and eternal salvation. Ensconced within a religious community that unequivocally condemns homosexuality as against God's teachings, these people, like the woman above, feel great anxiety and shame about their sexuality. They can also experience an overwhelming fear for their souls. In these situations, people often must endure great struggle to resolve the conflict between homosexuality and their faith.

In retrospect, though, what was most striking about this woman's account was not the struggle per se. Instead, what was most notable was that she was able to admit this struggle so publicly within a social space purposefully created for such discussion. This ability and these public spaces are relatively recent developments. Prior to the 1970s, Christians who struggled with homosexual desires had very limited options for dealing with them. During the 1950s and 1960s, only a few major metropolitan areas had gay organizations, such as the Mattachine Society and the Daughters of Bilitis, and these were secular organizations devoted to educating people about homosexuality and advancing gay rights, not spaces for reconciling faith and sexuality.

One such space began to take shape in 1968 with the formation of a gay-affirming religious organization, the Metropolitan Community Church (MCC), a group that believes that homosexuality and Christianity are wholly compatible. MCC is a rather unique evangelical denomination, one that has roots in conservative Protestantism but espouses some positions consistent with more liberal theology. MCC retains an evangelical emphasis on biblical authority, on personal salvation through Christ, and on engagement with individuals and the culture to exert a redemptive influence. (For characteristics of evangelicals, see Hunter 1983; Smith 2000, 13; Noll 2001, 11.) However, MCC also asserts that homosexuals are created by God as persons of equal worth and that homosexual practice is consistent with biblical teaching as long as it is done within the confines of other biblical mandates (e.g., within a committed monogamous relationship/ marriage). As such, MCC offers a potential haven for Christians struggling with homosexuality. However, MCC and the similar Catholic (Dignity), Episcopalian (Integrity), and Jewish (Beth Chayim Chadashim) groups that soon followed were initially small and concentrated in cities. Outside of these urban areas, homosexuality, though certainly stigmatized, was largely invisible in churches and the public sphere. As a result, through the early 1970s, most Christians who were gay had little choice about how to handle their struggle; they could risk being ostracized and leave their churches or they could hide their sexuality, struggle alone, and continue as church members.

Over the last three decades, however, the options for dealing with this struggle have expanded a great deal, due largely to the ongoing heated social and religious debates surrounding homosexuality. Throughout the 1970s, as the gay rights movement took hold and homosexuality became an issue for public discussion, churches were pushed to take a formal stand on homosexuality. The earliest statements from religious groups, like the Unitarian Universalist Association and the Lutheran Church in America, were fairly sympathetic, calling for compassion and arguing against discrimination and criminalization of homosexuals (Wilcox 2001, 93). These early statements were quickly followed by more absolute statements condemning homosexuality. For instance, the Methodists (in 1972) and the Southern Baptists (in 1976) issued resolutions stating that homosexual practice was a sin incompatible with Christian teaching. It was also during this time, in 1976, that Exodus, a Christian ministry designed to heal homosexuals and restore them to godly heterosexuality, was created. Like MCC, Exodus is an evangelical organization, but, in contrast, it maintains the conservative theological position that homosexuality is sin. Exodus holds that the divine mandate for sexuality includes only heterosexual marriage and that homosexuality is the result of psychological damage created by sinful behavior. This damage, according to Exodus, can be repaired and heterosexuality restored through healing prayer. Exodus and the like groups that followed came to be known as "ex-gay" ministries and offered an opposing alternative to MCC's gay-affirming theology for Christians struggling with homosexuality.

These cultural developments helped to set the stage for the current debates between and within denominations, and in society more generally, about how to deal with homosexuality and how to treat homosexuals. These debates have increased the visibility of homosexuality in society and helped to form public spaces in which the issue can be discussed and homosexuals can find support. MCC and Exodus have emerged as important, though competing, venues in this arena. Each has grown tremendously since its inception, expanding in terms of membership and geographic distribution; they have become the largest, and arguably the most potent, religious groups developed explicitly to negotiate the conflict between conservative Christianity and homosexuality. As such, they are integral parts of the debate over homosexuality, both as a reflection of it and as influential forces that shape it. These groups present solutions at opposing ends of a spectrum of how homosexuality might be handled within Christianity. On the one side, homosexuality is perceived as given by God and is entirely reconciled with conservative Christian belief. On the other, homosexuality remains a damning sin, and the individual's sexuality must be transformed to fit into traditional Christian doctrine. In this way, these groups provide options for those who struggle with these issues, options that go beyond forfeiting conservative Christian belief or passing as straight.

The importance of the construction of these venues and expanded options should not be treated lightly because it is within such spaces, spaces that have in the past been difficult to cultivate, that stigmatized groups can give voice to their experiences and develop oppositional resources. Examining what people *do* within these cultural venues, however, is critical to gaining some insight on the likely impact of such spaces on individual lives, groups, and society. Understanding why individuals choose one option over another, how these solutions get integrated into and influence individuals' lives and relationships, and how such work collectively effects social institutions will help to shed light on the social, psychological, and interactional dynamics that create, sustain, or impede social change.

This research explores these issues through an ethnographic study of two groups of Christian men at the epicenter of the debate, one gay group consisting of members of two Bible studies that were linked to a MCC congregation and the other composed of members of an ex-gay ministry affiliated with Exodus. Specifically, this study analyzes how people who share a common problem—how to reconcile homosexual desires with the religious belief that homosexuality in sinful and damning—can arrive at and adopt such opposing solutions. This kind of analysis requires an exploration of the struggle experienced by Christians with homosexual desires, the conditions under which people are likely to choose to become a gay or ex-gay Christian, the process by which these resolutions are adapted to individual lives, and the resources (e.g., supportive relationships, ideologies, etc.) necessary for successful change. Such an examination enables assessment of the likely consequences of these groups for individual lives and the larger cultural landscape.

Beginning the Study

This examination did not begin with a plan. My attendance at the gay and lesbian student meeting when Creech was speaking was not a first step in a carefully crafted research design, nor was it compelled by a personal or scholarly interest in homosexuality. Instead, I was initially fulfilling a requirement for a graduate seminar in social psychology. But that meeting did launch this study. In the days and weeks that followed the meeting, I found that I could not stop thinking about Creech's talk or the woman's story. What was it about homosexuality that made Christians kick other Christians out of churches and daughters out of homes? How did Christians who experience homosexual desires deal with the conflict between that desire and church teachings? I wanted to make sense of all this conflict, so I began to explore ways of finding answers to these questions.

In his talk, Creech had briefly mentioned MCC, explaining that this denomination offered an affirming spiritual haven for gay Christians and was working to diminish the heterosexism within Christianity. So MCC seemed like a good place to start. After a brief Internet search, I contacted the pastor of a MCC congregation located in the southern United States to set up a meeting. We met in the MCC church building, where, after a brief tour, the pastor told me a bit about MCC's mission, its history, and his congregation. Before I left, he agreed to set up a focus group consisting of five male members of this congregation so that I could find out more about how people experienced being gay and Christian. A few weeks later, I listened as these men told their stories and shared their common struggles before finding MCC. All described how much their lives had changed for the better after joining. One man mentioned he had been in an Exodus ministry for a while in an effort to become straight. I had never heard of this group and spoke to him about it when the focus group was over. He told me that Exodus was a ministry designed to transform gays to heterosexuals, which was, in his opinion, "absolute crap." Nevertheless, if I was interested, he could give me the name and number of a former Exodus leader. I found a pen.

I called this former leader, who agreed to meet with me to explain how Exodus and its ministries worked. By the end of our discussion, he also agreed to arrange a focus group with four current Exodus members. A short time later, I again heard how hard these men struggled with their sexuality and faith and how helpful ministry meetings had been for them. Both groups had described the same problem, but they were working toward entirely different answers. It was even more intriguing that the men in both groups found these answers helpful and satisfying. How was it possible that people with the same basic religious beliefs and the same problem could arrive so convincingly at such opposing solutions?

It was this question that drove subsequent research. To systematically address this question, I returned to the MCC pastor and located an ex-gay ministry leader to ask if I could attend Bible study and ministry meetings to learn more about how people reconciled homosexuality and their faith. After negotiations, I was granted access to both groups, on the condition that I actively participate in the meetings by studying the Bible/group materials and discussing the assigned passages. (For particulars on gaining access to research sites and participant observation, see the appendix.) Within the MCC church, I attended two Bible study, or what were referred to as "cell," groups that were subsets of the congregation. The first cell group I attended was a twelve-week Bible study, called *Homosexuality and the Bible*, that was recommended for new members. I chose this group because it was specifically designed to help new members explore Scripture and its interpretation and to introduce them to MCC's theology. Given this group's purpose, I hoped that my participation in this group would allow me to observe how gay Christians began the process of reconciling doctrine and homosexuality.

This group was composed of six white men and one Asian man, all between the ages of thirty-three and fifty. All of these men had conservative Protestant backgrounds—Southern Baptist, Church of God, Assembly of God—except one who had been raised as a Jew but had become a Baptist as a young adult. The men met biweekly to study the eight biblical verses commonly used to denounce homosexuality and the four verses considered to be gay friendly. As a group, these men worked to determine what the Bible "really says" about homosexuality and discussed how they felt about these interpretations.

I also attended a second cell group, which I refer to as *Accept*, for approximately fifteen months. Approximately thirteen to eighteen people attended Accept meetings. Most were long-term (over two years) MCC church members, providing me with an opportunity to observe how more established members utilized MCC's theology. The group consisted of mostly white men (one black man and a few women attended sporadically) between the ages of nineteen and sixty. Again, the majority of group members were from conservative Protestant backgrounds, though two Catholics and one Mormon attended regularly. This group met to discuss the Bible, pray, and talk about their lives. In addition, I went to this group's social events (e.g., movie nights, dinners, Christmas parties, etc.) and their charitable functions (e.g., making AIDS baskets). At this point, because these particular groups were almost entirely male and I had established a relationship with them (there were other women's and co-ed groups), I decided to focus only on how Christian men dealt with their homosexuality.

Within Exodus, I spent approximately nine months attending the weekly meetings of an ex-gay ministry, referred to here as *Expell*. The Expell ministry operated out of an interdenominational, evangelical church, and its board of directors consisted, in part, of several church leaders. Of the approximately fourteen to seventeen people who regularly attended Expell, however, only about four were members of this church. All other attendees were members of local conservative Protestant churches, including Southern Baptist, Assembly of God, Church of Christ, and other interdenominational evangelical churches. Again, most participants were white men (one woman attended regularly) whose ages ranged from mid-twenties to mid-fifties. About a third of the men were married and often attended with their spouses.

Expell meetings generally included praise and worship sessions, teaching sessions to help members learn Exodus's approach to homosexuality, and small group discussions about members' life experiences. During these small group discussions, the group leader would occasionally divide us into groups by sex, usually, it seemed, to allow married men a chance to talk openly without their wives beside them. When this happened, I ended up in a small group of wives listening to their account of what was difficult for them about their husband's struggle and how they coped with it. At first, though I chafed at being cut out of the men's discussions and worried that I was missing key information, I was intrigued by the women's talk and took good notes. Later, as I interviewed the married men in the group, I began to recognize how important a role these women played in their husbands' efforts to become ex-gay Christians.

Put simply, the women were important sources of support and motivation for their husbands as they moved through the "healing" process. The wives provided emotional support and kept the men "accountable" for their actions. The men's love for their wives and their desire to uphold the marital vows they made before God also gave the men incentives to stay in the group; they did not want to add divorce to their list of sins and failures. Given the importance of the wives' help, and that Expell was designed to facilitate heterosexuality and heterosexual relationships, the wives' cooperation was critical to their husbands and the group. But why would women choose to stay in such marriages? How did they cope with being married to gay men? How was their cooperation elicited?

Answering these questions was important to building an understanding of how this subset of ex-gay men renegotiated their sexuality and faith. To find these answers, I wanted to interview wives of ex-gay Christian men, but Expell did not have a formal support group for wives, and the leader denied my request to interview the wives who attended. (For more details about gaining access and samples, see the appendix.) Instead, I e-mailed ministry leaders located throughout the United States asking for volunteers. Though few responded, one ex-gay ministry leader agreed to post a description of the study and my request for volunteers on an e-mail listserv for spouses of ex-gay Christians. I got twenty-three responses, fifteen of which led to interviews. Most of these women were married (two to pastors of churches); only three were currently separated or divorced but were still working on the marriage. All of the women were white, conservative Protestants or Catholics whose ages ranged from twenty-five to fifty-eight. Two women had been married less than a year, while the other thirteen had been married from four to thirty-four years. Given that these women were spread all over the continental United States, practicalities and funding required that I do about half of these interviews by phone.

Collecting Data

The data for this study come primarily from field observation and interviews. Most of the fieldnote excerpts in the following chapters are from my participation in Homosexuality and the Bible, Accept, and Expell group meetings. I also attended two conferences, a MCC regional conference consisting of prayer and workshops and an ex-gay ministry school designed to teach ministers and lay leaders how to administer "healing prayer" and help those struggling with homosexuality. In addition to observing meetings, I interviewed sixteen gay Christians, fourteen ex-gay Christians, and fifteen wives of ex-gay Christian men. (For a more detailed description of interview method and content, see the appendix.) These interviews lasted from an hour and a half to over four hours and, once transcribed, yielded well over a thousand pages of transcripts.

As a supplement to fieldnotes and interviews, I read the pamphlets, newsletters, and listserv posts that MCC/Accept and Exodus/Expell made available to members. In addition, I read books on the MCC recommended reading list (Piazza 1994; White 1994; Williams 1992; McNeill 1976) and on the Exodus list (Dallas 1996; Bergner 1995; Davies and Rentzel 1993; Payne 1981, 1985). I also read two booklets, available through a link on the Exodus Web site, that discussed wives' experiences dealing with their husbands' sexuality (Brown 2000; Hill 1998).

Throughout this study, I found it difficult to manage my dual role as researcher and participant in meetings. To do participant observation well, I had to become so much a part of the group that other members would cease to monitor themselves around me, even though they knew they were part of a study. It worked. Over time, group members relaxed and spoke openly, treating me as an insider. I also felt very much a part of both groups, and I shared many of my own personal feelings and experiences with them. They were kind. I knew the regular members well, I liked them, I appreciated their willingness to allow me to be part of their lives, and I wanted things to go well for them. In short, they felt like friends I should support—not examine critically and write about. So when I analyzed what they did, felt, and thought and drew conclusions, some of which I knew they would not like, I felt like I was betraying friends. An ethnographer's obligations, however, extend beyond the group under study to identifying problematic social patterns, with the hope that understanding might help to bring about useful change. My largest comfort in this struggle, then, was that some of what I found might eventually help to make their lives a bit better.

Why Does This Study Matter?

Most of what is popularly known about MCC and Exodus ministries comes from each group's media releases or from partisan organizations supportive of either gay rights (e.g., Human Rights Campaign) or the Christian Right (e.g., Focus on the Family). This information tends to construe these groups as complete opposites and as adversaries, obscuring their common purpose to help gays struggling with homosexuality and their similar theological and evangelical commitments. Further, there is limited scholarly research about how the groups really work, what they do, what they mean to the people who are actually part of them, and how they impact the larger

society. This research gap is particularly evident with regard to Exodus and ex-gay ministries. Of the sparse social scientific research undertaken to examine these ministries, most scholarship has focused
primarily on the effectiveness of the groups in orchestrating a change
in sexual orientation (Haldeman 1994; MacIntosh 1994; Spitzer 2001a,
2003). Such research has typically been done by surveying participants
on a one-time basis, providing only a snapshot of participants' experiences at a given moment in time. As a result, this research has provided little opportunity to explore the emotional and cognitive
processes associated with group membership and attempts at transforming sexual orientation.

At present, only one study has utilized sustained, in-depth field
research to examine these processes. Ponticelli's (1999) study of ex-
lesbians in an Exodus ministry examines the process of sexual identity reconstruction among members, revealing how important the
adoption of new discourses, ideological frameworks, and biographical accounts are to identity changes. As participants in this study for-
mulated new ways of thinking and talking about their situations within
the ministry group, the meanings of those situations, and of themselves,
were altered, and they began to see their homosexuality and its "cure"
in ministry terms. What is missing here, however, is an examination
of how participants were convinced to let go of old ideological frameworks and of the exact processes by which they were able to learn
new ones. Further, given gender differences and the greater stigmatization of homosexuality for men (Herek 2000), it is quite possible that
the process of sexual identity reconstruction may vary between men
and women. If this is the case, then how men experience the process
of trying to alter sexual orientation remains relatively unexplored.

In comparison to ex-gays and Exodus, gay Christians and MCC have
been studied somewhat more extensively. Much of this research focuses on identity integration; that is, on whether and how gay Christians can merge their religious and sexual identities successfully. These
studies (Thumma 1991; Mahaffy 1996; Rodriguez and Ouellette 2000;
Yip 1997; Comstock 1996; Wilcox 2003) have consistently shown that
gay Christians often, and not surprisingly, experience some cognitive
dissonance, whether it is internal (contradictions in one's own beliefs/
feelings) or external (contradictions between self beliefs and beliefs
of surrounding others). Mahaffy (1996) notes that reactions to this dissonance include changing religious beliefs, leaving churches, or

accepting the dissonance as a life condition. Studies of MCC congregations illustrate that most participants successfully integrate their religious and sexual identities by using religious and social resources within the MCC community to alter their beliefs (Rodriguez and Ouellette 2000; Yip 1997, 2002; Wilcox 2003).

Some scholars, particularly Scott Thumma (1991) and Andrew Yip (1997), have examined the process by which gay Christians achieve this integration, agreeing that integration is negotiated through the following steps. First, individuals must come to see that they can revise their religious beliefs. Often, this capacity emerges as people, usually through interaction with a gay-affirming religious group, discover flaws in existing interpretations, making them invalid. Second, individuals then learn a new theology that is gay positive, usually one that asserts that God made homosexuals and that homosexuality should thus be accepted as a gift from God. Finally, this new theology must be applied to the individual, creating an integrated identity of gay Christian. This integration often results through positive spiritual experiences and interactions with other Christians who accept the identity. These studies have greatly enhanced scholarly understanding of how gay Christians are able to integrate two disparate identities, particularly with respect to the kinds of cognitive changes that must be made to facilitate integration.

To date, there is little or no published sociological research that analyzes gay and ex-gay Christian groups in relation to one another, an important task given that the groups are theologically and socially connected and often define themselves in opposition to each other. Only one study, an unpublished master's thesis (Thumma 1984), undertakes this kind of comparative work. In this study, Thumma compares two groups, Good News, an evangelical gay Christian group, and Becoming, an ex-gay Christian group affiliated with Exodus. Much like the groups in this study, Good News and Becoming, despite their completely opposing views of and solutions to homosexuality within Christianity, are remarkably similar. Both are conservative Christian groups designed to help individuals who share a desire to be good Christians cope with the conflict between Christian doctrine and homosexuality. Most striking is that both groups use the same processes, similar to those outlined above, to accomplish such different goals. Again, however, this study emphasizes cognitive processes and does not examine emotional experiences in detail. Given that individuals must confront the feelings that the conflict between faith and sexuality generates as part of the reconciliation process, discovering how emotions are managed and transformed is critical to building a nuanced understanding of how this struggle is negotiated and how these groups function.

The present study both supports the findings of previous research and extends them by also examining how individuals, caught in these identity struggles, manage their beliefs and emotions in ways that support (or impede) their ability to cast off old notions, create new ones, and adapt these ideas to the self. To do so, this book provides an in-depth examination of both groups, focusing on how people experience their struggle with faith and homosexuality, why they decide to join either a gay or an ex-gay Christian group, how they came to (albeit different) terms with their homosexuality within Christianity, how involved spouses responded to this struggle, and the probable social consequences of it all.

Exploring the dynamics of these two groups will help us to understand the relationship between religion and inequalities related to sexual orientation. As the most widespread and, perhaps, the most potent moral force in Western society, Christian doctrine holds tremendous sway over what is defined as moral sexual behavior and who is considered good or bad. At present, Christian theology is one of the primary tools used to prescribe, reinforce, and maintain heterosexism. Analyzing how these opposing groups work within this doctrine to attempt to alter the meanings of homosexuality will help to identify the possibilities for and barriers to sexual equality within Christianity and society.

The infusion of these groups' ideas into culture is also important more generally. Christians who experience homosexual desire are not the only group of people to have stigma imposed on them by the dominant culture. Like other marginalized groups (e.g., women and racial minorities), gay Christians have had to struggle to create satisfying lives under cultural and political conditions that foster psychic and material disadvantage. Studying their thoughts, feelings, and behaviors in relation to these conditions can provide us with valuable insights into how stigmatized groups adapt to, reproduce, and challenge their oppression.

Studying these two groups further offers an opportunity to examine the process of social change. To maintain their cherished Christian identities, participants in MCC and Exodus have had to work within traditional theological frameworks to renegotiate what it means to be gay and Christian. In doing so, they not only have generated new ways of thinking about spirituality and sexuality, but also have helped to create and sustain new identity options for those who face such issues. Analyzing how they were able to construct and maintain new cultural spaces and understandings, in spite of serious ideological constraints, has the potential to help us learn more about how we make and change our social world. In sum, studying these two smallish and specific groups can provide a lens through which to view and understand the larger social world.

This book is meant to be a critical analysis of how these groups help members cope with their homosexual desires within the context of their faith and of the larger social consequences of their activities. It is not my intention to argue for one side over the other, nor do I begin or end with any conviction about the theological basis for dealing with homosexuality. Given the sensitive and divisive nature of this topic, I am pretty sure that there is something here to anger gay Christians, ex-gay Christians, and their proponents alike. My purpose, however, is not to undermine the groups but to make sense of them within the current cultural and political context. The courageous struggles of the people who attend these groups matter, and I want to show how and why. My hope is that both groups, and anyone interested in sexual politics, inequality, and social change, will benefit from taking a closer look at this part of the social picture.

The story that unfolds in the following chapters is largely the story of how these men were able to resolve such a complex dilemma. It is, to use the men's language, a "testimony" to their creativity, their courage, and their conviction. But it is more than just the men's story. It is also the story of True Believers trying to make sense of homosexuality in a way that preserves their faith in a society divided over the meaning of homosexuality.

I pick up this story in chapter 2 by providing an overview of MCC and Exodus that includes their organizational missions and histories as well as their theological positions. Chapter 3 examines the men's identity dilemmas, highlighting the cultural conditions and personal experiences from which these conflicts developed. The next chapter then addresses how and why the men, who struggled with the same dilemma, made opposing decisions to join either the gay or ex-gay Christian group. Chapters 5, 6, and 7 analyze what the men did within these groups to resolve their dilemmas, how they experienced their participation, and how membership in the groups changed their lives.

Chapter 8 explores how wives whose husbands are engaged in this sexual struggle both cope with the enormous pressures placed on their marriages and try to ensure their husbands' successful transformation to heterosexuality. Finally, the last chapter examines the implications of these groups for the individual and the larger society, analyzing their triumphs and limitations in terms of their efforts to redefine the meaning of homosexuality within Christianity.

2 Alternate Theologies
Sins and Solutions

The Universal Fellowship of Metropolitan Community Churches is a Christian Church founded in and reaching beyond the Gay and Lesbian communities. We embody and proclaim Christian salvation and liberation, Christian inclusivity and community, and Christian social action and justice. We serve among those seeking and celebrating the integration of their spirituality and sexuality.

Mission Statement of UFMCC

Proclaiming to, educating and impacting the world with the Biblical truth that freedom from homosexuality is possible when Jesus is Lord of one's life.

Exodus International—About Exodus

The above two mission statements clearly reveal the key difference between MCC and Exodus; MCC works to integrate homosexuality into Christian life while Exodus seeks to purge it. In accord with these contrary missions, the groups are also on opposing sides of the debate over whether homosexuality is innate (MCC) or chosen (Exodus) and split on the issue of whether people can change their sexual orientation. Certainly, each group's purpose reflects and helps to form the cornerstone of belief within each organization, and these differences are critical aspects of the groups. It can therefore be tempting, as mass media presentations of these organizations have done, to characterize the groups as polar opposites, pitting one against the other and aligning MCC with political and theological liberalism and Exodus with conservatism. Conceiving of these groups as entirely different and conflicting entities, however, is a mistake.

In spite of their obvious disagreement about how homosexuality should be handled within Christianity, these organizations have significant theological and organizational commonalities. In fact, these groups emerge out of and are grounded in similar religious traditions, sharing a great deal more doctrine than might be expected. They also reach out to the same population to cope with the mutual problem of homosexuality within Christianity, and they do so using remarkably similar processes. If we are to grasp how and why individuals who experience homosexual desire and who share similar religious beliefs can resolve a common conflict between their faith and sexuality in such antithetical ways, then we must first understand the groups' similarities and complexities, rather than just noting their opposing conclusions.

Without a full understanding of the theological or ideological context of these groups, we are also likely to misinterpret members' speech and behavior as bizarre or overtly political, rather than as conformity to a set of religious beliefs. Such misinterpretation would not only preclude a valid examination of these groups and of their functions and consequences, but it also risks ignoring or discrediting people's experience of homosexuality within Christianity, allowing heterosexuals to fill in the blanks as they imagine. To develop this understanding and to lay the foundation for the subsequent study, this chapter provides an overview of each group's organizational history, religious roots, existing theology, and approach to homosexuality. Readers will no doubt be tempted to side with one group or the other. My purpose, however, is not to decide which group is "right" or to evaluate which offers a more persuasive explanation of homosexuality. Rather, the intent is to understand the groups on their own terms. Only then is it possible to make sense of how the men were able, through participation in these groups, to resolve their struggles so differently. Doing so also allows for analysis of the larger societal consequences of this struggle.

Metropolitan Community Churches
In his book *Don't Be Afraid Anymore* (1990), the Reverend Troy Perry tells the story of the founding of MCC. It begins on a summer night in 1968 when Perry goes dancing with his friend

Tony at a large gay dance bar, called the Patch, just south of Los Angeles. At the time, uniformed and plainclothes police were known for infiltrating gay bars and hassling patrons, and this night was no different. So, when another man slapped Tony's butt playfully, both were charged with "lewd and lascivious conduct," arrested, and taken to jail. The bar owner, who was fed up with police harassment, organized his patrons into a protest group to go get the two men released from jail. The group stood at the jail wearing or carrying flowers, singing "We Shall Overcome" throughout the night until the men were released in the early dawn. Perry found this experience empowering because it forced him to recognize that gay people could demand their rights.

For Tony, however, the experience was devastating. Being arrested and taunted by police and other jailed men made him feel "like a freak in a sideshow" and a "dirty queer" (Perry 1990, 33–34). When Perry tried to reassure him, telling him that God cares and he would be all right, he responded, "God doesn't care. Be serious....[M]y priest said I couldn't be homosexual and a Christian, so that was the end" (1990, 34). Perry urged him to pray, to reach out to God, but he simply could not. In spite of all Perry's efforts, Tony left that early morning deeply sad, hurt, and alone.

Upset by his encounter with Tony, and yet aware of an odd, growing excitement, Perry was unable to sleep. As a former Pentecostal preacher, now defrocked because of his homosexuality, Perry did what came naturally to him—prayed urgently. As he prayed for Tony and for a church that would help him and all those who felt outcast, he suddenly knew that creating this church was his calling (Perry 1990, 35). It was in these events—the discriminatory acts of police and the church, collective resistance to such acts, the emotional distress of being stigmatized, outcast, and afraid of God's condemnation, and earnest prayer—that the idea for MCC emerged and grew.

Perry became progressively more certain that his mission from God was to start a new church that ministered to the gay community but included anyone who believed in God's love and forgiveness. As he clarified his vision for the new church, Perry was able to name it: *Metropolitan,* because it would serve the large urban area of Los Angeles; *Community,* because it would be an outreach into the gay community and would create a sense of camaraderie and familiarity; and *Church,* because it would be a house in which God could enter and work. With his vision of the church coming into focus, Perry placed an ad for the first church service in the September 1968 issue of the *Advocate.*

On October 6, 1968, Perry held his first worship service in his living room. Twelve people attended, a diverse group (though mostly men) consisting of a heterosexual couple, a Latino, a Jew, Protestants, and Catholics. That day, when Perry outlined his vision of MCC to his tiny congregation, he explained that they were *not* a gay church, but a Christian one, a Protestant church devoted to including all people. He stressed that their homosexuality did not define them; their humanity and faith did. Their mission, as he described it, was to build a theology of love and inclusion, freeing people from the hurt of exclusion and others from their feelings of hate.

Perry's first sermon, entitled "Be True to You," emphasized the importance of being true to who you are and believing in yourself as a child of God. He used the biblical story of Job as an example of a man who was steadfastly certain of his inherent worth and God's love, in spite of all the terrible things that befell him and others' suggestions that he must have sinned to deserve such a fate. Job's faith, Perry said, was rewarded.

Perry also drew on the story of David and Goliath, highlighting David's dire predicament and his constant faith to show that we can trust God to protect and help, even when circumstances look bad. He closed the sermon with a familiar quotation from Philippians 4:13: "I can do all things through Christ, which strengthen me." The central message of Perry's sermon was that, regardless of what the world shows you, you must be true to and believe in who you are because you are a created child of God. Do this, and have unswerving faith in God, and God can help and protect you. The events that led to this sermon, and the sermon itself, were small acts of resistance to discrimination, and no one knew then just how powerful they would become in thousands of lives as MCC later blossomed into one of the largest gay organizations in the world. As of 2004, MCC had about three hundred congregations in twenty-two countries, totaling approximately forty-three thousand members (www.ufmcc.org).

MCC's beginning, however modest and simple, born out of one man's desire to help those estranged from traditional Christianity, nonetheless contained most of the ideas that would later become the building blocks of a theology of inclusion and social justice. The goals and theology of an older, more mature and established MCC still mirror Perry's purpose on that fall afternoon in 1968. As noted in chapter 1, MCC is a theologically conservative, evangelical Protestant denomination that proclaims that there is one triune God, that the Bible is the divinely inspired Word of God, that Christ is the route to salvation, and that the Holy Spirit indwells the believer. It further emphasizes the importance of conversion (rebirth) and of sharing the faith (evangelizing).

MCC's theology, however, also merges aspects of Pentecostalism and elements of liberation theology with this conservative belief, facilitating the development of a gay-affirming doctrine. According to Warner (1995), Perry's Pentecostal background, one that emphasized the experience of God's love, influenced how he addressed scriptural prohibitions against homosexuality. First, Perry noted that Jesus exempted Christians from the Levitical rules in the Old Testament, including those that condemned homosexuality. Then, Perry placed Jesus's overarching message of love in the New Testament above all else, creating a Pentecostal "vision of grace with which to subdue a judgment of law" (Warner 1995, 87). This vision seems to have been shaped by, and enacted through, an adaptation of liberation theology. Put briefly, liberation theology rests on three key premises: (1) theology must be culturally contextual; (2) sin is defined as structural oppression of others, not simply individual wrong doing; and (3) salvation is construed not as a reward in the afterlife but as the construction of a just society in this life (Nepstad 1996, 110–111). By the end of the 1960s, this theology, as Wilcox explains, "set an example on a Christian theological level for other oppressed minorities who were working to gain their rights" (2001, 90), including MCC. As we will see, the influence of liberation theology and Perry's "vision of grace" are unmistakable in MCC's theology, programs, and activism. That said, it must also be noted that contemporary MCC congregations are diverse, reflecting variation in belief, worship style, and ritual (Wilcox 2003).

MCC's overarching mission is supported by and advanced through an affirming theology that rests on two simple, yet incredibly powerful, interrelated religious tenets. The first is non-condemnation of difference, or the idea that God made people diverse to fulfill divine purposes. As a result, MCC contends that people of all genders, sexual orientations, classes, races, and ethnicities are to be similarly valued and given the opportunity to participate fully and equally in their faith. With regard to homosexuality, this tenet means that God made gays as they are and loves them as such; therefore, gay must be good. Change is not possible or even desirable because doing so would work against God's creative intent. The second tenet is all-inclusive love, built on Jesus's example of extending love to all people. In what follows, I sketch out the details of these tenets more fully, noting their religious origins and providing some examples of MCC's interpretations of key biblical passages to illustrate how such tenets are supported. This sketch is by no means exhaustive, nor does it evaluate the validity of this interpretation. Theologians and biblical scholars have done this work elsewhere. (For pro-gay theology, see Boswell 1980; Scroggs 1983; Edwards 1984; for opposing views, see Yamamoto 1990; Dallas 1996.) My purpose is simply to provide an overview of MCC's doctrine.

One of MCC's core ideas, which reflects liberation theology's indictment of elites who cause suffering for the marginalized and its emphasis on context, is that condemnation of groups of people is the result of human prejudice and failing—not God's mandate. This idea is important because it allows MCC proponents to call existing, conservative biblical *interpretations* into question without undermining the integrity of the Bible or the belief in biblical *truth.* In other words, some existing biblical understandings are seen as human misinterpretations, colored by human bias in ways that condemn others to suit some powerful people's agendas, but the Bible is still God's truth. Specifically, MCC contends that conservatives have historically used the Bible to oppress and exclude certain groups of people from the ranks of "good Christians" and from the Kingdom of Heaven. Their attack on homosexuals and homosexuality is presented as another instance of conservative intolerance. To provide evidence for this claim, MCC cites slavery and the subordination of women, practices which the Bible was once used to justify. Consider the following two excerpts from an MCC pamphlet, *Homosexuality: Not a Sin, Not a Sickness:*

> For many centuries, the Christian Church's attitude toward human sexuality was very negative: sex was for procreation, not for pleasure; women and slaves were considered property to be owned by males; and many expressions of heterosexuality, like homosexuality, were considered sinful. Such tradition often continues to influence churches today. Many teach that women should be subordinate to men, continue to permit forms of discrimination against people of color, and condemn homosexuals. They say all homosexual acts are sinful, often referring to their interpretation of scripture.

> There are vast differences in doctrines between various Christian denominations, all of which use the same Bible. Such differences have led some Christians to claim that other Christians are not really Christians at all! Biblical interpretation and

theology differ from church to church . . . [and] from time to time. Approximately 150 years ago in the United States, some Christian teaching held that there was a two-fold moral order: black and white. Whites were thought to be superior to blacks, therefore blacks were to be subservient and slavery was an institution ordained by God. Clergy who supported such an abhorrent idea claimed the authority of the Bible. The conflict over slavery led to divisions which gave birth to some major Christian denominations. These same denominations, of course, do not support slavery today. Did the Bible change? No, their *interpretation* of the Bible did! (Eastman 1990, emphasis in original)

These excerpts show how MCC uses the link to history and the emphasis on interpretation to challenge the conservative version of biblical truth. In the first excerpt, Eastman grounds contemporary racism, sexism, and heterosexism in Christianity's alleged history of racism, misogyny, and puritanism. He links condemnation of homosexuals to other forms of discrimination carried out in the name of Christianity. If all that was said was that the church had historically oppressed homosexuals, then one might suppose that homosexuality was uniquely condemned by Scripture. Instead, Eastman is careful to point out that this ongoing condemnation is tied to an "interpretation of scripture," just as other forms of oppression are or have been.

The second excerpt emphasizes historical variation in biblical interpretation, specifically citing slavery as an example of men claiming biblical authority to oppress others and then later recognizing their mistake. Eastman notes that the Bible had not changed, only its interpretation. The parallel drawn between resistance to slavery and the contemporary struggle of homosexuals is clear. Just as the church once used biblical misinterpretation to condone slavery, something very few churches would support today, it was now misusing the Bible to condemn homosexuals. The point is that the Bible, and therefore God, does not condemn homosexuals—people do. MCC thus asserts that while homosexual relationships are subject to the same biblical rules as heterosexual ones—no adultery, promiscuity, etc.—homosexuality in a loving, monogamous relationship is no sin.

Making this sort of claim carries weight only if it is supported by biblical examples. To give proof of their charge of misinterpretation, MCC systematically examines the biblical verses typically used to condemn homosexuality (e.g., Deuteronomy 23:17–18, Genesis 19:4–11, Judges 19, Leviticus 18:22–23, Leviticus 20:13–14, Romans 1:24–27, 1 Corinthians 6:9, and 1 Timothy 1:10) and illustrates how each verse has been misinterpreted. In some cases, MCC asserts that conservatives have simply misunderstood the verse. In others, MCC asserts that misinterpretation has resulted from either a mistranslation of key words in biblical passages from the original language or a failure to consider the verse in context with the rest of the Bible and/or the cultural understanding of the time. In what follows, I provide two examples to show how MCC typically refutes the belief that homosexuality is condemned in the Bible.

In the first example, found in the Old Testament story of Sodom and Gomorrah (Genesis 19), we see how MCC corrects, using a textual strategy that still relies on a literalist interpretation, what they believe is a misconception of this account. For those unfamiliar with the story, I'll briefly summarize it here. God plans to destroy the cities of Sodom and Gomorrah because of the wickedness of the people, but Abraham pleads for the lives of the righteous in these cities. So God sends two angels to Sodom to assess the situation. Lot, Abraham's nephew, meets them at the gate, persuades them to stay in his house, and makes them a meal. Soon, all of the men of Sodom surround Lot's house, demanding the visitors be brought out so that they "could have sex with them" (according to the New International Version) or "may know them" (according to the New Revised Standard Version). Lot begs them not to do such a wicked thing and offers his two virgin daughters instead. The men, however, persist in their attempt to do harm to the strangers, and the angels blind them. Lot and his family are sent away, and God destroys the cities. As the family flees, Lot's wife is turned into a pillar of salt for defying instructions and glancing back at the burning cities. Later, to continue their family line in the absence of other men, Lot's daughters make Lot drunk, have sex with him, and become pregnant.

According to MCC, the conservative interpretation of this passage, that God destroys the cities for the sin of homosexuality, is completely distorted. Instead, MCC proponents employ a literalist strategy to first note that God rendered judgment on the cities *before* the men of Sodom demand the strangers be handed over to them. Thus, the judgment could not be a result of the homosexual incident at Lot's house. Second, they argue that the sin of Sodom had nothing do to with sexuality. Any kind of gang rape, whether homosexual (of the strangers) or heterosexual (of Lot's daughters), would be sinful. Lot's incestuous sexual relations with his daughters would also be sinful. Yet, no later reference of this story in the Bible raises the issue of sexual sin, homosexual or heterosexual. The sin of Sodom, MCC asserts, is therefore injustice and inhospitality, or the failure to treat strangers fairly and with kindness (as Lot does and is thus saved from destruction). The emphasis in the story of Sodom, to MCC, is not sexual and certainly does not condemn adult, loving, monogamous homosexual relationships.

To illustrate how MCC deals with what they consider to be misinterpretations based on faulty biblical translations, we next examine a passage from the New Testament, 1 Corinthians 6:9, which reads: "Know ye not that the unrighteous shall not inherit the kingdom of God? Be not deceived: neither fornicators, nor idolaters, nor adulterers, nor effeminate, nor abusers of themselves with mankind" (King James Version). For many conservative Christians, the King James Bible is the authoritative translation, and they have no doubt that the "effeminate" and the "abusers of themselves with mankind" in this verse refer to homosexuals. That they are included in the list of the "unrighteous" marks homosexual behavior a sin and condemns the homosexual. MCC, however, asserts that these two Greek words in this verse have been incorrectly translated to refer to homosexuals. From MCC's perspective, the first word in question, *malakos,* which has been translated as "effeminate" or "soft," actually refers to someone who lacks moral control or discipline. The second word, *arsenokoitai,* has been translated as either "catamite," referring to boy prostitutes, or "sodomite," which, according to Scanzoni and Mollenkott, refers to an "obsessive corruptor of boys" (quoted in Piazza 1994, 48). MCC contends that this word only appears in this verse and in Timothy 1:10, and it is not one of the Greek words that usually described homosexual behavior. Using these distinctions, MCC then points to the translation of this verse in the New International Version as a more correct alternative, noting that it trades "male prostitutes" for "effeminate" and "homosexual offenders" for "abusers of themselves with mankind." From these aspects of (mis)translation, MCC suspects that the Bible condemns those immoral enough to engage in sexual relations with boys—not adult, loving, and monogamous homosexual relationships.

These two examples illustrate what MCC contends are the problems with existing interpretations of all the biblical passages commonly used to denounce homosexuality. Human bias against homosexuality has kept conservative (and some of mainline) Christianity from seeing what MCC claims is the truth of these passages—and thus the evidence that supports MCC's belief that homosexuals are not condemned in Scripture. Further, MCC finds the biblical accounts of same-sex relationships between Jonathan and David (In 1 Samuel and 2 Samuel) and Naomi and Ruth (In Ruth) supportive of homosexuality. While MCC does not assert that either same-sex pair necessarily engages in sexual activity, the committed love that each shares is seen as a model for same-sex relationships. MCC pastor Michael Piazza explained it this way: "Their [Jonathan and David's] story is clearly a covenant of love and models for the world that two people of the same gender can and do make loving covenants that they keep and that keep them" (1994, 66). Here, MCC makes a radical break with conservative religious tradition, perceiving that Scripture is not just neutral with regard to homosexuality (in that it does not condemn it), but is affirming, providing models of same-sex love and celebrating them as sacred. Within MCC, homosexuals do have a place in the Kingdom of God.

MCC's assertions that Scripture does not condemn homosexuality and that gays are included in God's plan are only part of the story, a part that makes most sense when it is considered in the larger context of the whole of MCC theology. The linchpin to this theology is Perry's "vision of grace" (Warner 1995, 87), or the idea, taken from Jesus's words and example, that the most important divine concept is to love God and other people unconditionally. This idea is most closely associated with Matthew 22: 34–40, in which Jesus was asked to specify the most important law. He responded: "'Love the Lord your God with all of your heart and with all of your soul and with all your mind.' This is the first and greatest commandment. And the second is like it. 'Love your neighbor as yourself.' All the Law and the Prophets hang on these two commandments" (New International Version). In addition to this explicit statement about the importance of love, MCC proponents point to Jesus's example to highlight how he enacted this love, reaching out to the weak, the injured, and the sinner. Jesus, according to MCC, did not just extend his love to a subset of worthy people; rather, his love was all-inclusive, and he was careful to attend to those who had been ostracized or hurt. This example is the overriding model for MCC and a cornerstone of their belief.

MCC does not simply give lip service to this belief, nor do they use it only to advance the cause of gay Christians. Certainly, the spiritual needs and rights of gay people are a central concern, but MCC also works hard to ensure inclusivity and justice for all people, an effort that, in some ways, aligns them with liberal Protestants and echoes liberation theology's goal of a just society in this world. For example, according to the MCC pamphlet *Metropolitan Community Churches Today,* MCC strives to put "faith into action by creating a global community of healing and reconciliation, and by confronting the injustices of homophobia, sexism, racism and poverty through Christian social action" (Cherry 1994). Further, as a denomination, MCC has a department for "People of Colors" designed to identify and advance the needs of racial/ethnic minorities as well as to support reconciliation with whites. Importantly, a subset of this department is a program called "White People Healing Racism," which promotes white awareness of and responsibility for racism, what whites do to perpetuate it, and what can be done to end it. Similarly, MCC is concerned with sexism and has adopted inclusive language guidelines for congregations, which, among other changes, has resulted in referring to God as a Parent—not a Father. The denomination believes that inclusive language is necessary to "promote justice, reconciliation and love, the agenda to which we Christians have been called" ("Why Inclusive Language?" 1995). In short, MCC is serious about inclusion and is working toward a just society.

While MCC's theology is thus rooted in conservative Protestant doctrine, it also obviously contains aspects more closely related to liberalism and characteristic of liberation theology. Within the denomination's emphasis on love, inclusion, and social justice, there is an implicit, and sometimes explicit, notion that those who judge and who work to exclude people from the Kingdom of Heaven do not conform to an image of Christ and are thus unworthy. In effect, this theology indicts the conservative Christian who condemns others. At the same time, MCC uses a literalist interpretation of the Bible to celebrate love and inclusion. In fact, proponents of MCC believe that it is only through their spiritual relationship with God that they can attain salvation, stand firm against injustices, and heal the scars of hatred. As we will see, there are striking similarities between this gay-affirming, "healing" theology and the theology of healing homosexuality that Exodus promotes.

Exodus International
Attempts to learn about the origins and founding of Exodus inevitably lead to the discovery of the sensationalized and

misleading story of Michael Bussee and Gary Cooper. In this version, widely circulated by gay rights advocates, Bussee and Cooper are the most famous co-founders of Exodus, notable primarily because they later denounced Exodus rather spectacularly. By this account, these two men were instrumental in organizing the first Exodus conference, later referred to as the Exodus Summit Conference, in Anaheim, California, in September of 1976. At the time, both men considered themselves to be ex-gays and worked together at EXIT, the EX-gay Intervention Team at Melodyland Hotline Center in Anaheim, counseling people struggling with homosexuality. They were both married; Bussee had one child, and Cooper had three children.

Yet, approximately only three years later, in spite of their attempts to develop heterosexual attractions, the two fell in love. In the documentary *One Nation under God* (1993), Bussee and Cooper explain that they finally professed this love to one another on a plane to Indianapolis, where they were scheduled to address the United Church of Christ General Senate regarding homosexual change. After pronouncing their mutual love, they rewrote their speeches to advocate the church's unconditional love and acceptance of homosexuals. Their revised speeches drew surprised applause from gay protesters at the back of the room and withering looks from everyone else. In time, they divorced their wives and, in 1982, participated in a commitment ceremony, exchanging vows and rings. Their relationship (marriage) ended in 1991 only when Cooper died from AIDS.

After leaving Exodus, the couple drew on their personal and counseling experiences to declare, in multiple interviews and media appearances, that ex-gay ministries are fraudulent and dangerous. In a telephone interview with Kurd Wolfe of the Gay Broadcasting System, for example, Bussee spoke of his counseling experience with hundreds of people: "I had no success with them....[N]ot one person said, 'Yes, I am actually now heterosexual.'...There may very well be out there people that I talked to who are dead now because they committed suicide because of the guilt I inadvertently heaped on them" (O'Neill 1990). In *One Nation under God* (1993), Bussee and Cooper tell a horrifying story of a man who repeatedly slashed his genitals with a razor and poured Drano on the wounds because he could not change his homosexual feelings. These stories are haunting and memorable, and it is easy to see how Bussee and Cooper became central figures in existing cultural misconceptions of Exodus's founding.

While this dramatic account of Exodus's founding certainly contains much truth—Bussee and Cooper were involved in the founding, they did fall in love and leave, and they did renounce ex-gay ministries—it also leaves out critical details that alter our perspective of the relevance of the Bussee-Cooper defection from and condemnation of Exodus. To begin to fill in these details, we must first recognize that Bussee and Cooper neither invented ex-gay ministries nor were alone at the First Summit Conference. Instead, Bussee's greatest contribution to the formation of Exodus was his role in facilitating the first conference. In 1976, he was one of the leaders of the EXIT Hotline from Melodyland Christian Center. Prompted by a rapidly increasing number of calls, Bussee and others contacted multiple independent ex-gay ministries and decided to gather the leaders together for a weekend conference. So Bussee was instrumental in initiating the first Exodus meeting. Cooper's role, however, was much smaller. As a ministry volunteer, he helped with the logistics of the conference. While both men thus contributed, to a greater or lesser extent, to the founding of Exodus, they were only a part of the story.

The rest of the story involves the approximately fifty to sixty ex-gay ministry delegates (reported numbers of delegates vary) who attended this conference. It is important to note that some of these original delegates, like Frank Worthen (founder of Love In Action) and Ron Dennis (Transforming Congregations), remain ex-gay and have continued to play an integral role in Exodus and related ministries. Their success in the ex-gay movement reveals the commitment and dedication of the founders of Exodus and should not be overlooked or overshadowed by the Bussee-Cooper story. This original group, composed predominately of male ministry leaders from conservative Protestant denominations, discussed their ministries and their shared visions of homosexuality. For the first time, ministry leaders, who often felt unsupported by the larger Christian community, could share their experiences and encourage one another. They decided to form an organization of ex-gay ministries, called Exodus, devoted to Christian outreach to gays and lesbians. They also created a unifying statement of intent: "EXODUS is an international Christian effort to reach homosexuals and lesbians. EXODUS upholds God's standard of righteousness and holiness, which declares that homosexuality is a sin and affirms His love and redemptive power to recreate the individual. It is the goal of EXODUS International to communicate this message to the Church, to the gay community, and to society" (Davies 1996, 2). Further, the delegates agreed to hold annual conferences so that they could continue to come together to advance their ministries and their message. In sum, this group laid the groundwork for an international organization that would evolve into a conservative Christian authority on homosexual issues, providing information and help to an estimated 250,000 people worldwide (personal e-mail from Bob Davies, executive director of Exodus, 2001a) by 2001. By 2002, Exodus had established about 150 ministries in seventeen countries (Chambers 2002). Because of its promise of anonymity, the exact number of members is unknown.

From its initiation to the present, Exodus has been firmly grounded in a theologically conservative, evangelical Protestant tradition. Like MCC, Exodus upholds a belief in one triune God, in the redemptive power of Christ as the only route to salvation, in the Bible as the inspired Word of God, in the Holy Spirit as an indwelled guide, and in the importance of rebirth and saving souls. In contrast to MCC, however, it has also consistently reiterated conservative Christian arguments against homosexuality; homosexuality is clearly condemned in the Bible as a sin that defies God's will (as illustrated by the destruction of the biblical city of Sodom), and homosexuals are perceived to be among the unrighteous, listed in 1 Corinthians 6:9, who "shall not inherit the kingdom of God[.] Be not deceived" (King James Version). The general consensus of Exodus leaders, according to Bob Davies, a past executive director of Exodus, is that "the homosexual orientation is an expression of humanity's sinfulness—and cannot comfortably coexist within the context of a total commitment to Jesus Christ" (1996, 4). Exodus does, however, assert that homosexuality is ordinary sin, no worse than any other, and that Christian response to homosexuals has been wrong. The church should work to help homosexuals, not cast them out.

Exodus's focus, then, is on how Christians can aid homosexuals, namely, by helping them heal their homosexuality. This emphasis on healing is, perhaps, related to when Exodus emerged as an organization. Prior to the 1980s, the charismatic movement had shifted the emphasis of evangelicalism toward "the experiential aspects of Christianity, a sense of closeness to Jesus through the Spirit dwelling within, and toward its therapeutic aspects," as reflected in the upsurge of prominent televangelists (e.g., Oral Roberts, Jimmy Bakker, Pat Robertson, etc.) who promised healing through Christ (Marsden 1991, 78–79). Exodus's theology of healing shares this emphasis. The core Exodus belief is that, through a close and right relationship with God, homosexuals can experience God's redemptive love and healing, freeing individuals from homosexuality and allowing them to reassume their true heterosexual identities. It is this idea—that individuals can be freed from slavery to their sexual sins—that is captured in the organization's name.

At first glance, it might appear that Exodus is simply repeating a conservative Christian position on homosexuality; homosexuality is a sin, so those who experience homosexual desire should pray earnestly and God will take away such desire—a strategy that countless gay Christians have tried. In a very loose and general way, this statement does sum up Exodus's approach to healing homosexuality, but there is much more to Exodus's healing process than wanting/praying for homosexual desire to dissipate. According to Exodus, individuals must both come to understand the roots of their homosexuality and establish a proper relationship with God if they are to be healed. The following sections outline Exodus's explanations for homosexuality and describe this proper relationship.

Root Causes of Homosexuality

Exodus does not believe that homosexuality is innate or consciously chosen. Instead, Exodus traces homosexuality, like all sin, to the fallen state (e.g., the fall in the Garden of Eden) of people and their correspondent sinful natures. Homosexuality, itself a sin, thus results from other sins—the individual's sins and/or sins committed against that person. But which sins and how do they manifest as homosexuality? To help answer such questions, ex-gay leaders adapted aspects of psychoanalytic theories of development, which they saw as consistent with biblical teachings, to homosexuality. From this perspective, homosexuality is seen as the result of particular kinds of breakdowns or disruptions of important relationships (especially parent-child) at critical developmental junctures, or can be associated with molestation or other forms of sexual abuse. The psychological trauma of this disruption or abuse impedes normal development and thus can create varied disorders, including homosexuality.

For this reason, leaders of the ex-gay movement and authors who endorse and explain an ex-gay perspective usually refer to homosexuality as the result of psychological, emotional, and spiritual brokenness, labeling it, for example, a "homosexual neurosis" (Payne 1981), a "cannibal compulsion" (Payne 1985), a "sexual identity confusion" (Foster 1995a, 1995b), and a "symbolic confusion" (Bergner 1995). The brokenness described by all of these neuroses, compulsions, and confusions is, regardless of the circumstances out of which it emerges, characterized by the sexualization of unmet emotional or psychological needs.

In the most common scenario, a child does not achieve an emotional bond with a same-sex parent. This failure to bond can happen for any number of reasons—divorce, sexual or physical abuse, or even parental emotional detachment—and, according to Davies and Rentzel, results in a "separation anxiety" or an "overwhelming drive to connect with and find their identity in another person" (1993, 45). The child then unconsciously searches for this connection among same-sex peers as he grows up, seeking in other relationships what he missed from his parents. However, without a close bond with a proper gender role model, the child can engage in inappropriate behaviors (i.e., become "tomboys" or "sissies") that result in teasing and isolation from same-sex peers, making the child feel as if he/she does not "belong" with this group. This lack of same-sex friendships further erodes gender identity and intensifies gender insecurities.

Exodus contends that these kinds of insecurities in a gender identity can coalesce at puberty. During pubescence, these emotional needs become confused with burgeoning sexuality, giving rise to homosexual attractions and feelings. In other words, during puberty, a boy misinterprets his emotional need for male bonding as sexual attraction. The following excerpt from an ex-gay ministry study guide, *Sexual Healing,* explains the most typical scenario for the development of homosexuality:

> A homosexual inclination [develops when] the child has a distant and cold parent of the same sex, and no other significant same sex figure to take the place of this parent in the emotional bonding process that must take place in the life of every child, somewhere between the ages of 3–10. The child fails to receive an *emotional* (not sexual) bonding—the emotional assurance that he or she is a full and acceptable member of his or her own gender. A concomitant result is that they also miss the modeling of same sex behavior that accompanies such a bonding process.
>
> Their inability to replicate proper traits and behavior of their own gender often results in ridicule and rejection by the prime models of sexuality in their peer group, which results

in a further sense of alienation from the idealized state of masculinity or femininity. Those who have been deprived of emotional gender-bonding sometimes become obsessed with discovering proper sex-identified behavior for themselves and begin a lifelong, "secret" examination of idealized models of their own gender. Soon, they find themselves staring at these "idols" for no apparent reason—always subconsciously looking for that magic key in other "successful" peers that will show them what to do to become similarly acceptable.

At about the same time, puberty takes hold, and this examination begins to zero in on the physical evidences of sexuality that have begun to display themselves in the school locker room, or on TV, or in movies they watch. This is where pornography can be particularly damaging. In the unconscious search to find points of identity and modeling, they'll find themselves looking at members of their own gender in the movie sex scenes, or locker room, more so than the opposite sex—a behavior that will convince them all the more that they must be homosexual.

In these ways and others, their basic "emotional" needs have become sexualized, and they naturally begin to confuse the emotional pull that they feel toward members of their own sex with their emerging sexual drive. (Foster 1995a, 62)

In short, Foster argues that same-sex emotional bonding is the key to being affirmed in a gender identity and to developing/learning appropriate gender behavior. In the absence of a proper role model, gender is not correctly constructed, and a weak gender identity results in not acquiring proper gendered behaviors, including those related to sexuality.

In addition to the "typical" scenario presented above, Exodus posits that several other experiences could also contribute to the development of homosexual inclinations:

- Sexual molestation, incest or rape by opposite sex—victim develops a hatred for the opposite sex and/or associates heterosexuality with shame and violation. Homosexual attractions can result.
- Sexual molestation, incest or rape by the same sex—victim becomes "scrambled" and believes they are "meant" for same sex satisfaction.
- Masturbation at a young age (especially with a mirror) or expo-

sure to homosexual pornography—child learns to associate same sex organs with sexual desire.

- "Opinion of Society"—"Fleshly excesses" lead people to be curious about and try homosexual sex.
- Overbearing authority figure of the opposite sex—ridicule child's gender while endorsing behaviors of their own. (Foster 1995a, 63–64)

In each case, homosexuality is said to stem from some emotional or psychological trauma that "twists" the appropriate sexual feelings and behaviors that should have emerged naturally from a proper gendered identity. Such twisting or distortion is held to be a consequence of some form of sin, committed by important others, against the child. In this sense, ex-gay proponents perceive that homosexuality is rooted in human defiance of God's laws, though not, as mainstream conservatives often contend, through the conscious choices of homosexual individuals to live a sinful lifestyle.

The Process of Healing Homosexuality

If homosexuality is, at the most basic level, created by sins or living outside of God's will, then the cure is found by learning to live in accord with God's laws and developing a proper spiritual relationship with God. All healing, Exodus asserts, must be done through God. While there are accounts of instantaneous healing, Exodus cautions that healing is usually a long process that spans several years and takes place in incremental steps as the individual matures in his/her relationship with God. The overarching goal of this healing process is not termination of homosexual behavior, heterosexual marriage, or even changes in sexual thoughts or desires; rather, these are "side effects" of the larger goal of becoming more closely "conformed to the image of Jesus Christ" (Davies 2001b, 14–17). Although each individual's healing process is supposedly unique, it is still largely a process of conforming to this image.

Exodus offers no checklist of sequential steps to be taken to be healed of homosexuality, nor does it suggest that every individual will achieve the same level of healing. Instead, they assert that the healing process is composed of several common elements that bring one into right relationship with God. In the words of ex-gay ministry leader David Foster, "The beginning and the end of everything that we need to do [to be healed] can be summed up as: 'the pursuit of a relationship with the God who saved us and who heals us and who has a future for us'" (1995a, 9). To pursue this relationship, the individual must first develop the spiritual conviction that homosexuality is against God's will. Then, the individual must be convinced that God can heal and become willing to do whatever it takes to follow God's Word and become more Christ-like. Further, the individual must recognize that God has all the power and authority and that they cannot heal themselves with their own strength. What makes this step so difficult and important, according to Exodus, is that it requires the individual to truly and unconditionally surrender himself/herself to God, trusting in and living from God's grace.

Grace, as a Christian concept, refers to God's unconditional love for humankind. It cannot be earned or lost through one's actions but rather is freely extended and constant. Learning to accept and trust in God's grace and love is seen as an act of considerable commitment, one that Exodus says is essential to enabling God to begin healing the brokenness of the homosexual. In other words, Exodus asserts that it is only when the homosexual submits to God entirely that the healing process can begin. A gay Christian who attempts healing in an Exodus ministry will be required to undertake many difficult steps toward healing, including unveiling his/her struggle to others, breaking off personal relationships associated with homosexuality (e.g., gay lovers, friends), and resisting or coping with powerful attractions and emotions. Exodus believes that it is only through submission to God that a person can confess his/her struggle, persevere in the face of pain and temptation, and be patient as healing progresses. All this is possible, according to Exodus, because submission enables the person to trust in God to give them the strength to do so. For Exodus, it is God's power that allows the homosexual to resist temptation, and it is God's healing touch that mends psychological damage.

To further build this proper spiritual relationship with God, Exodus cultivates an image of God as the ideal father. In this image, God is presented as a completely trustworthy caretaker who unconditionally loves and protects his children, allowing them to struggle only because of what it can teach them. An analogy presented in the video version of an ex-gay ministry manual, Sexual Healing, helps to clarify the image of God that Exodus promotes: "God's grace is like a father trying to teach his son to ride a new bike. The father pays a lot of money for the bike. When the boy gets on, he wobbles and falls down, scraping himself up and denting the bike. An ungodly father would condemn the boy for wrecking the bike he paid so much money for. But a godly father, or God the Father, comes over and kisses the boy's wounds, puts him back on the bike and teaches him how to ride it" (Foster 1995b). In this analogy, it is evident that God as Father allows his children to be wounded as a consequence of sinful actions so that they can engage in better behavior. However, God is also the key agent in healing and learning from those wounds. In addition, Exodus suggests that God sometimes allows injury to bring his children closer to him. Bob Davies explains, "Like a good father, God chastises his children, disciplining us so that we will return to him, so that we can experience his love" (2001b, 47). This image of God as Father thus modeled the proper relationship of a child's unconditional trust in and submission to an all-powerful but loving Father who can and will fix any problem or hurt, demanding in return only love and obedience.

Given that Exodus roots homosexuality in failed parent-child relationships and the absence of proper gender role models, this image of God the Father is thought to be especially important in the healing process. When Exodus's participants establish the appropriate relationship with God as Father, God takes over the parental role—what Davies (2001b, 58) refers to as "reparenting"—healing the psychological and emotional brokenness caused by distorted relationships and enabling normal development. Further, God is the ideal gender role model who can restore a secure sense of gender identity. This is not to say that those who attempt healing simply sit around and wait for God to do the work. They must study the Bible, earnestly pray, listen for God's guidance, and follow it. Exodus also prescribes the development of healthy same-sex friendships and a Christian support network.

Whether there is variation in belief and practice across Exodus ministries simply is not known at present because there are so few studies examining these groups that comparisons cannot be made. A review of affiliated ministry Web sites and literature, however, suggests great similarity and a shared emphasis on the relationship with God as the foundation for healing. For Exodus ministries, only God can truly meet emotional needs, heal brokenness, and mend the psyche and spirit.

———

Despite MCC's and Exodus's radically different convictions regarding the religious meaning of homosexuality, the groups share many fundamental conceptions. Both groups share a theologically conservative foundation and perceive that the problems that homosexuals face originate in human failure to live by God's laws (sins); though for MCC this failure refers to the structural oppression that arises from the human propensity to exclude and condemn, while for Exodus it refers to an individual's failing to enact the proper human relationships. Both groups share an image of God as a heavenly Father (Exodus) or Parent (MCC) who unconditionally loves his (her) children, and both believe that their purpose is to allow for healing, via God's strength. Finally, both groups advocate a similar resolution to these problems— establish a proper relationship with God and live in accord with divine laws, always conforming more closely to the image of Jesus Christ. "The image of Christ" varies, however, from the MCC version of *unconditionally loving and accepting* to the Exodus version of *helper on the path to obedience and righteousness.* In sum, the groups share a basic problem-solution model.

Yet, even while the groups share the same religious foundations and the same general problem (sin) and solution (be like Christ) model, they have found little room for compromise or common ground. In fact, each seems to regard the other with great animosity—seeing them as a primary antagonist—perhaps precisely because of their religious similarities. Challenges from those most like you can be the most threatening because such challenges tend to come from within a shared worldview and can thus destabilize a valued way of seeing and making sense of the world and the self. Some of this hostility might also have emerged because the groups are competing for members. Given that these groups are designed to minister to the same population, they must, to some extent, define themselves in opposition to the other to gain adherents. Comprehending how these groups appeal to and aid a common population, in spite of such opposing resolutions, first requires an examination of this population and of their struggle with faith and homosexuality prior to joining a group. Developing an understanding of how this struggle emerges, what kinds of implications it has in individuals' lives, and why individuals choose to stay in a faith that condemns them will help to illuminate the role of the groups in providing solutions to individual struggles. It is these issues to which we turn next.

3 | The Dilemmas of Christian Men Who Desire Men

One summer evening, after an Accept Bible study meeting, Chris and I stood in an apartment parking lot talking about childhood memories of the summer. At one point, he paused and then said, "You know, every once in a while it is still a little weird and scary to say the words 'I am gay.' I'm okay with it now, even glad, but still." When I asked him why those words had been, and still could be, so difficult, he explained:

> I did not want to be gay. It certainly wasn't the plan. I didn't know a single gay person growing up. All I knew was that kids at school called other kids "faggots" if they seemed at all wimpy or different. It wasn't a good thing to be. Mostly, I wanted a good relationship with God, to be a good Christian, and to lead a Christian life and have a wife and kids. I thought being gay would end all that, so I stayed in denial about my sexuality for a pretty long time and tried to push all those feelings away. Finally, I had to admit it; I had to say the words 'I am gay.' But I was also a Christian, and that is so important to me. They didn't go together. It was like—great, now what do I do? Show me Lord.

Chris's memories are poignant and recall a litany of powerful emotions surrounding the recognition of his homosexuality: fear, anxiety, trepidation, confusion, and helplessness. That his faith, which was "so important" in his life, "didn't go together" with the homosexuality he could no longer deny put Chris in an untenable situation, one in which he held two contradictory identities. This contradiction, once noted and felt, initiated an intense struggle to reconcile the mismatch between these identities. This struggle was shared by all the men in this study. Like Chris, they found the initial realization that they were gay and the resulting conflict between their Christian beliefs and sexuality to be incredibly difficult—cognitively and emotionally. These difficulties, as we will see, reveal the kind of dilemma the men faced and illustrate its gravity and complexity.

Chris's explanation of why it was so hard to name his sexuality (and to label himself) also reflects three common characteristics of the struggle that the men in this study endured to resolve the conflict between their faith and homosexuality. First, this struggle emerged from a process in which the men came to recognize that their homosexual desires were more than a passing phase and that they were gay. Second, all of the men initially had the sense that homosexuality was bad, so bad, in fact, that being gay would adversely impact their entire lives. This negative perception was rooted in the stigma imposed by a heterosexist dominant culture and by conservative Christian prohibitions against homosexuality. Finally, each man wanted, first and foremost, to be a good Christian and echoed this gay Christian's sentiment: "I am a Christian first. Everything else I am or do must be guided by that fact." Yet, each found sexual desire an incredibly powerful impulse, one not easily ignored or diminished. As a result, they felt they could not control the sexual desires that collided with their Christian beliefs, making being a good Christian a seemingly impossible task.

The struggle to accomplish this task began well before the men joined either Accept or Expell. In some cases, they wrestled with their sexuality for only a year or two before they found a group. For others, the struggle was already decades old. Regardless of differences in duration of the struggle, each man's struggle began through a gradual realization of his homosexuality, which sparked fear, anxiety, and shame. This realization led each man to the same dilemma: How can I possibly be a good Christian when I desire to have sex with men? To define this dilemma clearly and to understand why it was so important to the men, we must examine its cultural and religious underpinnings as well as how it emerged in the men's lives. This chapter explores the dynamics of this dilemma, focusing on the social conditions and interactions that helped to shape it.

Cultural and Religious Origins

Stereotypes of gay men fluctuate from feminine or "sissified" images of men with limp wrists, a swishing walk, high-pitched voices, and an impeccable sense of fashion and design to "hyper-masculine" images of muscle-bound men dressed in leather, boots, and studs or other overtly masculine apparel. These images emanate from the common cultural conception that gender and sexuality are inextricably linked and the concordant assumption "that gay men and lesbians are gender *non*conformists—lesbians are 'masculine' women; gay men are 'feminine' men" (Kimmel 2000, 253). Clearly, the exaggerated femininity represented in the first stereotyped image reflects this assumption, while the embellished masculinity in the latter image can be seen as a reaction against it. The flip side of this assumption, of course, is that heterosexuals are appropriately gendered. This association between gender and sexuality has profound implications in our society, though the focus here is on gay men.

In our culture, masculinity has been linked to highly valued characteristics—rationality, strength, competitiveness, and aggression—that are thought necessary for success in the public sphere, while femininity has been linked with less valuable traits like emotionality, nurturing, and cooperation. These distinctions undergird the power and advantages men have over women, and, as Lorber points out, "men have justified the privileges of these gender-segregated social worlds by their masculinity" (1994, 62). Being able to claim a masculine identity, then, is to be able to tap into an important resource, though not all masculine identities are equally powerful. Social scientific research has shown, for example, that men who are racial minorities or who are poor are marginalized and do not share the same level of privilege as upper- or middle-class white men (Connell 1995; Nonn 2001). Scholars further agree that one of the key signifiers of hegemonic, or the ideal, most dominant form of, masculinity is heterosexual desire and prowess (Connell 1987, 1992, 1995; Segal 1990, 1994; Lorber 1994; Fracher and Kimmel 1989). Not only do gay men obviously lack the ability to credibly signify masculinity this way, but homosexuality is also positioned "at the bottom of a gender hierarchy among men . . . [as] the repository of whatever is symbolically expelled from hegemonic masculinity . . . [and] is easily assimilated to femininity" (Connell 1995, 78). Male homosexuality is thus marginalized through its socially constructed link to femininity, and gay men (at least those who are openly gay) are stigmatized as inferior and denied access to the power and privilege of straight men.

In addition to having to cope with a stigmatized sexual identity, gay people must also endure a society in which heterosexuality is normative and embedded in institutions and practices (Phelan 2001; Jakobsen and Pellegrini 2003). Our idealized traditional family structure and our gendered division of labor are organized around heterosexual relationships (Lorber 1994; Coltrane 1997). Legal rights surrounding marriage, families, and health care are structured to protect and serve heterosexuals. Tax policies, insurance policies/benefits, and retirement benefits also privilege heterosexuals. Homosexuals can face employment and housing discrimination or be overtly excluded from participation in specific groups or professions (e.g., the Boy Scouts and the military). Certainly, gay people experience harassment, verbal abuse, and physical violence (Franklin 1998). Our culture and the structure of its institutions thus not only reflect a presumption that everyone is (or should be) heterosexual, but also provide heterosexuals with rights, protections, and advantages not offered to homosexuals. Given the stigma of a gay identity and the loss of power and privilege, being gay in our culture surely makes life a lot harder. A gay man has to reconcile his differences from hegemonic masculinity, forfeit the protections and privileges of heterosexuality, and risk discrimination and potential physical danger.

Christian men who experience homosexual desire not only must cope with these difficulties, but also must come to terms with their sexuality in the context of their faith. Conservative Christian doctrine simultaneously emphasizes the importance of heterosexual marriage to God's mandated earthly order and labels homosexuality a sin, making homosexuality extremely threatening to believers. From this perspective, homosexuality defies God's order, and the homosexual can be perceived as a condemned sinner. For those affiliated with conservative denominations, like the men in this study, this conflict can be far more complex and troubling than any secular one because it has implications for eternal salvation.

Within conservative Christian belief, marriage is a key institution for structuring human society and relationships in a godly way. God is thought to have established marriage in Genesis 2 as a primary institution and the foundation of society. Conservative Christian author Jay Adams explains the importance of marriage this way: "God designed marriage as the foundational element of all human society. . . . Society itself in all its forms depends on marriage. . . . Marriage is also the foundation upon which the church as God's special society rests. This covenantal community is weakened as the 'house' or 'household' is weakened" (1980, 4–5). Instituted by God, marriage reflects the proper (e.g., divinely mandated) societal order and is thus perceived to be critical to the well-being of the church and society. Anything that threatens marriage can, as Adams asserts, be seen as an "attack upon God's order" (1980, 5).

Marriage, according to conservative Christian doctrine, is also decidedly heterosexual. For most conservative Christians, the creation story in Genesis (particularly Genesis 2:18–24) clearly indicates that God created men and women and intended for them to be joined together as "one flesh"—physically, emotionally, and spirituality—in marriage. Conservative commentators, as Bartkowski points out, assert that "men and women were not only created to be different from one another, but were designed by God to complement one another" (2001, 48). Through marriage, men and women are perceived to be completed, with the masculine qualities of "protecting, initiating, governing" merging with the feminine traits of "nurturing, responding, feeling" (Foster 1995a, 37–38). This merger makes each individual a richer, more complete person and fills what Adams refers to as the "loneliness," or unfulfilled gap, of "mere masculinity or femininity" (1980, 16). Clearly, conservative Christians view marriage not only as an institution of great importance but also as one God designed to complete individual persons through the merging of the masculine and feminine. Participating in marriage, then, is central to becoming a whole person and to complying with God's mandated societal order. The only acceptable deviations from this order are those who give their lives to God and remain celibate.

These beliefs, in conjunction with the command in Genesis 1:28 to "be fruitful and increase in number" (New International Version), sharply establish heterosexual marriage and family life as God's divine plan. These links and their importance are evident in the National Association of Evangelicals' "Christian Declaration on Marriage":

> We believe that marriage is a holy union of one man and one woman in which they commit, with God's help, to build a

> loving, life-giving, faithful relationship that will last for a life-time. God has established the married state, in the order of creation and redemption, for spouses to grow in love of one another and for the procreation, nurture, formation, and education of children. . . . Motivated by our common desire that God's Kingdom be manifested on earth as it is in heaven, we pledge to deepen our commitment to marriage. . . . By our commitment to marriage as instituted by God, the nature of His Kingdom will be more clearly revealed in our homes, our churches, and our culture. (National Association of Evangelicals)

The association between heterosexual marriage and participation in and commitment to God's order obviously poses tremendous difficulties for believers who are gay and perceive homosexuality to be outside the boundaries of God's mandated order. The disjuncture between what they believe is God's will for their lives and their lived bodily experience of sexual desire can be stark and frightening. To be good Christians, and to fully participate in Christian life and community, they should act in accord with divine dictates, but these actions would require the immensely trying task of changing or ignoring their sexuality (or choosing to remain celibate). Failing to do so, however, is to risk defying God.

This sense of being or acting outside of God's will is heightened substantially by conservative Christian interpretations of several biblical passages (such as the story of Sodom and Gomorrah, Genesis 19:4–11; Leviticus 18:22–23; 20:13–14; 1 Corinthians 6:9; Deuteronomy 23:17–18) that explicitly mark homosexuality as sinful and condemn the homosexual. Such interpretations underscore the incompatibility between "homosexual" and "Christian." These passages, in conjunction with belief in the spiritual importance of marriage and procreation, create a partial definition of a "good Christian man," one that requires heterosexuality, marriage, and children. Homosexuality, within this religious tradition, is seen as a threat to God's order and a sin, something good Christians reject. As believers, the men in this study, at least initially, felt homosexuality endangered their well-being, both in this life and the next. For these men, many important aspects of their lives, such as their sense of themselves as men and their spiritual success, hung on their ability to live heterosexual lives. The problem, the dilemma they faced, was that they were gay—in spite of the intensity of their desire to be straight.

The Development of a Dilemma

Given the above cultural and theological conceptions of homosexuality, it is easy to see why men, particularly those ensconced within a conservative Christian religious tradition, would have a hard time thinking of themselves as homosexual. From their perspective, Christianity and homosexuality were incompatible, and the men were stuck in the untenable position of cherishing their faith above all else and experiencing sexual desires that contradicted that faith. Because they placed such a high value on their faith, the men could not resolve their situation by abandoning it. Doing so was simply out of the question. For them, being able to claim a Christian identity meant being able to claim to be the kind of person they wanted to be—compassionate, righteous, virtuous, and saved. This identity helped them make sense of the world and themselves—what was right and wrong, who was worthy and unworthy, and how it all fit together. Most importantly, being a good Christian provided a sense of security; if the men were "right with God," then they need not fear for the future and their salvation. They perceived this struggle, at its core, to be about their souls. For these reasons, their Christian identities were too valuable to be cast off. As a result, the men found themselves stuck in a dilemma that felt enormously consequential. Explaining this dilemma fully requires an examination of what constitutes and characterizes such a dilemma as well as an exploration of how it emerged in the men's lives.

The problem, of course, began when the men's sexual desires made it impossible for them to follow the set of rules, or "identity codes," for acting like a good Christian (Schwalbe and Mason-Schrock 1996). Put plainly, identity codes prescribe the kinds of behaviors that will allow us to be seen, by others and ourselves, as a certain kind of person. A mother, for example, is supposed to love, nurture, and teach her children. Claiming the identity "mother" can then indicate that you are a loving, caring, and responsible person—but you have to do it right to be a fully creditable mother. While having a child may make you a biological mother, it is only by following the identity codes for mother—caring for the child's bodily and emotional needs—that you can be seen as a good mother and claim the specific virtues associated with motherhood. In the same way, these men wanted to claim the virtues tied to a Christian identity by living up to the identity code for being a good Christian—including heterosexuality, marriage and children—but could not do so in the face of their pressing homosexual desires. As a result, they did not feel like good Christians.

This is to not to say that every violation of an identity code disqualifies you from claiming a desired identity. People often violate the code. Sometimes, violations are small, relatively isolated incidents that can be ignored. For example, a mother might refuse to help with homework one night because she is too tired. As long as her refusal to help is not habitual, this one violation is no threat to her identity as a good mother. Sometimes, though, violations are more severe, and we have to do repair work. A mother might, for example, lose her temper over something silly and yell at her child. Good mothers do not hurt their children, and she will have to apologize and explain herself to get things back on the right track. At other times, however, such violations are so important and persistent that they must be corrected or we may be disqualified as a certain kind of person. The men in this study experienced the latter type of violation. For them, the discrepancy between who they claimed to be (Christian) and what they actually felt/did (homosexuality), over time, led to a chronic sense of inauthenticity—a sense of faking being a good Christian. This sense of inauthenticity is a consequence of what I am calling an identity dilemma. To understand the men's struggle precisely, we must draw distinctions between two kinds of identity dilemmas—performative and ideological.

Performative dilemmas arise when the codes for two or more identities demand actions that are simply hard to pull off, usually because they require more time, energy, skill, or other resources than an individual possesses. It might be nearly impossible, for example, to be both a full-time professor and an Olympic athlete, in light of the practical demands of enacting both identities in a convincing way. These kinds of dilemmas would seem to be fairly common. Though perhaps never easy to resolve, these kinds of identity dilemmas are readily escapable, at least in principle, by scaling back one's ambitions.

Ideological identity dilemmas constitute a deeper trap. These dilemmas arise when two different identity codes are not merely tough to live up to, but antithetical. One code, in other words, prohibits behaviors that are mandated by the other. The code for enacting the identity "Christian" is typically seen, in conservative churches, as prohibiting gay sex. To practice gay sex is thus to discredit one's self as a Christian by violating a key part of the identity code. Again, however, the dilemma arises not merely because of what any single identity code prescribes or prohibits. A Christian troubled by gay desire, or feeling ashamed for having gay sex, could, after all, seek relief by choosing permanent celibacy and/or atheism. The dilemma arises because of the preeminent desire to retain the identity "Christian" while also believing that sexual desire either cannot or should not be extinguished.

Ideological identity dilemmas are less common because people do not usually try to ground their identities in mutually exclusive ideological frameworks. If this happens, the contradiction is likely to be discovered post hoc, after commitment—by chance or choice—to one framework. Christians with same-sex desires do not commit themselves to "being gay" and then find a church in which they can feel miserable. They are committed to Christianity, often from childhood, as a matter of historical accident. The dilemma arises later, after a sexual awakening brings them into conflict with church teaching.

The men's identity dilemmas were not abrupt realizations. They did not experience a few episodes of homosexual desire and then worry about being bad Christians. Instead, their identity dilemmas formed over time as their homosexual desires persisted, forcing the men to recognize these desires as part of themselves. In other words, what the men felt and did had to consistently violate the identity code for good Christian before they began to feel inauthentic as Christians. The men's identity dilemmas emerged in a typical pattern, having distinct phases, in which the men gradually recognized their homosexuality as a permanent part of themselves. This gradual recognition resulted from what sociologist Andrew Yip calls "becoming," or the "continuous process through which one acquires an identity" (1997, 114). For these men, this process of becoming created both an awareness of their homosexual identities and a correspondent growing sense of themselves as inauthentic Christians. Once fully cognizant of their sexuality, the men became impostors, faking a straight identity and feeling like frauds. At this point, they experienced a full-fledged ideological identity dilemma.

Becoming

Men in both groups described periods in their lives when they felt homosexual desire, and sometimes engaged in sexual activities with men, without feeling inauthentic as Christians. These episodes occurred before the men labeled themselves as gay, and, in retrospect, the men saw them as having occurred during "periods of denial." During this time, the men engaged in homosexual activities secretly and disregarded these actions as meaningful. Instead, they participated in highly visible, customary heterosexual activities, like dating women, to indicate their heterosexuality. Because their heterosexual performances were public and visible, while their homosexual activities were kept hidden, the men could, at least for a time, conceive of themselves as straight, in spite of contrary desires and behaviors.

For example, during an interview with Ben, an ex-gay Christian, he told me his "struggle with homosexuality" began in 1986. When I asked him what was happening in his life prior to 1986, the interview continued as follows:

> *Ben:* I lived my life in a fantasy world, basically. I did my job and came home and paid bills and ate and slept. I lived my life with the people in my mind. I didn't really have friends. I was raised on farms. Four brothers and sisters, but I didn't have much contact with other people. In high school, I was president of my senior class, so I guess I was popular but I didn't really have any intimate friends. The exciting part about living in my mind was that I could think about sexual stuff almost always. Homosexual. I lived my sexual life in my mind.
>
> *Michelle Wolkomir:* Did you ever label or classify it as . . . ?
>
> *Ben:* What do you mean by classifying it? Like calling it a sin?
>
> *Michelle Wolkomir:* No. Did you ever say "I'm gay" or "I'm a homosexual"?
>
> *Ben:* I wouldn't admit it, no, but I knew I had that desire.

Ben further described this period of time as "a state of deception," in which he dated a few women but did not have a regular girlfriend. By dating, Ben put on a credible heterosexual performance, one that allowed him to take his homosexual fantasy life less seriously, at least for a little while. Similarly, Jared, a gay Christian man, remembered denying his desires for other men. When he described his sexual feelings in high school, he said: "I always thought it was really neat to get the really raunchy dirty magazines, you know, like *Hustler,* because not only did they have the picture of the women I was supposed to be masturbating to, but it had the guys in there too. And I found myself paying more attention to the guys than I did the women. But I really did not accept that; I was like, 'Oh, it's a sexual act thing, you know; yeah, that's it.'" With regard to his high school and first two years in college, Jared said, "I was thinking I was straight. I mean, I was still dating Lisa." Like the person who sees herself as honest, even when she tells a few lies, these men were able to see themselves as heterosexual men who occasionally desired, and sometimes had sex with, or fantasized about, other men. So while the men recognized that they had homosexual desires, these desires were not yet persistent and pervasive enough in their lives for them to see themselves as gay.

Some men never completely denied their homosexuality; instead, they perceived their same-sex desire as a "stage," something that did not seriously compromise their masculinity or their salvation because they did not consider it part of their real identity. Sean, a gay Christian, made it clear that at one time he felt his same-sex desires were fleeting. When I asked him, during an interview, if he had discussed his homosexual feelings with anyone, he said, "No, because I thought that this may be silly of me to do because you know, in time, this could change. . . . I knew that I was having the same feelings I had when I was thirteen or fourteen, and they didn't seem to be going away, and I couldn't understand this. . . . I still couldn't see myself as a gay person at that point [age twenty-four]." Sean, and those like him, initially perceived their homosexual desires or encounters as blips, fleeting moments en route to an otherwise straight sexual life. Because the men who denied their homosexuality or who saw it as a phase kept this desire invisible to others and did not consider it defining of their identity, their sense of being authentic Christian men was not yet threatened. By signifying heterosexuality through acts such as dating women, or, in some cases, by getting married, the men were able to disregard other violations of the identity code for straight men, though only temporarily.

Such violations, however, took on new meaning as same-sex desires persisted and strengthened over time. When homosexual desires and encounters intensified to the point that the men could no longer deny them or view them as blips, they reached a crisis in which these desires were experienced as more important violations of an identity code. Now the men began to see their sexual desires as indicative of who they really were and, therefore, began to think of themselves as gay. At this point, the way the men perceived themselves shifted; they had become, in their own eyes, homosexual.

This new perception created a sense of inauthentic Christianity. Whereas the men once saw their homosexual behaviors as temporary deviations from heterosexuality, they now perceived that they were homosexuals—the line between being a good man doing something bad and being a bad man was crossed. Brandon described this experience as coming to realize "that these feelings that I had had since I was thirteen were not going away, and I did have this attraction to men, and now I had come to realize this as being homosexuality. And I remember rising up in bed one night and screaming at God to deliver me from these feelings. . . . I thought that I needed to get rid of these feelings to get on with my life." Brandon wanted God to end his homosexual desires so he could "get on with his life." Clearly, these feelings were an unwanted piece of himself, and he saw them as an impediment to living the life he had planned and being the person he wanted to be.

These feelings, shared by all the men, gave rise to this question: How can I be the man I want to be and know I should be when I also know that I am gay? This question, implicit in Brandon's belief that homosexuality will keep him from living the life he has planned, initiated his dilemma by bringing homosexuality into sharp and immediate conflict with the identity "Christian man." Men in this phase found themselves trapped by two seemingly incommensurable identity codes, and they began to feel like impostors.

Impostoring

Finally, the men fully developed identity dilemmas through interactions with other people. These interactions heightened their feelings of inauthenticity because most of their interactions were still based on a heterosexual identity. In an attempt to avoid the stigma attached to a homosexual identity, the men continued to stage a straight performance, lending a fraudulent quality to their personal relationships. For instance, one gay man explained that his relationships with family members did not feel "real," that he did not feel "known, almost like a stranger," since he had discovered—but not revealed—his homosexuality. Another gay Christian admitted that he avoided social situations and the possibility of building personal relationships after he realized he was gay: "As long as I could maintain my anonymity I was OK, but once people tried to get to know me better, it made me feel uncomfortable. I wanted no part of being in any of these men's groups at church or anything like that. I just didn't feel comfortable getting involved in those." This man, like the others in this study, worried that his sexual identity would become known and he would be rejected, or that he would establish a relationship built on a false heterosexual identity. These men felt like they were living a lie in passing themselves off as Christians.

As self-aware impostors, the men's sense that they were fakers became more acute, intensifying their identity dilemmas and the feelings surrounding them. Interactions with others highlighted their fraudulence by marking the discrepancy between who they claimed to be and who they really felt themselves to be. This discrepancy, and the emotional havoc it created, became a preoccupying concern in the men's lives. An ex-gay Christian man, Ed, described this period in his life: "My worlds were starting to collide. I was a mess emotionally. I was feeling really guilty about going to church Sunday morning, going to the altar and crying my eyes out, but, as soon as even that afternoon, going to the bookstore for sex, being out the night before having sex, going to church the next morning, you know, things like that. Having these two faces and stuff and praying to God that no one from church ever saw me at these places—I felt myself as an outsider. I looked at myself as an outsider." This man partitioned himself into "two faces" and his life into discrete worlds, one Christian (heterosexual) and the other homosexual. He feared discovery as an impostor because discovery would deny him full participation in Christian life. But already he felt like and saw himself as an "outsider." His continued interaction with others, predicated on a heterosexual identity, began to create a chronic sense of inauthenticity and anxiety. As the men became impostors in an attempt to retain their place in a Christian community, they felt less and less deserving of membership in this community.

During this period, as a response to these emergent identity dilemmas and their increasing sense of fraudulence and alienation, seven of the thirty men interviewed in this study got married, believing that the "right woman" would cure them of their homosexual desires and that marriage would force the issue by taking away any choice of sexual partner. Further, because marriage was an established route to participating in "God's order," the men hoped that getting married would once again allow them to feel like authentic Christians. If they could not create legitimate heterosexual lives by wishing or praying unwanted homosexual urges away, these men decided that they would structure heterosexual lives with the hope that doing so would curtail wayward sexual desire. This plan, shared by all of these men, is perhaps best expressed in the words of an ex-gay Christian who was explaining how he planned to cope with his inability to get rid of unwanted homosexual feelings: "Basically, the plan was to get married, and they'll [homosexual desires] go away. I'd thought about marriage for a long time. In fact, part of my cover [as a heterosexual] was being engaged. I'd been engaged three times, but every time I had to back out of it. . . . As a Christian, I'd prayed for years to get married and have children, and I wanted to marry the right person. She felt like the right person; I loved her as a friend, but I wasn't attracted to her sexually. But I felt like I could make the commitment, that once I was married I would be able to change, that I would have to change." For these men, marriage was an attempt to resolve their identity dilemmas, and they sincerely believed that getting married would cure them. When it did not, their dilemmas were heightened in one of two ways. Four of these men, three who would later join the cell groups Accept or Homosexuality and the Bible and one who later joined Expell, ended up divorced, an event that strengthened their notions of themselves as failed Christians. Not only were their attempts to change their sexuality unsuccessful, leaving them with the same identity dilemma, but they had also added divorce, compounding their sense of failure and despair. The other three men, who would later become ex-gay Christians, stayed married, but their marriages were not the healing salves they had anticipated. Instead, these marriages were (prior to joining Expell) additional sources of pressure and shame. Not only did these men have to perform sexually as heterosexuals, but when they felt homosexual desire, they had to contend with the sinfulness both of these desires and of thinking about (or engaging in) adultery. They loved their wives "as best friends" and did not want to hurt or lose them. Still, they desired men. Marriage, regardless of whether it lasted, inflamed the men's identity dilemmas and served only to make the search for a solution more pressing.

In sum, the men's identity dilemmas arose out of a social environment in which homosexuality was stigmatizing and threatening, and they emerged over time as the men's feelings of inauthenticity intensified and forced them to confront the contradiction between their spirituality and sexuality. It was in interaction with others that the men began to experience themselves as fakers. Once the men acknowledged the discrepancy between their gay desire and straight Christian identity, every interaction became an occasion for experiencing themselves as frauds, or "two-faced outsiders." While the men constructed these two faces to try to protect their Christian identities, they simultaneously deepened their sense of inauthenticity and heightened their emotional turmoil. These men were afraid of discovery, rejection, and damnation. They felt isolated, anxious, and ashamed. It was these feelings that drove them to seek solutions in either Accept or Expell. But how and why did men with the same religious beliefs, feelings, and dilemmas choose to resolve them in such opposing ways when they joined one or the other group?

4 | Choosing a Path to Resolution

I'd met a few folks from MCC. They were good people, and they told me about MCC and how it had helped them. When I finally got up the courage to go to a Sunday service—not knowing what to expect—I was surprised by the love and joy in that place. I knew God was at work and it felt right for me. I guess I never really considered an ex-gay group.

Interview with Sean, Accept member

I knew I couldn't join a gay Christian group like MCC. It was just never an option for me. The whole idea of it's okay to be gay and Christian felt wrong, and I didn't want to be wrong. When I heard about Expell and talked to the group leader, it felt like I was finally in the right place.

Interview with Matt, Expell member

In these excerpts, Sean and Matt described their reactions to discovering Accept or Expell as right and/or wrong feeling and indicated that their decisions about joining were predicated on these feelings. When initial contact with a group "felt right," Sean and Matt took this feeling as evidence that they had found the "right place" in which to resolve their struggle. Like Sean and Matt, all of the men in this study based their decisions about which group to join on their emotional reactions, with good feelings serving as proof of an appropriate choice. None of the men were concerned with, or even noticed, the theological and conceptual similarities between MCC and Exodus. Instead of seeing the groups as closely related, they saw only the groups' opposing solutions to the homosexuality/ spirituality problem. As a result, when the men chose a group in which to resolve their dilemmas, they did not experience the choice as a rational weighing of the potential costs and benefits of two possible options. For each man seeking a way to resolve his dilemma, only one option seemed viable at that time. So, while most of the men knew general information about both groups, they did not gather specific information about each and use it to decide which to join. Their decision was not deliberative; one group simply "felt right," and they explored this option alone and then joined. But what made one group feel right for some and wrong for others?

As we will see, which group felt right to the men was linked to the particular biographical and social conditions under which the men first committed themselves to Christianity and joined Christian communities. The men's emotional and psychic needs that prompted and were fulfilled by their initial commitment to Christianity also influenced their later choice of group. Earlier in their lives, joining conservative, primarily evangelical, Christian communities gave the men feelings of self-acceptance, self-esteem, and belonging. For those who grew up in these communities, biblical dictates were a basis for assessing self-worth. For those who joined later, as adults, biblical dictates were a way of fitting in with others, of eradicating difference. For the few men who joined these communities in the midst of crises, biblical dictates provided a way to assure themselves that they were good men worthy of good lives, as long as they followed the rules. Either way, biblical dictates, as defined by the community, were initially resources for the men to measure their moral worth, protect their present well-being, and secure their eternal futures. Ironically, when the men's homosexuality became visible and their dilemmas emerged, these communities turned into potential sites of rejection and alienation, propelling the men to seek resolution in either Accept or Expell. Which group the men chose, to a large extent, was contingent on the kind of existential needs they fulfilled through participation in a religious community. In what follows, I show how the men's original reasons for investing in their faith and their current life situations also shaped their feelings about Accept and Expell, making only one group feel right for them.

Paths to Gay or Ex-gay
Christian Communities

Understanding why one group (or the other) "felt right" to some of the men and not others requires an examination of the men's initial commitment to Christianity to discern how and why their faith was important in their lives. All of the men in this study experienced God as the focal point of their lives and perceived God's Word, the Bible, as conveying the absolute truth about how to live a righteous life and about the consequences of not doing so. For them, the Bible was a guide to the proper Christian behavior that makes a person worthy of salvation and the love and fellowship of other Christians. To behave otherwise threatened the soul and community membership. In sum, the Bible prescribed a moral code, and the men perceived that there were desirable rewards for adhering to it. The rewards the men reaped for their adherence varied, however, according to the individual emotional needs that emerged from their life experiences. Some men felt isolated and needed a sense of belonging, some required a sense of safety in a dangerous and unpredictable world, and others needed to feel worthy within their communities.

These varied emotional needs formed the foundation of three distinct biographical paths the men traversed initially to become committed members of Christian communities and greatly influenced how they chose to resolve the conflict between their homosexuality and faith. In the first pattern, which I refer to as "belonging," the men joined these communities later in life to achieve a respite from feelings of isolation and difference. Because they were first drawn to Christian communities as a way of being accepted and escaping their sense of difference, these men did not later feel comfortable joining the gay Christian group—a group that is decidedly different and often stigmatized. In the second pattern, called "bargaining," a few of the men joined a Christian community to find help when their lives spun out of control. God helped them improve their lives, they believed, because they finally agreed to live by divine mandates. Joining the gay Christian group was not an option for these men because it risked their bargain with God, placing them back in a precarious position. In the final pattern, "meeting expectations," the men were born and socialized into these communities and wanted to feel acceptable by community standards. Which community standards (gay or ex-gay) were important to them, however, was heavily shaped by the personal relationships in their lives when they were choosing a group. These relationships, their beginnings and endings, became signs that indicated what course of action was acceptable to God, one's self, and others. All of the men who joined Accept and six who joined Expell indicated that they felt "led" to their respective group in this way. Ex-

ploring these biographical differences will help create a better understanding of the men's choices and the way they experienced joining
these groups.

Belonging

For some of the men, joining Christian communi-
ties provided a refuge from lives that had otherwise been lonely and
disconnected. Six of the fifteen ex-gay Christians described feeling like
outcasts from childhood through adolescence. Their peers ridiculed
various personal characteristics; they had few, if any, intimate friends
or close family relationships; and they felt different, rejected, and afraid.
They sought acceptance and love, fearful they would never find it. At
some point in their lives, they met a Christian person (usually, though
not exclusively, an evangelical Christian) who offered them this acceptance, and/or they attended a church service where they felt wanted
and important. This sense of being accepted, given their prior isolation, was a welcome and provocative feeling that drew the men into
the religious community.

Perhaps because of the emphasis in evangelical Christian communities on creating a just Christian society through the development of
"personal relationships to allow God to transform human hearts from
the inside-out," each of these men felt he received great attention upon
joining this community and felt accepted and loved (Smith 1998, 188).
There was only one requirement—accept Jesus Christ as a personal
Lord and Savior and live by God's Word. In addition to the group's
compelling invitation, Christianity also held out the promise of unconditional love and acceptance from Jesus, who wiped clean sins
(what the men saw as wrong with themselves) and offered salvation.
All the men had to do to receive this love and acceptance, or so it
seemed, was to grant and live by the authority of God's Word. Initially,
for men who had sought to be accepted their whole lives, this trade-
off was an easy one to make.

The following examples from the lives of two ex-gay Christian men,
Ed and Matt, illustrate this biographical pattern. In each man's life, I
trace the feelings of rejection and isolation they experienced as children and young adults, and then show how joining a Christian community and accepting the Bible as an authoritative source appeared
as a resolution to this search. To begin, consider Ed's account of his
early life. He traced the isolation he experienced prior to joining a
Christian community to an incident that occurred in first grade when

he was punished for misbehaving by having to play with the girls at recess for a week:

> The stuff in parochial school started, the real stuff started from that incident and on. After that, the guys started calling me girly, and I was also heavyset. I mean I was heavier than most guys, but I wasn't that fat, but guys called me fatso anyway, cause I was definitely fatter than them. They started calling me girly and fatso then. This is like first grade, and it progressed; it stayed that way. I didn't play much with other guys because they wouldn't pick me for their games, so I was left off to one side. I was heavy, heavier than most, and this was the height of the President's Physical Fitness Program, so I had to do all these things I never had to do before: run, chin-ups, push-ups, squat thrusts—you know, all these agility tests— throw a ball, kick a football. I'd never seen a football, let alone kicked one. I was a target—open, open, open season—and so I cried a lot during those years.

Ed also spoke of being "scared to death" of his parents and never fitting into any of the groups he joined in college. Of his drama club experience, he said, "I just didn't fit in there, so I just turned to; I stayed behind the scenes, you know, to make others look good." Ed wanted to fit in, but in all areas of his life he felt continually relegated to, as he put it, "staying off to one side" or "behind the scenes."

Ed finally got a role on the stage—and moved from misfit to community member—when he joined Campus Crusade and the Baptist Student Union, two competing groups, in his later college years. He explained: "I wanted so much to be with them, you know. That was really my desire because these were people who didn't make fun of me or anything. Christians did not make fun of me; they were very, you know, they wanted so much to improve me and include me." At first, it might seem odd that Ed would feel accepted by a group that wanted to improve him, but in this case "improve" meant to become more Christ-like, a goal that he *shared* with others in the group. For the first time, Ed felt he was being taken seriously; the efforts to improve him were experienced as concern for his well-being, and he was able to participate fully.

But what made Ed look into Christian groups as a source of acceptance in the first place? While he grew up going to church every Sunday, religion was not yet a crucial part of his life. During our interview, I asked Ed if he had ever felt close to God as a kid. He said no, but that as a teenager he had met a young minister who strongly affected him: "He was a neat fellow, probably in his early twenties, but to me he was, you know, so much more mature. He'd lead me through the prayer, and he was the sweetest, he had the warmest, the most wonderful smile, the gentlest disposition anybody had. And me being much the loner that I was, the kids making fun of me over the years and stuff, it was like I was just drawn to this person, and wanting so much what it was he had." While it is unclear whether Ed had a crush on this minister, it is obvious that this man was kind to and accepting of him. Leading someone through a prayer is an act of concern, and Ed was touched by this gesture. Yearning for acceptance, Ed felt strongly pulled toward this person and believed that if he were like this person, then he would be liked too. In college, when Ed experienced rejection from other groups, he sought out Christian groups, hoping to find the acceptance this young minister had once shown him. Before joining Christian groups, Ed explained, "[I] felt like an outsider, knowing [I] lacked a lot of what other people had and being very desirous of it." His membership in Christian groups made him "feel really accepted and safe." The price of this feeling was a commitment to Christianity and to living his life in accordance with its dictates. The Bible thus became an authoritative guide to making decisions about his life.

Like Ed, Matt also felt rejected and alone for much of his early life. He recalled never feeling very close to anyone in his family, except his sister, because they "were kind of like the black sheep" of the family. He remembered only one good friendship as a child and adolescent, a friendship he described in the following way:

> I liked Jason; he was different. He wasn't afraid to stand out in a crowd. He wasn't afraid of what other people thought of him. He was everything I wasn't. I mean, I was afraid. I mean, I literally did not want to do anything to be different, and I think a lot of that was just from growing up. I was always really kinda chubby. I wasn't ever really fat, but I was always chubby, and I, I think in my mind, I was always just this beast, you know. [I've] always felt different, and I was never good at sports and all that kind of stuff. I just wanted—I just was trying to fit in like everybody else. I mean, that's like, my whole life was about fitting in, not standing out, fitting into the

mainstream. What I liked about Jason was that just didn't matter. He could be whoever he wanted to be. I think that was probably the draw that was there.

In much the same way that Ed was drawn to the preacher he met as an adolescent, Matt's sense of being different, while wanting so badly to be like everybody else, drew him to a person who was different, but did not care. He was trying to either learn to disregard the "beast" in himself or fit in. He accommodated this desire in his late teenage and early adult years by becoming part of the "party crowd" because "if you hung out with the people that were drinking, that's what you talk[ed] about and that was something [I] could do. That's how [I] kinda learned to fit in with people."

Because of his desire to fit in, Matt's growing awareness of his homosexuality was terrifying. It was, to him, a shameful form of difference that would make him profoundly unacceptable. So, he decided in high school that he would never be gay. He explained, "I may be acting out like a gay person, but I am not going to choose that as my lifestyle. My whole thing was, if I'm gay, that means I'm different, that means I stand out, and that's the last thing I want to do." His fear of being unacceptable to others led him to Christianity. During a small group discussion at an ex-gay ministry meeting, Matt told the group that he would "never have become a Christian if he wasn't gay because he could not imagine needing God if it were not for this issue." But needing God seemed to follow as the result of needing people. Consider, for instance, Matt's account of how he became a member of his first Bible study group: "The more I understand about the whole thing [Christianity], the more I want to be like that [Christ-like]. I think when I first like started going to BSF [Bible Study Fellowship], part of the reason I went is because of people like Bill and Peter [co-workers], who I saw that were together, you know. They had problems, but they didn't have to go out and drink and party and all this stuff to be accepted in a group, to be manly or whatever. That kind of drew me there. But then the more I found out about—you know, it's all about Christ, and about being like Christ." Just as he was drawn to his high school friend, Matt followed Bill and Peter because they seemed to have something he lacked and wanted desperately to find. His decision to join BSF was predicated on what he saw in those he admired, on the ways he perceived them to be accepted and "manly." His desire for and acceptance of Christ and his decision to grant the Bible authority in his life were, at least partially, a consequence of his search for a place where his perceived differences could be controlled and negated. By accepting Christ and the Bible as authority, his life became dictated in exactly the same ways it was for others in the group. Unwanted feelings of difference could be eradicated, it seemed, by doing what the Bible said to do.

The biographical paths of these men, their sense of rejection and abnormality due primarily to their perceived inability to convey a respectable masculine version of themselves to others, prompted them to seek acceptance from a group that gave the appearance of granting acceptance easily—Christians. When they met other Christians, men who seemed to have what they lacked and wanted, these men sought to gain these characteristics for themselves by joining Christian communities. It was only after the men joined and committed to the group's interpretation of truth, and found some level of acceptance, that they experienced an identity dilemma. If they embraced the group's version of truth—a requirement for acceptance—then their homosexual desires and actions threatened both their group membership and their notions of themselves as legitimate group members, making them once again vulnerable to rejection.

Because of these feelings and their desire to maintain a sense of normalcy and belonging, the men could not turn to the gay Christian community, where the difference they had fought to overcome would be center stage. They chose instead to become ex-gay Christians, at least in part, because they were unable and unwilling to risk their sense of belonging, of finally being included in a dominant group. Choosing to become an ex-gay Christian was, for these men, a way of maintaining conformity; it was an adaptation that allowed them to acknowledge their sexuality without challenging dominant Christian beliefs and thereby risking the label of outsider yet again. One of these men, in his description of how his religious community viewed homosexuals, explained: "So, if you come up and, say, two guys—it's right and it's fair. It doesn't fit. It doesn't fit the model. If a person comes into that kind of situation and they are in a gay lifestyle, and they are not giving spiritual and mental assent that this is wrong and not the best God has for them, then they won't be accepted [in his community] at the deepest level." This man, like the others who traversed this biographical path, believed that full acceptance required fitting the "model," that deviations, such as "two guys" who were "in a gay lifestyle," meant rejection. This sentiment, held by each of the six men who fit this pattern, was echoed in another ex-gay Christian's explanation of his decision to join Expell: "I had found a group that I could, you know, fit in with, and they accepted me, and, and you know, I wasn't about to decide to, you know, abandon that because this is probably the first time in my life that I had that. And so I knew I didn't want to be gay, 'cause I knew I didn't want to fall back into that whole thing, not being, not fitting in, not being accepted. And most people I knew would not have accepted that."

These men believed that trying to assimilate their sexuality into their faith would mean facing yet another rejection, something they could not risk in light of their own biographies. Importantly, the men, while they noted that homosexuality did not fit God's model for the world, did not cite this model as the reason for their choice. Instead, the men chose a path that enabled them to conform to the voices and opinions of ordinary people, thereby fulfilling their own need for acceptance and avoiding what they anticipated would be further shaming.

Bargaining

A few men turned to Christianity in an attempt to "bargain" for a better life. Three ex-gay Christian men (one who had fluctuated between the two groups but had decided to identify with ex-gay Christians at the time of this study) turned to religion when they felt helpless in the face of dire life circumstances. When their lives seemed to have hit bottom, when they felt unworthy, unloved, and helpless, they turned to God for answers. For each of these men, the decision to trust God was not much of a decision at all; rather, they perceived that turning to God would enable life, while continuing as they were literally meant dying. In short, the men made a bargain with God that worked something like this: "If I believe in you and live by your Word, then you will help me to fix my life and make me happy." The following two examples from the lives of Expell members illustrate how brushes with religion in childhood suggested answers to later problems. Coming back to God and giving his Word authority in their lives provided the men with a way to understand and cope with their current predicament.

Tim, an Expell leader, retrospectively accounted for his life's failures and successes as direct consequences of his belief in God and his (dis)obedience to God's Word in the Bible. He was introduced to religion in an orphanage, where he lived from age five to eighteen, and explained that he believed in God from this point on, though the belief was "buried." From the orphanage, Tim joined the military and found a homosexual partner, eventually moving from the South to the Southwest. This partner not only was physically and emotionally abusive, but also was an alcoholic who took drugs. Tim himself became dependent on progressively more dangerous drugs. Finally, a co-worker approached him and said, "You need to go back to where your joy is."

As Tim contemplated her words, he heard a voice in his head say, "If you stay here, you will die here. If you leave from here, I will give you life." Tim believed God had spoken to him. He soon found himself driving back to the South and ended up staying in a friend's trailer, with no money, no job, no drugs, and no prospects. He described it as a "crash situation" in which he "did everything but burn." After another failed attempt at a homosexual relationship, Tim resorted to praying. He recalled finding a piece of Scripture, 1 Corinthians 6:11, on "a beautiful day, June 21st," and explained his reaction to "that one piece of Scripture. No one ever told me I needed to be healed. Those words were so powerful to me. It meant that he could heal me." First Corinthians, chapter 6, discusses sexual immorality, including "homosexual offenders" and incites the believer to "honor God with [his/her] body" (verse 20). Though the "wicked will not inherit the Kingdom of God" (verse 9), the chapter offers a way out: "But you were washed, you were sanctified, you were justified in the name of the Lord Jesus Christ and by the Spirit of our God" (verse 11). Similarly, chapter 11 tells believers to uphold Jesus's teachings and to recognize that "when we are judged by the Lord, we are being disciplined so that we will not be condemned by the world" (verse 32).

For Tim, these chapters explained his struggles and offered a way for him to attain his salvation. God had been "disciplining" him so that he would not be condemned. How wonderful it seemed to Tim that God had been watching out for him the entire time, making him struggle to bring him to belief so that he could be saved. According to Tim, God said, "The world will kill you. I will give you everlasting life." Given this choice, Tim eventually went to a church, one that had an ex-gay ministry. Here, he reaffirmed his faith, and the group placed him in a Christian home for newly aspiring ex-gay Christians. Suddenly, he had a home, friends, and a job, which Tim perceived as rewards from God for his choice to believe. Tim explained all the positive changes in his life as a result of his rediscovered faith: "They [good changes] are gifts to me as I have been obedient in following what I believe are God's desires for my life. Only Christ could have done it. Only him. Only he. Period. You will never be able to convince me that it was anything different than the power of the Spirit, because in my own ways of being human, I can make bad choices just like that." This post hoc interpretation of contingent events legitimated Tim's decision and proved to him the reality and benefits of his bargain.

Tim still remembered the date on which he read the passage in Corinthians (and where he was sitting when he read it) because he saw this textual encounter as marking a turning point in his life. Prior to reading this passage, Tim felt that his life was a string of bad choices that he could not help but make and that had left him distraught, depressed, and angry. When he no longer knew how to help himself, he found in the Bible a promise that he could be healed, that God could remedy this whole situation. Tim then interpreted his troubled life as the result of living in disobedience to God, who had allowed him to "fall far enough" that he would return to the fold and be saved. This interpretation gave new meaning to Tim's life. The losses and pain he suffered were vehicles to bring him to God, a way of teaching him. In an interview, Tim said that he tried to remember this past, "Lest I ever forget what God has done for me. He told the Israelites, 'Remember what I have brought you from.' It's important for me. My life has meaning because of this issue."

Another ex-gay group member, Josh, also rediscovered God when he felt he could no longer control his own life. While his family sporadically attended church when he was growing up and he even had a powerful religious experience one summer at a Bible study camp, he did not become "convicted" until he felt he could no longer help himself. His downward spiral began when he started drinking and taking drugs, dropped out of high school, and joined the military. Here, he fed his addictions, going to parties to do drugs and to have sex (heterosexual and homosexual). He explained: "I was just getting more involved in drugs, and more involved in alcohol, and I was at a party, and they were passing around what is called White Cross speed, and we were gobbling it up like candy, you know, and I OD'd on it. I finally somehow made it out of that apartment and got back to my barracks, and this deep conviction just hit me, and I fell to my knees, and I cried out to God. And I said, 'God, my life is a mess,' and I said, 'God, I need you,' you know, and I just felt this burden lifted off of me, and I felt this peace." When Josh turned to God in a moment of despair, he found peace. Like the hope Tim felt when he believed he could be healed, this sense of peace offered an alternative to the "mess" of Josh's life. His initial reaching out to God came at a moment when he was close to destroying himself, but the peace, the easing of the burden of controlling his own life, was what prompted him to pursue God. In this pursuit, he joined a church community and came to understand that his problems were the result of demons he had let in by not living a Christian life. The answer, the path to peace, could be found in the Bible.

Like the men who joined Christian communities to feel accepted, these men experienced their homosexuality as a threat to their newly established commitment to Christian doctrine. These men worried that their homosexual desires and behaviors not only would risk their good standing as members in these communities, and thus the assistance and support of other members, but also would jeopardize the bargain they had struck with God. Thus, their homosexuality was more than just shameful; it was frightening because it threatened the positive changes in the men's lives and their sense of peace.

For these men, the ex-gay Christian group provided a way to deal with their identity dilemmas, a way that did not threaten to break their bargain with God and thus their newly acquired sense of security. By joining Expell, they illustrated their commitment to God's Word and their willingness to struggle to overcome any barriers to adhering to his Word. The men believed absolutely that God would help them, making it possible for them to hold up their end of the deal and retain feelings of safety.

Choosing to join the ex-gay group was thus a way of ensuring the men's futures. As they saw it, joining a gay Christian group would mean breaking their end of the bargain (i.e., adhering to God's Word) and, therefore, would threaten their current positive life conditions and newfound security. It simply was not a viable option. One of these men, Tim, used a metaphor of the potter and his clay to explain how he perceived this bargain with God: "As the potter is the master of the outcome of the clay—he can make it and shape it and crush it, make it and shape it and crush it as many times as he needs it to make it the way he wants it to be. I believe that that is what happened in my life. I don't believe that anything is happenstance. I believe that God is a sovereign God. Though the world may not understand what his desire and design is, he knows what it will take to draw those to him who are his own. Why would I want to even question that?" Thus, Tim perceived that God had "crushed" him—that is, put him through the wringer—as a way of creating him as he wanted him to be. Now that his life was going well, Tim was not about to get off the path God had set for him, lest he be crushed again. The only legitimate option these men felt they had to cope with their homosexuality was to join Expell—or it might have seemed like they were trying to wriggle out of the bargain they had struck with God. And to do so would have put them at risk of more suffering at God's hands.

Meeting Expectations

The final pattern, which I refer to as "meeting expectations," characterizes the largest number of the men, all of the gay Christians and six of the ex-gay Christians. This pattern, while similar to the first in that the men shared a desire to be acceptable to themselves and to other people, differs because these men were already part of a Christian community and did not need to seek one out. Instead, these men were born and raised in communities where Christianity was an expectation, part of what it meant to be a community member. For instance, one gay Christian, when he described the genesis of his struggle, explained: "I really don't try to question the way I got here. I think offhand I would say that being raised in the South, being raised in the town I was raised in, being raised in a very conservative, fundamentalist home, fundamentalist church, and then again, the fear of being disliked, all of those things. I was taught so much to obey authority and the preacher is always right; [gays] were perverts and abominations, absolutely hopeless." This man's account of the biographical roots of his struggle is representative of those raised in religious communities. These men explained that Christian beliefs were a taken-for-granted feature of individual and communal life. They believed that to be an upstanding member in their communities of origin, they had to profess belief, attend church, and participate in other church activities. Much of their social life revolved around the church. In short, church membership was mandatory for acceptance and respect in these communities.

As a result, these men, often as young children, automatically invested the Bible with authority, without a great search and struggle. From childhood on, they embraced their religious communities' message that a good person was a Christian. For them, the tenets of Christian belief were guidelines for being a good person and for feeling acceptable to others, God, and one's self. Their struggle with homosexuality arose out of these beliefs.

The two representative accounts of the men's lives that follow not only reveal what the men saw as the behavioral expectations that characterized their lives within these communities, but also illustrate how the men used these expectations as guidelines for acceptability. In the first instance, I consider Alex, a gay Christian in his mid-thirties who just came out over the last three years. Alex grew up in a small, southeastern town that he said had a "very established way of life." He described it as follows: "I want to say it [life in this town] was ritualistic; that's not really the word I'm looking for, but just sort of that familiar pattern. You know, you got up every morning, every Sunday morning, and you got dressed and went to church, and everything was pretty much the same way. If it wasn't, everybody complained, so everybody wanted everything to be very much the status quo around there. I was always involved in Sunday school and grew up with a certain set of friends who were there, you know, the whole time I was growing up. Church played a pretty pivotal part, really, in sort of my social life at that time." Here, Alex saw the community he grew up in as having a very specific way of life that centered around Christianity. He felt that residents policed the community to maintain the status quo and complained when there were any deviations from the established order. Alex's "certain set of friends" were familiar with and lived under these same expectations. Thus, to Alex it seemed there was a unified set of expectations that had to be met in order for him to be accepted. Alex discussed these expectations in an interview:

> *Alex:* I've always been driven a lot by expectations put on me, living up to the expectations of my parents, of the church, of friends, work and school, and society and everybody, you know.
>
> *Michelle Wolkomir:* When you think about those expectations, which ones come to mind?
>
> *Alex:* Always make good grades; don't go out and party and be wild; be a good boy; dress up on Sunday and go to church every Sunday. Living up to everything; not necessarily considering if it's the right thing for me to do personally, but letting other people tell me where I was needed. And I've kind of had the same model of God, I think, because of that. God had all these expectations of me, and I

always felt a little bit like if I did not match all
those expectations, then I couldn't face God.

Alex felt that he had grown up under a highly restrictive model of
what it meant to be a "good boy," a model that included Christian beliefs and behavior. At that time in his life, disregarding this model
would have threatened his standing in his community, as well as his
own sense of himself as a good person. God, too, Alex believed, would
have disapproved of any deviation. As Alex saw it, communal and
divine expectations were synonymous, making his homosexuality a
threat to acceptance in this life and the next.

For Todd, an ex-gay Christian, Christianity and a fulfilling social
life were also linked from a very early age. He grew up in what he
called "a strong Baptist family" in a small, Midwestern town, where
his family was heavily involved in church and church activities. His
mother taught Sunday school classes, and his father was the pastor
for several country churches. Todd was an only child and spent a lot
of his childhood helping his parents with their church activities, as-
suming his own responsibilities at an appropriate age. When I asked
if he liked being this involved, he responded, "I guess I just didn't
know any other way, and yeah."

As a pastor's son, Todd was usually positioned as a leader, whether
officially or in terms of status among his peers and church members.
He believed that his acceptance and status in this community, while
granted no doubt because of his parents' roles, were contingent upon
feeling and acting "right," professing Christian belief and behaving in
accord with that doctrine. As Todd became increasingly aware of his
homosexual feelings, he became afraid of "being unacceptable" and
"made fun of" and of "disappointing [his] parents." Acting on these
feelings seemed "very wrong, sinful, and very contrary to the lifestyle
[he] wanted to pursue." Later in his life, after his short marriage ended
in divorce, Todd felt that he had failed and sinned so badly by di-
vorcing that he might as well try to have a homosexual relationship.
He seemed to believe that since there was no hope for him to be a
good Christian, he might as well default to his own desires. He explained, "I just gave up on trying to do things the right way; pretty
much I decided I didn't care. I was just tired of doing things the right
way and trying to please everybody."

Like Alex, Todd's sense of rightness was linked to the expectations of his religious community and family. His own sexual feelings

were wrong in that they contradicted these expectations and threatened his sense of being acceptable to a religious community and to himself. When he felt that hope was lost, he consciously chose to behave the "wrong" way and to please himself. However, because of the ties between his religious beliefs and his social relationships, this adaptation left Todd feeling more lonely and miserable than ever. When he ended a homosexual relationship, Todd described his feelings this way: "I had at least a partial understanding of how far I had allowed myself to fall from, from my own, you know, the moral standards that I had set for myself, and that my family had set for me, and just how far I had fallen from God's desires for my life. That hit me really hard, too, just the loneliness. I just felt at that time that there was more of a void in my life, more of a, you know, an absence of God than there was at any time in my life. [I just] tried to get myself involved in everything in church I possibly could to replace him and fill up the empty space." Todd perceived his failed relationship as a reminder that he had defied his own, his community's, and God's standards for his life. As such, he felt a huge "void," one that he defined as an absence of God. His return to church and church activities to "fill the empty space" was an attempt to re-establish this community and, through that connection, to find God again. Todd, like Alex, closely connected his religious community's standards to God's during this time in his life, and both perceived that being acceptable in these communities and in heaven depended on their close adherence to these communal/biblical codes of behavior.

Like the men who turned to Christian community to feel accepted, these men also experienced a sense of inauthenticity as Christians when they acknowledged their homosexual desires. They, however, were already accepted members of a community and had neither searched for acceptance nor experienced any sense of initial resolution to this search. Instead of their sense of abnormality being connected to the secular world, it was centered in and tied to their religious communities. Consequently, these men left their initial religious communities, ultimately moving to new towns to seek answers to their dilemmas. Some of the men eventually found answers at Accept, while others turned to Expell.

At first it seemed odd that these men, all of whom shared similar biographical experiences in their initial commitments to Christian community, would make varied decisions about how to cope with their homosexuality within the context of their faith. These decisions, however, originated from the same belief, learned in these first communities, that they would be acceptable as people only if they followed the path God made for them. Given their uncertainty about the meaning of their homosexuality in relation to their faith, choosing a group that felt right meant that the men had to discern God's will for their lives. To do so, they used the status of important personal relationships and their feelings surrounding these relationships as signs, from God, of his desire for their lives. For some, the end of a relationship (e.g., a death or breakup) was evidence of God moving them to a particular path, while for others a deeply felt need to protect or sustain a relationship fueled a decision. In a few instances, the men interpreted casual friendships or chance encounters as God placing people in their lives to push them in the right direction. In each case, the men perceived their personal relationships as a kind of map that directed them in accord with God's will.

For some of the men, the end of a valued personal relationship was experienced as a catalyst—what one man referred to as "a wake-up call from God"—for rethinking their lives, including the way they were coping with their homosexuality. For instance, one gay Christian man, Sean, got married while he was in college, believing that marriage would be "the end of it [homosexual desire]." For twelve years he stayed in his marriage, having homosexual encounters, without acknowledging that marriage was not the solution to his problem. He explained: "I should have realized it [marriage was not the solution] sooner, but I didn't realize it till I was thirty-two. That's when I just stopped and made myself deal with it." I asked him what happened when he was thirty-two. He responded:

> I really think the catalyst was when my mother died. I realized how many things in my life I had done because other people wanted me to do them. I realized that there had not been many decisions in my life that I had made on my own, through listening to God. So that was a big contribution to it. The frustration with being dishonest. The frustration within myself that was just growing. The years and years of frustration and dishonesty had just grown to where I had to wrestle with it a lot. A counselor and a friend said you need to . . . be true to yourself because you're never going to be true to anyone else until you do that. And that kind of slapped me in the face. That was the moment I actually began to deal with this.

Sean's father had passed away years earlier, so when his mother died, he was freed, in a sense, from his parents' expectations of him. He was therefore able to realize how his own actions accorded with their expectations but not his own desires or even God's plan for him—he had been "dishonest." He believed the life he was living was not one that fit his true self (e.g., God given), and he decided he must "deal with" and accommodate his homosexuality. His confidant in the above passage was a gay man who suggested that Sean attend the gay Christian church. He did, just "to see what it was like," and found it "supportive" and "helpful." Soon after, and because he believed God had arranged this sequence of events to "show him the way," Sean divorced his wife and became a church member.

Similarly, Jason, an ex-gay man, believed that the breakup of his long-term homosexual relationship prompted him to rethink his participation in a homosexual lifestyle. Jason, a well-read, well-educated man, met his partner, a graduate of a divinity school at an Ivy League university, at the gay Christian church. He felt they were well-suited to one another, and they moved in together soon after. They were active in the church, doing many things together. For the three years they lived together, Jason was happy. When his partner ended the relationship suddenly, Jason was devastated. He gradually stopped attending the gay church and started what he called "a period of spiritual searching at that time." This search enabled him to realize that "at very deep levels [he] was very dissatisfied [with homosexuality]." This dissatisfaction, he contended, was God's way of pushing him away from a gay lifestyle because it was at this point that he "prayed and knew to define [him]self in different terms." At the charismatic church he had begun to attend, he was directed to an ex-gay ministry and became a member. Just as the death of Sean's mother was seen as evidence he needed to change his life and pursue a gay lifestyle, Jason's loss of a romantic relationship was interpreted as divine direction which resulted in his membership in an ex-gay ministry.

The men believed these losses were signs of divine providence. By taking someone away from them, the men believed that God was showing them the direction he wanted their lives to take. Sean, for example, believed that God allowed him to stay married for so long to "keep him safe" until he could "be responsible as a gay person" because Sean believed he would have been "very promiscuous" and "the '70s were a very dangerous time to come out." His mother's death was eventually interpreted as a signal that he was ready to handle coming out. In a casual conversation after our interview, Jason also explained that he believed God had put him in this relationship initially to reveal to him that homosexual relationships, no matter how compatible, were inherently flawed and unnatural. If God had not put him in this relationship, Jason felt he might have always wondered about whether he could have a good homosexual relationship. For Jason, the relationship had failed not because of some lack on his part but because it was inherently wrong. This reinterpretation enabled him to feel better about himself, and he believed that he must reject homosexuality if he was to have a successful relationship. In short, he interpreted his relational difficulties as signs of what God desired for his life.

Two other ex-gay men, Todd and Peter, also experienced the failure of important relationships as divine direction, but in a slightly varied form. Both men married in their early twenties, convinced that marriage would cure them of their homosexual desires. When it did not, their marriages ended in divorce, and both men experienced their divorce as "failing as Christians." As a response, they tried to have homosexual relationships.

Todd's relationship was abusive, and Peter never established a serious relationship. The end of Todd's relationship caused him to reflect on how far he had fallen from his own moral standards as well as his community's and God's standards for his life. Peter had a nervous breakdown. He concluded that "God allowed [him] to experience what divorce was like" and to "realize that something's not right here [in the gay community]" so that he would seek help and healing. Here, it was the dissolution of relationships that prompted them to choose a particular path. Instead of turning inward and contemplating their responsibility for the failure of these relationships, both men shifted their attention to external circumstances. If a straight relationship did not work, it was because God wanted them to be gay. If a gay relationship did not work, it was because God wanted them to be straight. Again, the concept of divine providence seemed to both guide and legitimate the men's decision-making processes.

Conversely, three of the ex-gay Christians I interviewed chose to join the ex-gay group because they did not want to lose their wives or children. They believed God put them in this situation (the struggle with homosexuality) to reveal and solidify the importance of family and living a heterosexual life. When the men's homosexuality threatened their extended family connections, jobs, and places in the community, the men realized these aspects of their lives were God's gifts and they could not trade them for homosexuality. Because they loved their wives and saw their marriages as God's will, staying married was particularly important to these men, and they came to believe that God had given them their wives to help them overcome their homosexuality. One of these men, Charles, explained his decision to join the group by saying, "I don't want to get divorced. I want to stay married. I want to keep my family together. God has used my homosexuality to show me what he truly desires for my life, and I now desire it too." Another ex-gay man, Andy, described his struggle and decision in the following way: "That struggle was just crazy. I mean, I was going through a depression about it; it was getting harder and harder to say no to this [gay] lifestyle, and I knew that if something didn't happen, I was either going to kill myself or have an affair. If I had an affair, I'd end up getting divorced. I just happened to listen to a Christian radio station, and they were interviewing the leader of the Exodus group— and yes, homosexuals could change. I jotted down the number and actually called and talked to the leader." Soon after, Andy claimed that God told him, "This is a way out for you, a way for you to follow the path I have made for your life," and so he joined Expell. For these men, the prospect of losing their families and straying from God's design for their lives was, at least initially, much more daunting than denying their sexual desires. The feelings that emerged at the prospect of losing valued family relationships were interpreted as indicators of God's will for their lives, signs to the men to choose an ex-gay resolution.

In other instances, the men's decisions were influenced by chance encounters with others, believed to be God's messengers placed strategically in the men's lives. The men perceived those they encountered as divine trail guides, showing them both the path God desired for them and how to traverse it. These encounters quieted the men's fears surrounding their acceptance by others because their guides modeled and normalized a particular choice of group. By sharing another person's experiences, particularly when that person appeared successful and normal, the men's fears that they were weird or unacceptable were eased, and they now saw a path they could choose to resolve the negative feelings surrounding their homosexuality and spirituality. Consider Chris's account of how he was introduced to the gay church. When he first suspected he was gay, he thought: "Oh my God, maybe those kids were right. And then, could it be? Could it be? 'Cause, I mean, in church you were constantly taught, no, that cannot happen; that's not it. I mean, there was always, you know, Pat, who walked up and down the street [in his home town], who everybody said was gay. I was like, ach, I'm not that way at all. That was the only concept of anybody being gay that I knew, was Pat, and I mean he was just, like, a really weird person." Aside from Chris's awareness that his homosexuality was contrary to biblical teaching, he could not imagine being gay because the one gay person he knew was nothing like him. He sought to avoid being "a really weird person." Because he knew only Pat, his notions of being gay were linked to weirdness. But then he met Marshall, a gay man who was financially successful and respectable, and this encounter gave Chris a new image to contemplate. He explained: "There was somebody, this guy Marshall. I mean, he drove a Mercedes Benz, and, I mean, he's the vice president of this stock brokerage firm. I mean, a really great person, and he sent me this letter and said, 'I know what you are going through and I'd like to help you. Here's my 800 number at work; call me and let's have dinner and talk about it.'" Eventually, Chris called Marshall, who took Chris to his first gay bar, his first bookstore, and even to his first service at the gay church. Though they never dated, Chris said that Marshall "was God's way of telling me what to do. He took me to the [gay church] for the first time, and I don't know that he really taught me anything, but he kind of pointed me in the right way and showed me what God wanted me to do. . . . I've been at [the gay church] ever since." Marshall, because of his visible markers of successful masculinity, his wealth and prestige, seemed "normal" and less threatening to Chris. Chris could even aspire to be a success like Marshall. As a result, Marshall could guide Chris to a path to begin the resolution of his identity dilemma.

In a similar manner, Mack found a friend who normalized his struggle and pointed him toward a path for resolution, one he believed God meant for him. Mack said:

> My friend Dion took me to lunch one day and shared with me his story, which was that he was struggling with homosexuality. As soon as he told me that, I just—it was like this whole, like, new, newness came along, 'cause it was like, here was Dion, who[m] I had known at work and who was a really good friend, and [I] knew that he was a good Christian,

and I knew all these things about him, and he said he could struggle with this; you know, other people did struggle with it. And he talked about Expell, about going to counseling, that there was help for it, and began to shed a whole new light on the whole thing, that not only was it not totally crazy to have this struggle but that there was a Christian way to deal with it. You know, that all Christians didn't just think that all homosexuals were going to hell. God was using Dion to give me answers. I started going to see a counselor, and then I started going to Expell.

The "newness" that Mack described was the dawning of a new perspective, a more amiable light being cast on the specter of his sexual struggle. If Dion, a man Mack knew and trusted and saw as a good Christian (meaning a good person), could have this struggle, then Mack's own struggle felt less scary, less like a judgment that he was a bad, unredeemable person. That Dion's struggle was not "totally crazy" transferred to Mack's perception of himself, and he learned that other Christians share this same perspective. Even better, he believed that Dion was on a divine errand to point him to a path that promised resolution to his struggle as God wished. He followed it faithfully, beginning with counseling and the support group Expell.

For some men, then, the decision to follow a gay or an ex-gay path to resolution depended on whom they met during this time. When the men interacted with someone they perceived as having admirable qualities, this person's acceptance and advice normalized a particular path and made it both visible and viable. For others, the decision was tipped by fear of losing an important relationship, or the actual loss of such a relationship. The pain of losing a significant other got reinterpreted as God's hand in their lives, guiding them to a specific resolution. Conversely, some acted to keep families intact, both because of their love for these people and because of their belief in the biblical model of the family.

Whether the men chose to resolve the conflict between their faith and sexual orientation in the gay or ex-gay Christian group thus depended largely on individual biographies, interactions with people, and the emotions that arose from these interactions. While individual life circumstances generated specific psychic needs, the men shared a desire to feel like good Christians, acceptable to themselves, others, and God. Though attempting to achieve this acceptability took varied forms because of their diverse biographies, the men's choices were uniformly motivated by emotional and social need for a sense of belonging, security, and goodness. The men found what they thought of as divine direction in the feelings generated in interactions with ordinary people—not words taken from Scripture. These interactions were decisive in setting the men on one or the other path.

Choosing a path to resolve their conflict and joining a group, however, were just the beginning of reconciling their faith and sexuality. Selecting a group to join was only the first step in becoming a member; the men still had to learn their respective group's explanations of homosexuality and theology and fit these explanations to their own lives in satisfying ways. While the men were not undertaking a conversion process—they remained Christians with neither a "dramatic change in master status" (Bankston, Forsyth, and Floyd 1981, 282) nor a switch in perceived source of authority (Travisano 1981)—they did have to construct a revised form of Christian belief that accommodated their sexuality. In many ways, the men, at this point, had simply chosen a blueprint to use for the healing process they still had to undertake. This healing process would require commitment to the chosen group, a willingness to revise their understanding of biblical truth, and the strength to manage their emotions. Much hard work still lay ahead.

PART II

The Resolution of Dilemmas and the Transformative Process

5 | Challenging Traditional Meanings

One night, about a month into my fieldwork with the gay Christians, I offered Terry, whose car was in the shop for repairs, a ride home from an Accept meeting. Like me, Terry was a newcomer and had only been attending meetings for a short time. During the drive to his home, we initially made small talk and joked about local happenings. Then Terry suddenly got serious and asked, "Michelle, do you *like* going to these meetings?" I was startled by the question. I had not considered whether I enjoyed the time I spent with the group, so it was difficult to answer his question. I did, however, recognize immediately how important his question was; if attending the group was not rewarding, then it would be very hard to keep doing so—for me or anyone else.

I answered Terry as honestly as possible. Yes, I liked attending the group. I enjoyed the warmth, the camaraderie, and the exploration of sexual and spiritual issues. I also explained that I did not feel this way at the very beginning. As a heterosexual woman from a Jewish family, I initially felt strange and out of place, worried that I could not fit in or that I might unwittingly offend. These fears dissolved, however, as group members made real efforts to include and get to know me. Attending the group became fun. Terry interrupted me here: "But that's just it. Because you're straight, you don't have to worry about what will happen to you. You can just make friends. For me, I'm scared. I'm joining a *gay* church. It will change my life, and I have to be sure I'm going the right way and that I am right with God. Going to group meetings is sometimes hard." When I asked Terry what was difficult about the meetings, he got a bit exasperated at my inability to grasp what he saw as obvious: "Look, I might live as openly gay for the first time in my life. I have no idea how my family, friends, or co-workers could react. Then, there's God. What if the group is plain wrong about homosexuality? There's just a lot I'm unsure about. Not the people there or anything, but what will happen if I go this route." Given such uncertainty, why did Terry decide to give the group a try? Because, as he put it, "The group may just be an answer to my prayers," a solution that would ultimately end the anxiety, shame, and fear that plagued him.

Terry's mixed feelings about joining a group were shared by many men in this study when they first became group members, regardless of which group they decided to join. On one hand, they were tempted and drawn in by the group's potential to help them resolve their long-standing dilemmas. On the other hand, they were anxious about the changes in their lives that membership required, whether they could accomplish those changes, and whether doing so was right with God. While new Accept members worried most about their rightness with God and new Expell members worried most about the possibility of changing, new members of both groups were tentative at first.

How new members resolved these initially confusing feelings (and whether they did) would have a tremendous impact on their ability to commit to their respective group, to adopt group ideas, and to learn to see themselves differently. If the men's anxieties and doubts persisted, their commitment, or determination to pursue an "increasing identifi[cation] with the group, its meaning system, and its goals," would be stymied (McGuire 1992, 51). As a result, they would be unable to whole-heartedly embrace group messages and unlikely to experience any individual change or remain group members. Their success, their ability to reconstruct themselves in a positive light as either gay or ex-gay Christians, hinged largely on creating and sustaining commitment to their respective group.

The challenge of self-transformation through commitment to a support group and its healing process is certainly not unique to gay and ex-gay Christian men. In fact, the groups in this study represent just a tiny fraction of support groups. Our increasing cultural emphasis on the self, feeling, and therapeutic intervention over the last three decades has led to the formation of an estimated 3 million support groups in the United States, attended by approximately 75 million people (Moskowitz 2001, 247–248). Similar to Accept and Expell, many of these support groups, and their therapeutic philosophies and practices, are generally geared toward the goal of self-transformation and reflect what has been referred to as our "therapeutic culture" (Nolan 1998, 2002; Furedi 2004). This culture is characterized, in part, by an intense focus on the self as a point of reference for understanding one's self and society and for structuring courses of action, as well as by the corresponding core belief that "the self must not be subordinated to externally imposed and collective demands" (Rice 2002, 84). Within this cultural framework, emotions are critically important indicators of the self (and its relative health) and a basis for understanding individual and social pathology (Furedi 2004, 24–30). Constrained or negative emotions are perceived as markers of injury and the repression of the true self—usually brought about by disease, abuse, and/or oppressive social institutions—and are thought likely to create individual problems (e.g., disorders, addictions, syndromes, compulsions, etc.) that can lead to social ones, such as domestic violence, sex crimes, and child abuse. The afflicted are conceived of as victims who can, through the open expression and therapeutic management of their emotions, overcome these disorders, rediscovering and embracing their authentic good selves.

Social scientific research has analyzed the processes by which support groups work to help people feel better through the construction of new, more positive self-understandings. In most cases, this kind of self-transformation requires that support group participants learn group ideas, adapt these ideas to their own situations, and thereby arrive at a new view of themselves that is affirmed by the group (Denzin 1998; Francis 1997a, 1997b; Karp 1992; Mason-Schrock 1996; Rice 2002; Sandstrom 1996; Taylor 2000; Thumma 1991). For example, a study of Alcoholics Anonymous (Denzin 1998) shows how members learned to think of their alcoholism as a disease that caused them to behave irresponsibly. As a result, members could understand their lives differently; they were not bad and irresponsible people, but they did bad and irresponsible things because they were afflicted by alcoholism. This reframing of their situations enabled them to separate the disease (the cause of their trouble) and past shameful actions and emotions from the sober, good person in the present, allowing good self-feelings to emerge. It is through this kind of therapeutic process that support group members are thought to fend off effects of disease (like alcoholism), abuse, and/or societal oppression and thereby begin to see themselves positively.

This kind of self-transformation, however, is more complex than it may at first seem. Support group members, in general, do not merely follow the steps in an instruction manual to learn new ideas and how to apply them to their situations—and then just feel better. Instead, self-transformation is often a lengthy, difficult, and taxing process because it usually demands that members confront and change their existing beliefs about the world, thus creating high levels of emotional stress as members let go of old ideas, adopt new ones, and cope with painful feelings. For these reasons, initiating the support group healing process requires that support groups gain potential members' commitment through the provision of both a persuasive ideological message and effective tools and strategies for coping with emotional duress. In fact, if members are to successfully adopt group ideas, then groups must help develop emotional incentives and rewards for doing so throughout an individual's membership.

Managing emotions effectively is particularly important for new members as they confront uncertainties surrounding their membership and are introduced to new and challenging ideas. Consider Terry's mixed feelings about Accept and his fears about the validity of the group. Without guidance and help managing these feelings, he could become overwhelmed by them, drop out, and be stuck in his old dilemma. If he and the other men in this study were to resolve their dilemmas, then they had to reconcile these mixed feelings and soothe fears, so that they could make an initial commitment to their respective group and its ideas. This chapter focuses on how Accept and Expell helped the men deal with initial uncertainties and constructed the emotional bargains that enabled the men to begin to dismantle their old beliefs and to seriously consider the group's ideological message. As we will see, the men's willingness to "test" or "try on" group ideas about faith and sexuality depended heavily on the emotional promises the group offered the men. Without this kind of emotional groundwork, the transformation process could not have begun.

Emotional Bargains

As illustrated previously, the men in this study experienced their homosexuality as psychologically discomforting and emotionally stressful. Their sense of being fraudulent Christians and of having two lives that would inevitably collide created great shame, anxiety, and fear. It was these negative feelings that, in part, pushed them to seek help and to try to resolve the conflict they faced. But negative emotions, no matter how powerful, serve only as catalysts for the general search for a solution; alone, they are insufficient to prompt membership in a *specific* group. The group must also convince potential members that it can deliver relief from oppressive feelings. In this sense, the act of joining and committing to a particular group results simultaneously from the desire to be rid of negative emotions and the perception that a group can fulfill its promise to help members do so. In what follows, I examine these emotional dynamics, showing how the men's emotions served as incentives to prompt them to seek resolution in either Accept or Expell and how the group's promise to meet these emotional needs facilitated the men's initial commitment to the group.

Developing Emotional Incentives

In the last chapter, we saw how the men traversed different biographical paths to consider either Accept or Expell as a resolution to their conflict. Regardless of which path the men took, their journeys were characterized by a common struggle—to understand their homosexuality and selves in the context of their religious beliefs—and by shared emotions. These journeys toward the groups were also marked by the men's sense that they were making little progress, a sense that intensified their bad feelings and made their search for an answer more pressing. Over time, the men's emotional distress heightened to intolerable levels, fueling an increasing sense of urgency to their search for answers and culminating in the recognition that they could no longer tolerate living with such a contradiction. At this point, the men felt they had to do something to end their struggle and, prompted by their feelings and what they perceived as God's directions, decided to join either Accept or Expell. The following three examples, from the lives of a gay Christian, an ex-gay Christian, and a married ex-gay Christian, respectively, illustrate how the progressive intensity of this struggle created emotional incentives for resolution.

Terry. When I first met Terry, he was in his late forties and had recently become a member of Accept. The struggle that led him to Accept, while somewhat longer than that of younger gay men who came out earlier in their lives due to changing social attitudes and increased visibility of homosexuals, reflects the shame and anxiety common to the men's lives before they joined the group. Like many of the men, Terry was born into a staunchly religious family in a small southern town. His father was a Southern Baptist minister. Not surprisingly, the family's life revolved around the church, and Terry remembers feeling "called" into some sort of ministry from the age of ten. In high school, he dated a few girls and remembers enjoying the experience. He continued dating in college and participated in overt heterosexual displays like "panty raids" in the women's dormitories. At the same time, he was attracted to boys/men and had had several homosexual encounters. He noted that these encounters left him feeling "really guilty," but he was not too worried about it at that time. As he explained, "What I did, I did discretely, so no one ever said anything to me or called me queer. I knew I was attracted to guys, but I never admitted more to myself because I was attracted to girls too. I just didn't understand back then."

His real difficulties began when other people began to notice his homosexual activities. Late in his college career, Terry served as the minister of music for a small church. In this capacity, he became close to a male high school senior, and the boy spent a night at Terry's home. Soon after, a deputy visited Terry and explained it was best if he left town; he was never given a reason. Terry moved and found another church. Soon, however, he began to have dreams that these church members also found out he was gay. He describes waking up in "sweats," with a sense of terror that persisted while he was awake. From that point on, he explained, "I always had the fear of somebody finding out, of someone knowing. I knew I could not keep my feelings a secret for long, so I got married. I did love her though, and I thought that once I was married everything would be fine. I'd be normal like everyone else. It was okay for a while. We had two kids."

His marriage was "okay" for a couple of years, but then he began having homosexual encounters and the shame and fear of being "found out" crept back into his life. Once again, Terry felt he had to move or risk hurting his family. This cycle continued for several years, until Terry's wife refused to move again. After their separation, Terry continued to have sex with men, but he again covered his homosexuality by dating women. He remarried a few years later, determined not to let his homosexuality ruin this marriage. He prayed and spent hours on his knees in church, begging God to take away his homosexual desires. When his desires remained, Terry became depressed; he was ashamed of his behavior and scared he would be discovered. His stress was so pervasive that he could not perform sexually and had to be taken to the hospital for severe chest pains on a few occasions. To make matters worse, he met a man about a year and a half into this marriage and fell, as he says, "completely in love." He felt incredibly stuck, pulled by his faith, his obligation to his wife, and his desire for a normal heterosexual life, but also drawn toward homosexuality by his passion and love for this man. His situation quickly became intolerable. The turning point in Terry's life was a dream. He explained his realization this way: "I woke up one night screaming and sweating from a dream. In the dream, I was walking down the sidewalk, and everyone who saw me saw a tortured and twisted up man. They turned away from the sight of me with repulsion or looked right through me. With no one to see me, I shrank in size until I ceased to exist. I was just gone. It was terrifying. I spent years begging God to take this [homosexual] desire away, and this dream was God's way of telling me I had to be the one to end the torture."

A few days after this dream, which forced Terry to recognize that he had to do something, he was unexpectedly forced to resign as an organist and custodian for the church he was attending because church leaders had become aware of his homosexuality. He was deeply hurt by the rejection of people he thought of as friends, and he felt afraid and alone. Around the time of this incident, he was also invited to listen to his son sing as part of a choir performing at a MCC congregation. He went and found the service "joyful," "worshipful," and "full of love for God," and he met others who were gay and Christian and "seemed blessed." He thought that God may have orchestrated these events to push him toward MCC; and because he "lost everything— wives, grandchildren, jobs"—he felt he "had nothing to lose" and was now willing to find out about the group, to see, as he put it, "if this ministry was where God was calling [him] to be."

Phil. Like Terry, Phil, at age forty-one, had endured a long struggle with his sexuality before he was compelled to seek help, though he joined an ex-gay group. His struggle began in the school halls and classrooms of the southern town where he grew up. Born into a conservative, evangelical Protestant home, Phil believed sex was reserved for marriage, and he shared this belief with his peers at school whenever they would talk about sex. His consequent unwillingness to enter into adolescent banter about sex, his disinterest in sports, and his gentle mannerisms resulted in predictable ridicule, and he suffered being called a "queer," a "homo," and a "faggot." He recalls that these labels, while hurtful in that he felt like an outcast, did not bother him at "a deep level" because he did not think they were true. He remembers thinking his lack of interest in girls was a result of his not being ready to be in a relationship and did not connect it in any way to homosexuality.

At fifteen, however, things changed. During a weekend retreat sponsored by the Boy Scouts, Phil remembers being "molested by an older boy." This boy was friendly to Phil and, during the course of a conversation, explained that he worked in a massage parlor. He offered and gave Phil a massage—one that turned into a sexual encounter. Initially, Phil thought the experience was "nice," but then he felt "a horrible fear come over [him]" and began to believe that "something was very wrong with [him]." This event, the idea that he had allowed the seduction to occur, led him to begin to believe what he called "the hideous lies" that he was indeed "a faggot." He began investigating homosexuality, visiting adult bookstores and looking at pornography. He felt ashamed by his behavior, but he did not know what to do about it. He prayed, alternating between asking for forgiveness and asking for God to take away his desires. In the meantime, he finished a technical degree and began to work as a technician in a big company. He felt at the time that he would just have to accept his homosexuality and live with it. Friends introduced him to what he called "the gay lifestyle," and he began going to gay bars. Soon, he was involved in a homosexual relationship that lasted for two years, ending only when his lover's alcoholism and abuse convinced him such a relationship was wrong. At this point, Phil wanted desperately to get out of "the lifestyle," but he could not rid himself of his homosexual desires. He grew more anxious and fearful. To add to his difficulty, he lost his job. A deep depression set in, and Phil started to see a counselor and take antidepressants.

Eventually, he found a job as an electrician, an occupation he chose because it was "more physical and masculine" and because it would offer him a chance to form "friendship" bonds with men. He felt these bonds would help him "grow out of homosexuality." So, when his coworkers did not accept him and often referred to him in homosexual terms, Phil became even more distressed. Further, he also attempted dating relationships with women, each ending in disappointment. He believed these relationships failed because of his emotional state. He explained how he felt at this point in this life: "I guess I wanted somebody to make me well. To make me anything but gay, anything but a homosexual. I hated it. It's twisted. It's a shameful thing. I felt ashamed. After all this stuff and my break up with my girlfriend, I had to take Prozac again because my nerves were really getting bad. . . . My emotions were torn up. I needed help." Like Terry, Phil had reached a point in his life where he was becoming overwhelmed by the feelings that emerged from his struggle to cope with his homosexuality. The intensity of Phil's feelings brought recognition that he "needed help," that he was no longer willing (or able) to live with such struggle. This recognition made Phil's search for help more urgent, and he finally confided in a friend whom he had heard give a testimony about her sexual struggle. This woman told him he could be healed and directed him to an ex-gay ministry, which he hoped "would be the answer to [his] prayers."

Charles. Just as Terry and Phil had done, Charles struggled arduously with his homosexuality before deciding to join an ex-gay group, though his situation was compounded by his love for his wife and children and his desire to stay married. According to Charles, his conflict originated in his Southern Baptist home located in the rural South. As the youngest of three sons, he was often left behind when his father and brothers went places and had no close friends or even a playmate. He described himself as "pretty much a loner" who was "detached from peer groups" and yet wanted male attention and "fantasized about spending time with guys." At age eleven, he realized he had sexual feelings for other boys/men, and the recognition felt simultaneously "sick," because he knew such feelings were wrong in God's eyes, and "good," while still "confusing." He enjoyed the attraction but knew it was wrong and could not understand why he experienced it.

In middle school, he started dating girls as a "cover-up" because he was "afraid of what was in there [himself]" and he did not want people to know he had these kinds of feelings. He told no one about his feelings and felt increasingly more isolated and detached. He was deceiving everyone, making him feel unworthy and always in danger of discovery. His self-image, as he explained, was "pretty nasty." What kept him hopeful and going forward was his belief in a good and loving God. While he wondered why God "let this stuff happen" and why God "didn't just stop it," he also "held onto that [his belief] because it was the only hope [he] had—that some day something was going to happen and God was going to fix this [his life]."

Charles continued dating women as a "cover" throughout high school and into college, even while he had occasional homosexual encounters. He was so serious about maintaining this cover that he had been engaged three times before he graduated, knowing that each engagement was "just a sham." He prayed constantly to God, asking for the right woman and conveying his desire to "get married and have children," believing that the right heterosexual relationship would end his struggle. Finally, he met Lucy and developed what he described as a "satisfying, comforting, solid" relationship. He felt God had sent her to him, and he remembered thinking: "I'm not attracted to her romantically, but I love her as a friend and I like her relationship with Jesus Christ and I can make a commitment and I will do everything I can to honor it." He told Lucy about his sexual desires for men, and she was touched he confided in her and echoed his belief that Jesus would change him after they were married. They married soon after, and Charles worked hard at the marriage. He managed to "perform" sexually, but "it [sex] didn't do it for [him]," though he loved and respected Lucy as a person. They had two children in the first three years of marriage, and Charles seemed to be managing. After four years, however, Charles met a man and had a homosexual affair. Eventually, he told Lucy, broke off the affair, and tried to get help from pastors and counselors. For a while, things seemed to be going better; they had two more children, and Charles stayed away from men.

Charles, however, was profoundly unhappy. He began having homosexual encounters, but he found anonymous sex to be dissatisfying and dangerous. He decided to find someone else in his position and to have a "relationship on the side." He met a single gay man and began a relationship that progressed and felt good and "natural." He remembered feeling so torn about what to do and guilty and ashamed. He "had gotten to the point where home was miserable, and [he] was tired of making home miserable. They [his family] did not have a clue what was going on, and Lucy did not want to think about the possibility of [him] being involved again, so she thought he was just having a midlife crisis." He decided to leave to "stop making the family miserable" and to get "whatever enjoyment possible out of life and then die and go to hell."

A week before he planned to move out, however, he met a pastor who asked him what was wrong. When Charles explained, the pastor told him that "nothing was too big for God" and that he knew where he could get help. Charles felt waves of grief at the thought of losing his family, and he knew then that he "wanted to stay married and needed to keep [his] family together." If Lucy was willing to work through this with him, he felt he had to try again. He told Lucy what was going on. She was, understandably, very hurt and angry, but she agreed that "she and God would work to heal him as long as he was honest with her." Charles knew he wanted to follow God's will for his life and did not want to lose his wife and children, and Lucy's support seemed like evidence of what God wanted him to do, solidifying his decision. He would take the pastor's advice and join an ex-gay group, believing that with God and his wife on his side he might "find peace."

The examples from these three men's lives are representative of the kind of struggle that the men in this study endured and the feelings it evoked as they tried to make sense of themselves and their homosexuality within the confines of their faith. Over time, when they made little progress toward a resolution to their problem, their lives seemed to become more complicated as people, relationships, and events were impacted by their dueling and mismatched desires. Fear, anxiety, and shame became prominent features of their lives, and they experienced debilitating emotional distress. This distress, and the need for relief from it, created the emotional incentives that prompted them to seek help in earnest.

Making Emotional Promises

While these negative emotions certainly propelled the men's search for resolution, they were not a sufficient reason to decide to actively participate in a specific group. Deciding to participate required that the individual believe that the group could actually provide effective help. The men joined these *particular* groups because each held out an emotional promise—either to rectify negative emotions or to allow for the enactment of positive ones—that pulled in the men. So, while the men's feelings were catalysts that pushed them to seek help, they were drawn into these specific groups because of the groups' promise to make them feel better, albeit in different ways. Accept promised a way to find acceptance and love as a gay Christian, while Expell promised a way to change the self to fit into the dictates of conservative Christianity. Both promises secured the men's initial commitment to the groups.

These promises were communicated to prospective members through group literature and videotapes as well as lessons taught by group leaders. But the two most common and powerful ways such promises were transmitted were interaction during group meetings (Accept) and personal conversations (Expell). When a potential new member came to an Accept meeting, the group leader would open the meeting with prayer and then welcome the new person, always thanking God for bringing the new person and giving him the courage to begin to seek truth, and through truth, to heal. Healing thus became a focal theme of the meeting, as the group leader asked veteran members to recount their stories. The following fieldnote excerpt is representative of numerous exchanges that occurred when new people attended meetings:

Leader:	(to potential member) Were you scared to come here tonight?
Potential Member:	Yeah, I tried to come for a long time, but I just couldn't. I kept praying about it, but I just wasn't sure, you know? Then, I felt so bad this weekend, so wrong, that I finally decided to just do it.
Leader:	(slight smile) Sounds real familiar . . . that wrong feeling, the fear. How about to the rest of you?
Old Member:	Yep, I can remember driving to meetings and parking on the other side of the street to watch people as they left to see if they looked normal, or if they were all weirdos or something. I was so scared I was going to a freak show, that I would be in an ungodly place and end up worse off than I was. But I didn't. I felt loved by God, by others, and finally by myself. Going to [the MCC church] was like going into a place where there's like a breath of fresh air because it was the first church I had ever been to, ever, that preached that God loves you, no matter what, period. Churches preach the love of God, but when you don't fit, the love goes right out the window. So that's what drew me, and what I'll always remember—God loves you as you are, period. No conditions, no qualifications, no nothing—God loves you. I

> was surrounded, finally, by all these people
> who were gay like me, and I was not alone,
> and they knew God loved us no matter what.

In this exchange, the group leader solicited the potential new member's feelings, acknowledged his fear and mixed feelings about the group, and then called on another member to give an account of his own past negative emotions and how he overcame them within the group. In this way, the confusing feelings new members experienced were acknowledged and explained. The promise, too, was clear: becoming one of us can make you feel better and turn what is wrong into what is right.

Expell's promise to potential members held this same message, but it was most frequently and powerfully conveyed to them in private conversations before the men came to a group meeting.[1] These sessions served dual functions. On one hand, they were attempts to ensure no one would bring a dissenting opinion or disruptive philosophy/theology to the group meeting. On the other hand, they were concerted efforts by leaders to create initial commitment to the group. Because these men were trying to live heterosexual lives, anonymity was critical and most would not risk coming to a group meeting until they were reasonably certain they wanted to join the group. In interviews, Expell members typically described their first meetings as secretive and frightening, yet as important turning points in their decisions to join:

> I finally called the group leader to find out about the ministry. He agreed to meet me at work. When he got there, I wouldn't let him talk until we were in the conference room with the door locked. Then, I told him if he couldn't answer one question to my satisfaction that we had nothing to talk about. I asked him if Christ could heal me. He said yes, without a shadow of a doubt. I asked how he knew. He said because Christ had healed him, taken him from a suicidal man with no hope to a man with a family and a Godly life. He was the first man I'd met who struggled too and who believed I could be cured. For the first time in a very long time, I felt less alone and somewhat hopeful, scared still, but there was hope.

This man shows us how important it was for him to know, before joining or, indeed, even talking further with the leader, that he could be helped. Without the promise of a "cure," he had no interest in the group. The leader's testimony and evidence (family) evoked positive emotions (hope, lessened isolation) and held the promise of a cure and permanent good feeling.

These excerpts not only illustrate how emotional promises were conveyed, but they also show us how the promise itself could spark immediate positive emotion. Meeting other people who had suffered in the same ways provided the men with some immediate vindication and lessened their sense of isolation. Such promises also created for the men, often for the first time since the inception of their identity dilemmas, hope that their negative feelings and their problem could be resolved. These good feelings drew the men toward the group and made them willing listeners to still others' similar accounts of how they had once felt the same way but now "were at peace with who they are." Such accounts reiterated the powerful and tempting promise to the men: if you become one of us, then all those terrible feelings you have been wrestling with will dissipate. Thus, simply having negative emotions was not enough to secure the men's participation. It was through this promise of emotional relief that the groups exerted a pull and recruited new members.

It was not surprising that the men who joined Expell were drawn in by the group's promise. Expell's explanation of homosexuality fit easily into and was consistent with the men's existing theology, requiring only minor changes. In short, the pull of Expell was that it promised to make the men what they wished themselves to be—heterosexuals with families. The gay Christians, however, pose a more interesting and complex case. Accept's theology contradicted the men's initial view of Christian doctrine. Prior to their introduction to the group, the men did not believe it possible to be gay *and* Christian—as evidenced by their identity dilemmas. Yet, even in the absence of this initial ideological affinity, the men were still pulled to join the group. The emotional promise "hooked" them, in spite of their skepticism, and compelled the men to stay and consider the group's ideological message. In sum, it was not what the men thought that drew them to the groups but how they felt. Their desire to be rid of troubling feelings and the group's promise to help them do so were enough incentive to secure a tentative commitment to their respective group. Becoming a gay Christian or an ex-gay Christian became seen by the men as an answer to their struggle, providing some immediate relief and holding out the possibility of complete satisfaction/resolution.

Finding Fraud and Flaws in Old Beliefs

Once the men believed that their respective group might hold the answer to their dilemma, they could make an initial commitment to the group and its goals. This commitment enabled them to begin the work of becoming a gay or ex-gay Christian. Such work entailed revising their existing Christian ideology to redefine what it meant to be a good Christian in ways that would legitimately accommodate their sexuality. In other words, the men now faced the task of altering damning aspects of their long-held Christian beliefs so that they could understand themselves and their homosexuality in new and more positive ways. For the men to accomplish this kind of revision, they would first have to challenge the validity of these damning pieces of conservative Christian theology. Launching such a challenge, however, was incredibly difficult and complicated for several reasons.

Dominant and traditional ideas are incredibly resilient and tough to change for three primary reasons. First, people usually encounter these ideas as a ready-made part of their lives, just simply "how the world works," and thus see them as something to be accepted—not challenged (Schwalbe 1998, 16). Second, ideologies, as sets of beliefs about how the world works, are used as "an interpretive system" that guides how people see themselves and their "conceptions of and actions in the social and political realm" (Fine and Sandstrom 1993, 24). Questioning such beliefs is hard because doing so requires that we relearn how to see ourselves and our environment. Finally, such ideas are hard to change because they are often held in place by and protect those in power.

An example will help illustrate how and why dominant ideas are so persistent. Consider our acceptance of the "achievement ideology," or the belief that those people who try hard enough will be successful. Because many of us are taught this idea as children, we often take it to be "the way things are" and tend to understand individual failures or successes as a result of what that person did or did not do. We rarely think about other factors, such as the design of a social system (e.g., education, job market, etc.), that contributed to a failure or a success (cf. MacLeod 1987). As a result, we see individual achievement as strictly a result of individual effort and try to work hard so we can be successful. When we succeed, we see it as a result of our work. When we fail, we think we "should have tried harder." Rarely do we think about how much help we receive from others or the opportunities that are given to us just because of who we are. Most importantly, we see successful individuals as those who worked hard enough and deserve their success. In this way, the success of those in power and the failure of others become legitimate; they got what they "deserved." The achievement ideology therefore not only structures how we approach attaining goals, but also protects the powerful by justifying their power as earned. In turn, the powerful can use their greater resources (i.e., money, media, and political clout) to perpetuate this ideology. This cycle makes transforming dominant ideas quite hard.

Dominant religious ideas, and the meanings they give to the identities constructed from them, have a peculiar characteristic that makes them even harder to question and change than secular ideas and self-understandings. Put simply, religious ideologies and identity meanings are anchored in the divine realm and in God's authority—not just the authority of powerful people—making them automatically legitimate for believers (Berger 1967; Mol 1976). This kind of anchoring is particularly firm, powerfully cemented by the idea of an immutable divine realm not subject to human doubt or whim.

By contrast, secular ideologies and identity meanings are anchored in the mundane, human realm and in human authority. Because humans are perceived as fallible, and our knowledge as partial and changing, it can be less difficult to challenge and alter secular ideology. For example, just a few decades ago, prevailing dominant gender ideology held that women were "the weaker sex" and could not endure or perform the same physical tasks as men. Accordingly, women were thought to lack the physical capacity to compete in marathon races and the belief was that doing so would cause them bodily harm. As a result, women were not allowed to enter marathons. In 1967, however, Katherine Switzer registered for the Boston Marathon using the name K. Switzer. When officials discovered, during the race, that Switzer was a woman, they chased her to remove her from the race. She eluded them, with the help of some male participants, and finished. Her finish sparked more women to run long distances, and this aspect of dominant gender ideology became suspect. Soon, in 1972, women could officially register for the Boston Marathon, and in 1984 a women's marathon was added as an Olympic event. In this way, these women challenged an aspect of traditional gender ideology through athletic performances that refuted a dominant idea. Here, experience could be used to reveal wrong human thinking, creating changes in gender ideology and the meaning of a feminine identity, at least to some degree.

A similar type of challenge, however, cannot be launched against an ideology that permeates conservative evangelical Protestantism because no human experience could effectively call divine wisdom and authority into question. Human experiences that contradict these religious ideologies are characterized either as wrong/sinful or as unable to be understood by mere people. Put bluntly, humans have a tough time arguing with God. Most importantly, perhaps, people, at least those who are believers within this tradition, do not want to argue with God. In fact, posing challenges to religious ideology can feel very threatening and risky. Believers, like the men in this study, use their religious ideologies to make sense of their lives, to structure their actions and feelings, and to discern right and wrong. To pose a serious challenge to these ideologies is to shake the foundations of how they understand the world. Further, tampering with this ideology can be seen as defying divine authority, an activity that may put one's eternal salvation in jeopardy. If challenging God's Word was so unlikely and undesirable, then how could the men successfully question the validity of the religious ideology that damned them?

Quite simply, a successful attempt to revise the men's Christian beliefs could not challenge God's Word or authority; God's Word remained the truth the men had to obey. Instead, the men in both groups focused on human (and thus fallible) interpretations of God's Word. To challenge existing conservative Protestant doctrine regarding homosexuality, the men examined the key aspects of traditional interpretation of the Bible that damned homosexuals, claiming that such conservative interpretations reflected *human* biases, not God's truth. By labeling the damning aspects of this belief as artifacts of human interpretation, the men pulled them out of the divine realm, where they were protected by divine authority, and set them firmly in the secular realm, where they could be challenged and changed. This innovative interpretive strategy was a form of ideological maneuvering—shifting of key pieces of ideology from the sacred to the secular realms—that enabled the men to discredit existing interpretations of homosexuality and homosexuals. In doing so, the men created within their religious beliefs a new interpretive space that they could later use to construct an alternative and affirming theology/ideology.

The extent to which existing interpretation had to be discredited varied considerably between Accept and Expell. Because Accept strove to make homosexuality and Christianity compatible, it had to reject all interpretation that labeled homosexuality as damning. By contrast,

Expell attempted to recast homosexual struggle as righteousness and, therefore, needed only to refashion the meaning of sexual struggle, redefining it as a moral, rather than as a shameful, activity. In spite of this difference, a similar process occurred in both groups. In what follows, I show how both groups maneuvered key pieces of interpretation out of the sacred realm and into the secular, thereby opening them to challenge and change.

Exposing Fraudulent Interpretation

In previous discussion of MCC's theology (chapter 2), we saw that MCC promoted the idea that condemnation of groups of people results from human misinterpretation of the Bible. MCC politicized interpretation and asserted that conservatives have (mis)used Scripture, and still do, to oppress others to suit their own prejudices and agendas. The idea here is that fallible humans have distorted the truth of God's Word. Whether this distortion has occurred is irrelevant to the focus of this study. Instead, it is important to recognize that this discrediting of existing interpretation was critical to MCC's ability to build a new and gay-affirming theology. Without invalidating condemning biblical interpretations, there was no theological room to develop an alternative interpretation. The same was true for Accept members; before they could learn and embrace an affirming religious ideology/theology, they had to make space in their faith by letting go of their belief in traditional and damning interpretations of key biblical passages. But given the duration and intensity of the men's belief in traditional theology and their desire to obey God's truth, it was not easy to convince them that they were victims of fraudulent renderings of God's Word.

To this end, the MCC congregation I studied had a special twelve-week Bible study for new members devoted to the explicit goal of uncovering what the "Bible really says about homosexuality." This study, to reveal the "fraudulence" of existing interpretation successfully, had to do two things. First, it had to transform the men's certainty that the Bible did condemn homosexuality into a question about what the Bible says about it. Second, it had to provide a convincing answer. To do both, the study group focused on translation, critiquing current translation and discussing how to engage in better biblical interpretation. By pointing out the weaknesses in existing translation, traditional scriptural meanings became suspect. Then, using what they thought of as better methods of translation, the men reexamined these Scriptures, arriving at the conclusion that they did not condemn homosexuality. The following examples, drawn from fieldnotes, illustrate how the men learned to discredit anti-gay interpretations.

To overturn the men's conviction that homosexuality was sin and replace it with the question of what was biblically said about homosexuality, the group leader drew on traditional forms of authority, such as religious experts and the Bible, readily recognizable and acceded to by the men. In this way, the leader did not appear to be imposing his own, non-expert interpretation; he was merely suggesting they take another look at the Bible to examine what is says about homosexuality. In fact, he demanded that group members *not* rely on his own words but hear expert discussion and read the Bible, guided by the Holy Spirit, to decide for themselves. This interpretive strategy is commonplace in many conservative Christian communities; religious authorities espouse or denounce a particular interpretation, point their audiences to the inerrant Scripture, and encourage them to see for themselves the truth. Kathleen Boone describes this strategy in her work on Protestant fundamentalist discourse, explaining that, while "all readers are to pray for guidance in interpreting the scripture and to accept the leading of the Holy Spirit in answer to such prayers" (1989, 78), telling "readers to consult the Bible to check a pastor's doctrine is to send them to the text with interpretive model in hand" (88). In other words, when experts tell non-expert readers what to look for, and sometimes where to find it, it is quite likely that they will find precisely what experts pointed them to, thereby giving authority to expert interpretation. While Boone is referring to fundamentalists, her discussion also applies to conservative evangelical Protestants' strategies of biblical interpretation generally and to Accept's and Expell's strategies specifically.

To utilize this strategy, the group leader used a video, *Homosexuality and the Bible* (Hawkes 1994), as a primary teaching tool. The main speaker in the video, who also served as a pastor at a MCC congregation in Toronto, Reverend Hawkes (M. Div., D. Div.), was cast as a religious expert. He spoke from his desk in a library surrounded by books. His academic credentials appeared at the bottom of our screen. He was dressed as a preacher and often placed his hands on the Bibles that lay before him on his desk, particularly when he hoped to emphasize a point about biblical interpretation. This staging showed us that he was both a man of God and a scholar, and thus a credible source.

His presentation emphasized modern scholarship on the Bible, claiming that recent discoveries had allowed better interpretation of the Bible. He urged his audience "to set aside *cultural* biases and take a more *scholarly* approach to the Bible [emphasis added]" and asserted that "we are blessed to be able to see the truth today." The idea here was that, while traditional interpretations were culturally biased, newer interpretations were more reliable because they were based on scholarship. He continued by explaining that "churches are human institutions torn apart by racism, sexism, and homophobia," but that the Bible "is not a threat. The Bible can be a friend" (Hawkes 1994). In sum, he assured us the Bible was not the problem; the men could continue to trust it as truth.

To support his claims that the Bible was the source of truth and a friend, Hawkes cited Galatians 5:1: "You shall know the truth and the truth shall set you free." He then told his viewers that the truth is that the church has historically supported various forms of oppression with scriptural misinterpretation, such as using obedience Scriptures to condone slavery or submission Scriptures to deny women equality. He urged us to see that these examples show that cultural biases can lead to misinterpretation because of the difficulties inherent in biblical translation: words get mistranslated, passages are taken out of historical/cultural context, and some translators do not consider meaning changes over time. For instance, the word "awful," which we now think of as conveying a very bad thing, was once translated as "full of awe," a very good thing. In sum, we learned that human biases provided the motive to create oppressive interpretations and that the difficulties of biblical translation enabled people to do so. For these reasons, he urged that we carefully translate, using different versions of the Bible to compare meanings and looking up words in their original language when there was disagreement.

Because the men knew the Bible was once used to legitimate slavery and the subordination of women, it seemed plausible that contemporary cultural biases had also led people to misinterpret Scripture as condemning homosexuality. They also knew that the meanings of words can change over time. For the first time, then, the men began to wonder if homosexuality was condemned by God as they had been taught all along or whether such teachings emerged from the biases of people. As one of the men put it in an informal conversation after this meeting, "I spent so long asking for forgiveness, asking not to be gay, but I never once really wondered whether being gay might be okay—not until now. I don't know what to think." What was once taken as biblical truth—homosexuality was sin—now became the question of whether homosexuality was sin. To find this answer, both Reverend Hawkes and the group leader insisted that the men turn to God's truth, to the Bible.

In their search to understand what the Bible said about homosexuality, the men, guided by Reverend Hawkes's conclusions and the direction of the group leader, engaged in a lengthy process of translation for each of the biblical verses commonly thought to condemn homosexuality. Generally, the process was the same for each verse. The men read the verse from the King James (KJ) version of the Bible (because it is the version most often used by conservative Protestants) and agreed that it seemed to support a traditional interpretation. They then compared this translation to the New International Version (NIV) and the Living Bible (LB) to note differences. They looked key words up in their original language to check on translations. In each case, the men found that existing interpretation was faulty. The following fieldnote excerpt illustrates this process, using the men's examination of Deuteronomy 23:17–18.

Dylan (the group leader) asked the men to read aloud and compare this passage from KJ and the NIV:

> There shall be no whore of the daughters of Israel, nor a sodomite of the sons of Israel. Thou shalt not bring the hire of a whore, or the price of a dog, into the house of the LORD thy God for any vow; for even both these are abomination unto the LORD thy God. (KJ)

> No Israelite man or woman is to become a shrine prostitute. You must not bring the earnings of a female prostitute or of a male prostitute into the house of the LORD your God to pay any vow, because the LORD your God detests them both. (NIV)

The group quickly agreed that the passage from KJ seemed to condemn both homosexuals and prostitutes as "abominations," but that the NIV passage seemed only to condemn male and female prostitutes. To work out such contradictory evidence, Dylan directed the men to look up the words "whore" and "sodomite" in Hebrew, the original language. They discovered that "whore" in Hebrew was "qdeshah," meaning "female prostitute"—a reasonable translation. However, "sodomite," translated from the Hebrew word "qadesh," was a poor translation and should refer to male temple prostitutes. From this work, the men agreed that that NIV passage was translated more accurately, leaving them to conclude that this scriptural passage condemned prostitution, male and female, but offered no condemnation of loving homosexual (or heterosexual) relationships.

As the men in this study used this same procedure to systematically analyze the biblical verses they once read as damning, they found, often to their amazement, that such condemnation was missing. Over weeks, as they concluded that one biblical verse after another did not condemn a loving, monogamous homosexual relationship, the men began to believe that the condemnation of homosexuality was not biblical truth, but a fraud perpetuated by humans. While there were still a few shreds of occasional doubt, these men had arrived at an answer to their question—and God did not condemn them. They had been feeling ashamed, afraid, and anxious, at least in part, because they were worried that being gay was against God's will. Now, they had discovered that the bad feelings they had experienced about themselves were the result of human intolerance and misuse of the Bible to promote discriminatory behavior.

This revelation, which clearly echoed a key component of therapeutic culture—that the self must be liberated from oppressive social influence (Nolan 1998, 3)—enabled the men to reframe their problem, shifting the blame for their struggles from an inferior self (e.g., not in obedience to God's Word) to an oppressive society, recasting themselves as victims. This shift convinced them of the wisdom and utility of letting go of their existing—and wrong—beliefs about homosexuality. One man explained after the final Bible study meeting: "I'm not sure I could have ever believed it [homosexuality is not a sin] and gone against what religious people had told me my whole life if I hadn't actually seen it in the Bible right in front of me. The truth was there the whole time." Because this reinterpretation was based on a direct examination of biblical verses in which the men actually did the translation, they felt like they had "tested" existing interpretation and, just as religious leaders associated with MCC suggested, discovered a biblical truth that had simply always been there. As a result, they did not see themselves as adopting a group perspective, but rather saw that they had wiped away a false picture and finally found truth. In doing so, they created a new interpretive space within which they could begin to build an affirming theology.

Exposing Flawed Interpretation

When new members joined Expell, they believed that a "good Christian" had to be strictly heterosexual in behavior and desire and that any homosexual urge or action was especially sinful. This belief made the men particularly shamed and left no theological room for building positive self-understanding. Like Accept members, the men in Expell had to create new interpretive space in which to construct more affirming meanings of homosexuality and sexual struggle. They too could only begin this transformation if they let go of some of their existing religious beliefs surrounding homosexuality. Their task, however, was less difficult and complicated than that of Accept members because they did not try to overturn traditional interpretation, but only to expose its flaws and remedy them.

According to Expell, homosexuality was still a sin, and homosexuals were sinners. The idea, however, that a group of people were sinners was not striking nor did it merit special attention. Like many conservative Protestants, these men believed that all humans were sinners and had, as one man explained, a "sinful nature" that was a result of the "fall" in the Garden of Eden. What was of concern, though, was the belief that homosexual sin was exceptionally detrimental. Expell members felt that the sin of homosexuality was somehow more damning than other sins and perceived that other Christians felt this way too. As a result, they felt they were more wicked than others and deserved worse condemnation. To offset this idea, Expell asserted that the extra attention paid to homosexual sin arose from human biases against homosexuality, not from God's Word. Because of cultural prejudices, Expell argued, people had elevated homosexuality to an extraordinary form of sin and therefore homosexuals were perceived to be extraordinary sinners. To combat this belief and open new interpretive space, the men had to learn that homosexual sin was ordinary sin on par with any other. If homosexual sin was normal sin, then the men were just sinners like everyone else. They could also more readily believe they could overcome normal sin and be forgiven for it.

To persuade Expell members that they were just normal sinners eligible for the same kind of salvation as other Christian sinners, leaders used an interpretive strategy and process similar to that of Accept. Group leaders called into question damning aspects of existing interpretation as *human* bias by providing an alternative interpretation and then asking members to turn to Scripture to discover truth for themselves.

When members did so, older, more condemning interpretations became human misinterpretations, thereby moving them from the divine to the secular realm. Once secularized, these aspects could be challenged through a reexamination of biblical passages, creating spaces for new theological ideas.

To begin this process of exposing flawed interpretation and redefining homosexual sin as no worse than any other, group leaders asserted that people's existing interpretation of the Bible exaggerated the significance of sexual behavior, magnifying transgressions into extraordinary sins. As the ex-gay group leader announced to the group, the "great social stigma attached to homosexuality has misled men to perceive it as somehow worse than any other sin, but sin is sin before the eyes of God." He further explained that, for those who struggled with homosexuality, it was very important they learn "the truth that homosexual sin is ordinary sin." Doing so marked the beginning of what he thought of as a healing process: "The first step in healing is to normalize homosexuality, to make the men realize it is no worse a sin than a white lie. I always tell them [the group] that men have distorted the biblical significance of sexuality. It gives them hope and lets them start to rethink their lives."

Telling new group members that homosexual sin was just sin and convincing them were two very different things. For the men to believe this was the case, they, like Accept members, had to see authoritative evidence. To support claims that the importance of sexual sin had been exaggerated by people, the Expell leader encouraged the group *not* to rely on his word but to read God's Word and see for themselves. While Expell members did not examine different versions of the Bible, analyze translations, or consider context, they did turn to the Bible as an authoritative source with which to assess the validity of the leader's assertions. The leader helped them to do so. For example, as an illustration of his assertion that homosexuality was just normal sin, the group leader urged the group to examine 1 Corinthians 6:9–11 of the King James Bible: "Know ye not that the unrighteous shall not inherit the kingdom of God? Be not deceived: neither fornicators, nor idolaters, nor adulterers, nor effeminate, nor abusers of themselves with mankind, nor thieves, nor covetous, nor drunkards, nor revilers, nor extortioners, shall inherit the kingdom of God. And such were some of you: but ye are washed, but ye are sanctified, but ye are justified in the name of the Lord Jesus, and by the Spirit of our God." This passage treats sexual sin as one item in a list. During the group discus-

sion that followed, Expell members noted that they were given no special treatment in Scripture, no extra punishment, and they concluded
that their homosexual sin was no worse than being selfish or gossip-
ing. And, just like the drunk or the greedy, the homosexual offender
was also "washed" and "sanctified." The men also read similar passages with the same conclusions. By the end of the meeting, the men
were amazed, relieved, and convinced by their reading of these passages. In a casual conversation during a short break in the meeting, a
man remarked: "It is so clear now; all the social pressures against homosexuals got put onto God's Word and made us think we were so
bad, but we are all just sinners. It's kind of a weird relief." After this
meeting, in a conversation on the way to our cars, one member said
to me, "People have made homosexual sin into such a big deal, but it
is a sin just like any other." Just as in Accept, Expell members employed a strategy common in a therapeutic culture, learning to shift
the blame for their intense shame and self-doubt from themselves to
a culture that unfairly castigated or oppressed them. They too were
victims. This shift, made through guided reexamination of biblical passages, enabled the men to reject the notion that homosexual sin was
especially damning.

If homosexual sin was ordinary sin, then the homosexual was just
an ordinary sinner, capable of being saved. To reach this conclusion,
Expell members, like their counterparts in Accept, shifted condemning pieces of traditional interpretation (homosexuals are uniquely
damned) out of the divine realm and into the secular so that they could
challenge them. In this way, the men detached the notion of homosexuality as extraordinary sin from divine authority, linking it to human fallibility. Once accomplished, this shift allowed them to see
traditional interpretation as flawed by human bias and therefore subject to modification. In doing so, they too created a new, albeit very
subtle, space in which to begin to redefine Christian ideology and themselves.

In many ways, opening this new interpretive space, while only
the beginning of the transformation process, was alone quite an ac-
complishment. It required discrediting existing and powerful biblical
interpretations through careful maneuvering of key aspects of theology between the sacred and secular realms, and the men had to learn
how to call on the higher authority of God to trump prevailing human interpretations. Using this interpretive strategy, the men maintained the integrity of the Bible and shifted the blame for their situations

to people who endorsed what the men came to see as oppressive and false (in Accept's case) or exaggerated (in Expell's case) doctrine. Because this ideological maneuvering was embedded in a process perceived of as seeking God's truth, the men felt their actions and subsequent conclusions were not heretical but righteous. Whether they learned to see traditional interpretation as fraudulent or simply flawed, the men perceived their activities as a quest to uncover and obey God's teachings, rather than as an attempt to resist dominant ideas and manage how they felt about homosexuality.

Further, the men's activities had implications for the importance of self and self-feeling in this context. In the process of opening new interpretive space, the men came to believe that they had to resist the stigma imposed on them unjustly if they were to discover divine truth and be who God intended them to be. Under these conditions, this belief imbued a key characteristic of and pursuit in therapeutic culture—the quest for a true self, unfettered by societal repression—with a sacred quality. Focusing on finding and living from the real self (the one God created) became an act of religious obedience—not self-absorption. Self-feelings and emotions thus could be perceived as signifiers, marking whether the men were moving in the direction God desired. Seen this way, the groups' strategies for initiating the transformation process provided a religious justification for the self focus characteristic of a therapeutic culture and gave more weight to the subjective experience of self as a critical guidepost by which to assess "right" living. Having cast off condemnation and opened space for new interpretations of situation and self, at least to some degree, the men were now empowered to begin the construction of an alternative, affirming ideology.

6 Learning to Be a Gay or Ex-gay Christian

An Expell member once commented, after what was a particularly difficult meeting for him, that "the road to becoming straight certainly throws you a lot of curves." During this meeting, he had confessed that he had, after several months hiatus, returned to visiting Internet sites containing homosexual pornography. In a small group discussion, he explained that, over the course of the last few months, he had been having difficulties at work and had also been remembering more details of a childhood molestation. He felt hurt and angry as he remembered these details and prayed to God to help him handle these memories and forgive. He tried reading the Bible when he wanted to get on line, but even this activity did not help. Eventually, in spite of his shame and desire to live a heterosexual life, he gave in and connected to a pornographic Web site. He was embarrassed, frustrated, and discouraged by what he called a "backslide," perceiving that his hard work toward progressing out of his homosexuality was not paying off as it should. By telling the group what he had done, he hoped to get the help and guidance necessary to navigate such "curves" so that he could continue down the road of an ex-gay Christian.

This man's "backslide" is an illustration of the kind of difficulties both Accept and Expell members experienced in their efforts to heal and become either gay or ex-gay Christians. When the men first joined the groups, newly convinced that their respective group could help solve their problems, and learned that damning aspects of their religious beliefs emerged from human bias and not God's law, they were energized and optimistic in their pursuit of a resolution. Persuaded that they were on the right track, the men imagined that healing would be a straightforward process; their respective group would simply fill in the newly created interpretive spaces by teaching them the proper understanding of homosexuality within their faith, and they would change and feel better. None initially recognized the enormity of the task of transforming their old thoughts, actions, and feelings into those appropriate for a gay or ex-gay Christian.

To accomplish this kind of metamorphosis, the men first had to learn what thoughts, behaviors, and emotions were appropriate; that is, they had to figure out what it meant to take on the identity of a gay Christian or an ex-gay Christian. Doing so required that the men understand not only the group's theological perspective and the way it fit homosexuality into Christianity, but also how to apply this perspective to their own lives. While the men found learning group explanations of spirituality and sexuality relatively easy, adapting them to their lives was tough work. As the men became regular attendees in their respective groups and got down to the business of healing, they began to struggle with old behavioral and thought patterns, finding them difficult to alter. Healing, they discovered, was not simply a direct process of learning and progressively feeling better.

The transformation that the men sought was complex and arduous work, requiring that they endure periods of intense uncertainty, anxiety, and struggle. These periods were psychologically and emotionally taxing for the men, leaving them discouraged and sometimes doubting their decisions to become group members. At this point, the group had to rally around the discouraged member, giving him strategies and tools to manage such bad feelings—or risk losing him. This chapter focuses on these ideological and emotional aspects of the transformative process of becoming a gay or ex-gay Christian, examining how the men learned new definitions of a good Christian and adapted them to their own situations, as well as the ways in which the group worked to help (or hinder) the men's ability to overcome obstacles during the process and to develop a sense of belonging that made their choice of group feel legitimate.

Redefining the Good Christian

In the last chapter, we saw how the men were able to discredit their long-held Christian interpretations of homosexuality by shifting these interpretations out from under the sacred umbrella of God's truth and into the secular realm of fallible humanity, thereby making them suspect and subject to change. At this point, however, the men knew only what homosexuality was *not;* it was either not sinful (Accept) or not especially sinful (Expell). They still had to come to a new understanding of what it meant to experience and act on homosexual desires within the context of Christianity.

To construct this understanding, the men in both groups worked to revise existing theology in ways that would accommodate their sexuality and cast them in a more positive light. This is not to say that the men were simply trying to make themselves look good, feel okay, or justify their behavior. They were sincerely trying to discern what it meant to be gay and Christian. Divine will was still the moral cornerstone of their lives and the guiding force that drove their behavior. The difference now was that the men were uncertain of the content of religious truth. Faced with such uncertainty and eager to make sense of their situations, the men, as group participants, learned how to draw on secular and religious cultural resources to redefine this truth. To transform traditional taboos against homosexuality, members of both groups combined aspects of secular culture with simple biblical precepts to create a revised version of theology, one that affirmed the men's sexuality (Accept) or their sexual struggle (Expell). Accept members learned to apply a social justice perspective to their situations to highlight the importance of including everyone in God's love, thereby creating a new theological framework from which the men could derive positive self-understandings. Similarly, Expell members constructed a revised and affirming theological framework by combining pieces of psychological theories of homosexuality with aspects of religious belief to reconceive of homosexuality as curable psychological disorder or disease. Both frameworks emphasized overcoming the sins of others to become the person God intended and offered a model of how to be a good Christian. In what follows, I show how group members used these cultural and religious resources to develop and adapt a more affirming theological truth.

God Loves Everyone

To develop this new theological framework, Accept members relied on both an essentialist understanding of sexual orientation and a principle of inclusion that combined notions of social justice with the biblical precept "God loves everyone." As we will see, this revised framework not only asserted that homosexuality was part of God's plan, making it just, but also emphasized the importance of love and inclusion within Christianity. In doing so, it rendered the human act of judging and condemning others as sinful.

Accept, and MCC more generally, predicated their revised theology, in part, on the belief that God created all people and all sexualities in accord with a divine plan. If God intended for a person to be homosexual to fulfill some divine purpose, then trying to deny or alter one's sexuality would be both futile and a direct contradiction of God's will. Sociologist Andrew Yip points to this same logic in his study of gay Christians, noting that "attributing one's sexuality to God's intended creation is the ultimate justification for its acceptability and unchangeability. If one's sexuality is God-created, it cannot, and most of all, *should not,* be changed. Attributing the responsibility to God renders any efforts to alter any sexual orientation morally reprehensible" (1997, 123). The belief that sexual orientation is an immutable part of the divinely created self means that being true to oneself is tantamount to being true to and obeying God.

Working from this essentialist position, Accept leaders tried to show new members that God had made them gay and that one of their mistakes had been to try to deny or change their sexuality. To illustrate these ideas during group meetings, leaders and longtime members routinely referred to their sexuality as God-given and described the troubles that had emerged before they came to this realization. However, given how contrary this belief is to the conservative Protestant notion of divinely mandated heterosexuality that the men had held for so long, members were often initially hesitant to accept it as truth. To overcome this hesitation, the group leader frequently drew on members' experiences and their testimonies to establish the legitimacy of this belief. The following example, drawn from fieldnotes, reveals how the group most commonly encouraged members to adopt this essentialist position.

One night, in the middle of a Bible study, group members turned to a discussion of when they most powerfully felt God's presence in their lives. Jamie, a longtime member, described feeling closest to God whenever he heard the hymn "Just as I Am" because it "filled [him] with a great sense of peace and warmth," reminding him that "God not only loves [him] as [he] is, but that God made [him] gay and desires for [him] to celebrate the gift of his sexuality." Then, Terry, who had only been a member for a few months at this time, asked, "How do you know God made you gay? I mean, I'm just not sure. I know God made me, but my sexuality is another thing." To answer Terry's question, the group leader gave a partial biographical account of coming to realize the origins of his sexuality, emphasizing how his emotions and positive experiences revealed God's hand in his life. He explained:

> I knew I liked to look at boys before I even knew what sex was. When I was like eight, I had a crush on the paper boy. I just liked seeing him, and I didn't feel bad about it because I had not yet been told it was wrong. Later, when I knew about sex, knew homosexuality was sin, I still felt drawn to guys, but I felt so guilty and ashamed about it. I prayed and prayed, begged God to take this from me. Then, one day, I was confiding to a Christian friend, who had a lesbian sister, how awful I felt about being gay and not being able to stop the feelings. He said, and I will never forget these words, "Maybe God wants you to celebrate the gift he gave you and be who he made you to be so you can fulfill his purpose for you." I was stunned. I never until that moment thought God made me gay. As I thought about it, I recognized that God makes all people, and they are so different in many ways, so why not sexually too? I prayed about it, and God brought memories of how it felt to be attracted before I was told it was wrong. It was like I got hit with a board; I realized it had felt right—before people told me otherwise—because it *was* right. God made me that way. The joy and peace I felt when I realized this convinced me. When you feel God working in your life, you just know.

This account, and others like it, presented homosexuality as just another difference in people created by God and encouraged doubting members to ask why they had not been able to change their sexuality. The answer, which was provided in almost all such accounts, was that altering sexuality is not possible because God makes gay people gay. Some members gave accounts that compared being made gay to being made left-handed or with some unique ability, and they believed that God made them different to teach them something or to use them to meet divine ends. Members could know that God created them gay, as the leader's story suggests, if they pushed aside all the human biases they had learned and paid attention to how they felt. When they were true to the self God made them to be, they would feel better.

This interlinking of self-fulfillment, good feeling, and God's intent had important implications for how the men understood their work and purpose in Accept. If they were trying to be the persons God made them to be, in order to fulfill a divine purpose, then their efforts, while focused on the self and feeling better, were not seen as self-serving but as an attempt to do sacred work. Linda Francis, in her study of Discovery, a Christian support group for those recovering from divorce, also observed this convergence. In this case, Joe, the group leader/facilitator, urged group members to see self-fulfillment and God's will as the same, explaining that he saw it this way "because [he was] not trying to do what [he] want[ed], but only what he who has sent [him] wants" (Francis 1997a, 89). Here, as Francis explains, "pursuing self-fulfillment is literally the way to heaven, because it is God's will (89). Through this kind of linkage, support group and individual goals become imbued with religious meaning and take on greater power and importance. For Accept members, including Terry and the other men who joined the group during the time I attended, adopting this essentialist position meant not only that their sexuality was an unchangeable aspect of themselves but that embracing it was critical to embracing God's will. As Terry put it during a conversation that took place a few months after the above Bible study, "I wonder if God thinks I'm dense; I spent so long fighting what he made me to be. So pointless. Why I couldn't see it before, I just don't know, but I know God has plans for me once I can be completely accepting of who[m] he wants me to be." Terry now saw his task as accepting himself so that he could fulfill God's purpose for him, making his transformation to a gay Christian a religious act.

In addition to asserting that homosexuality was God given, Accept (and MCC) promoted a principle of inclusiveness, based on the idea that God loves everyone. This inclusiveness principle was simple yet powerful. Because God created and loves everyone equally, regardless of race, class, gender, or sexual orientation, humans should also include everyone in their love and should not judge others. Based on divine example, and lodged in ideals already seen as true and good—that people should not be excluded because of color, sex, etc.—this belief in inclusiveness easily became seen as a legitimate and definitive marker of a good Christian. By combining social justice ideals with belief in God's all encompassing love, inclusivity became a key aspect of a revised version of Christian theology, changing what it meant to be a good Christian in a slight but important way. As we saw detailed in chapter 2, this revised view holds that good Christians include all others in their love, whereas excluders are seen as bad Christians because they fail this crucial test of morality.

Through their participation in Accept, the men learned this theology and used it as a resource to derive new biblical truths that placed their homosexuality, and themselves, in a positive light. This revised theology served the men in two ways. First, it recast their past struggles as the result of oppression, not their own failing, allowing them to understand their past feelings of unworthiness as the result of other people's exclusionary practices—others' failures to act like good Christians. Second, it gave them new ways to think of themselves as Christians. If the crucial test of morality was including others, then the men had a clear rule to follow: include everyone in your Christian love, and you can see yourself as a good Christian. In the following example, drawn from fieldnotes taken at an Accept Bible study meeting, we see how the men constructed the principle of inclusivity as a cornerstone of their theology and learned to use it as a communal resource to redefine situation and self.

One night, we began the meeting with a seemingly non-theological question: "What experience have you had with being tutored, or with tutoring others?" A few members answered this question by sharing stories of being tutored in specific academic subjects (i.e., math, languages), and they recalled being grateful for the help and attention, even if they felt a bit embarrassed by their inability to grasp subject material at times. The individual attention, they agreed, made them try harder instead of giving up and getting a bad grade. One member was tutored for a few years when he was in an accident and could not attend school. He remembered this as a lonely time, but tutoring allowed him to keep pace with his peers and eventually return to school in the right grade. Because of tutoring, he was not left behind. Finally, one of the men, Ben, described his experience tutoring two fifth graders. He explained: "I thought I would hate it. I thought they would be hard to control and that they were doing poorly because they had bad attitudes. Instead, I found it to be an incredibly rewarding experience. No one had ever really paid attention to these kids or cared how well they did. When they saw I wanted them to learn, they were grateful and tried so hard, tried to be so grown up around me to impress me. They did all the work, and they learned. So did I. It's kinda weird how important I felt when I tutored them." In these accounts, we see that tutoring, an act of concern in which the more knowledgeable help the less knowledgeable, has many benefits; people feel like they matter, they are more motivated, and they learn.

The study leader used this example of tutoring to point out the benefits of acting lovingly and inclusively without evoking the controversy that might have emerged had he begun the study talking about homosexuality. Specifically, he noted that three important lessons should be drawn from this discussion: First, when we tutor, we are giving special attention and care to those who are, in some way, struggling. Second, this extra concern shows those we tutor that they are important and that we want them to do well. Third, as a result, those we tutor often try very hard and succeed. The larger lesson to be learned here, according to the leader, is that if we include everyone in our love, giving more care to those who struggle to do what comes easily for some, then we enable people to grow, learn, and be successful. Conversely, writing people off as bad, incompetent, or unworthy is destructive.

The group next turned to the scriptural passage we were to study at this meeting, Acts 8:26–40, in which we see an example of God using a tutor to help a person excluded by men. Because this passage is quite long, I summarize it here. Philip is told by an angel to go south on the road from Jerusalem to Gaza, on which he meets an Ethiopian eunuch who had been to Jerusalem to worship but was denied entry to the temple. When Philip encounters the eunuch, he is sitting in his chariot reading Isaiah. Philip asks if he understands what he reads, and the eunuch replies, "How can I, unless someone guides me?" In response, Philip explains to the eunuch the "good news about Jesus" and baptizes him in water by the side of the road. The eunuch goes on his way rejoicing and proclaiming this "good news" to others. The group's discussion of this story went as follows:

> Scott: The Jews would not let the eunuch into the temple, so he must have felt excluded.
>
> Jamie: The eunuch is faithful, but he cannot participate in his faith fully as others do.
>
> Terry: He went to Jerusalem and the temple for guidance, so God sends Philip to resolve his quest after men deny him.
>
> Tyler: Yeah, he went looking for God and trying to understand his situation and must have left feeling alienated. In Jerusalem, he probably does not feel like God is with him, but after Philip baptizes him, he can rejoice.

Chris: God is always with you, even if you do not always know
    it. . . .

Scott: I think this passage shows that inclusivity is a big part of
    Jesus' ministry—including others.

Tyler: That's true; nothing can separate anyone from God's
    love; everyone is to be included.

Jamie: (sarcastically) Can we send this message to Jerry Falwell?

This exchange reveals how the men simultaneously constructed the
principle of inclusivity and applied it to their own lives. By noting
that God's response to the eunuch's exclusion (by men) from the temple
was to send Philip to guide or tutor the eunuch so he could also be
included in the "good news," group members create and affirm the
idea that inclusion is moral and divinely mandated behavior. In other
words, the men interpreted God's sending of Philip to baptize the eunuch as proof that *God* does not exclude anyone, in spite of what
people try to do. Seen this way, this scripture highlights the necessity of inclusion.

Further, the above discussion shows how the men used the principle of inclusivity, as the basis of their revised theology, to understand past feelings of alienation. Collectively, they likened their past
struggle with the church to the eunuch's rejection at the temple. Though
the Scripture does not say that the eunuch felt alienated, excluded,
or abandoned by God, the men "br[ought] their own predilections,
hopes, fears, and experiences into the story" (Scheub 1998, 4), revealing
how they felt when their "temple," or the church, rejected them. The
men could now interpret the rejection and alienation they once felt
as the result of others' (such as Jerry Falwell's) exclusionary (and sinful) behavior—not their homosexuality.

Taken as a whole, this Bible lesson, and similar others, taught the
principle of inclusivity and provided opportunities for group members to apply it their own lives. By introducing the lesson with a neutral
topic—like the discussion of tutoring—the leader was able to show
the importance of reaching out to those who struggle, without invoking the uncertainty that might arise in a discussion of reaching out to
those whose behavior could be seen as morally suspect. The importance of inclusion was then reiterated and linked to Christianity and
the men's lives through their study of the scriptural passage. This
reading of the Bible structured and affirmed Accept's revised Christian theology, in which inclusivity is a prime virtue. This principle,

in conjunction with the belief that homosexuality was God-given, ensured that homosexuality was no longer a basis to label people unworthy or to exclude them from the category of "Christian."

Sin and the Broken Psyche

Like Accept members, the men in Expell initially felt relief and excitement about their prospects for healing but were still uncertain about how to understand their homosexuality, what it meant about them, and how they were to resolve the issue. From their perspective, heterosexual monogamy (marriage) was the only form of acceptable sexuality, homosexuality was sin, and God certainly would not create them to be gay and then condemn them. Instead, they believed that God created them to be heterosexual, and, similar to Accept members, they felt that their struggles resulted from their failure to live in accord with their divinely created selves. They, too, connected self-fulfillment and feeling better with the religious work of becoming the individuals God made them to be.

Given these beliefs and their previous efforts to live heterosexual lives, how could the men understand their inability, to this point, to alter their sexuality? The Bible, as they saw it, declared their homosexuality a sin and humans inherently sinful, but offered no direct or explicit explanation for how they became homosexual. To make sense of their situations, members learned to incorporate aspects of psychological explanations of homosexuality into their religious notions of sin and redemption to create a new understanding of homosexuality as curable disease. To construct this new view, Expell drew on the pop psychology and psychotherapeutic discourse (cf. Rice 1996, 2002) that was grounded in the burgeoning self-help movement. This discourse, as Nolan notes, is characterized "by an elevated concern for the self, by a conspicuously emotivist form of discourse and self-understanding, and by a proclivity to invoke the language of victimhood and to view behaviors in pathological terms" (2002, 154). Using this kind of discourse, Expell built a revised religious framework that could explain the men's struggle and reframe the meaning of their homosexuality.

This framework merged the biblical notion of original sin and the "fallen" nature of humans with a psychological theory of the origins of homosexuality. According to Expell, and Exodus more generally, the core of this theory is that homosexuality results from emotional trauma caused by the sins committed against the sufferer by important people early in life. Put succinctly, this explanation, examined in detail in chapter 2, asserts that when some form of emotional, physical, and/or sexual abuse prevents a child from bonding emotionally with a same-sex parent or other role model during critical early periods of psychological development, that child unconsciously seeks this same-sex bond as he/she matures. At puberty, these same-sex emotional needs become sexualized, leading the person to develop homosexual proclivities. These proclivities can be overcome and psychological health (and heterosexual desire) reclaimed as the true (divinely made) self emerges through a healing process in which the right spiritual relationship with God is formed. As this relationship with God is formed, God, as the ultimate Father, will heal the psyche broken by others' sins and restore the self.

For Expell members, this explanation had tremendous appeal for a variety of reasons. First, it meant that they were blameless for their homosexuality. Using this explanation, they, like Accept members, could construe their struggle with homosexuality as a result of others' sinful behavior—not their own individual deficiencies. So, while they had to work hard to fix the "sickness" or "disorder" that resulted from what others had done to them, they were not the cause of their problem but were victims of others' wrongdoings. Second, this explanation also presented a seemingly simple and straightforward "cure." To be the heterosexuals they always wanted to be, the men could follow an established strategy: take responsibility for healing, engage in sincere prayer, resist homosexual desires, and deal honestly with their emotions. Finally, the men could use this explanation to reconceive their struggle with homosexuality as righteous behavior. Because this explanation framed the men's problem as not of their own making, and yet required them to struggle to overcome it, their efforts to be righteous were especially virtuous, providing evidence of their status as good Christians. Paradoxically, this reframing required that the men simultaneously distance themselves from homosexuality and embrace it as the temptation against which their mettle as Christians was measured.

The men learned this psychological explanation of homosexuality during Expell group meetings as they read the study guide, *Sexual Healing* (Foster 1995a), listened to the leader's teaching, and heard testimonials from those who had been healed. In this sense, the group provided models of how this psychological explanation could be fit to the men's lives and used to understand their homosexuality. In addition, at various times, a leader or a relatively old (long-term) member would help a newer member apply this explanation to his own life. In most instances, this help took the form of the older member showing the newer one how and what he came to learn about his own homosexuality and its origins. The example that follows illustrates the way experienced group members most commonly showed new members how to make sense of their homosexuality. This fieldnote excerpt begins with a new member describing his struggle and then shows how an older member used his experiences to offer an interpretive frame, consistent with the group's psychological explanation, to guide the new member's understanding:

> Mack, the newcomer, interrupted here and said: "I have been hesitant to talk because so many of you seem on the way out of the struggle and I am just in the beginning of it now. But I have something to share and I need your help and for you to keep me accountable. In the last week, I have been struggling with a desire to search the Internet to find pictures of naked men and to talk with other gay people, to kinda find a gay community to talk to. I have not done it, and I told my wife about it. She flaked out and went completely nuts. She has accepted that I slept with one other person, a man, and has forgiven me, but my continued struggle with this issue is too much for her. It is a near-death experience to tell her any of this, so I need you to keep me accountable and to help me get over this. [He started to cry here.] I have so many reasons not to sin: I have three beautiful children and my wife. I love my wife more than anything. I would die for her. This is not about her; it's about me, and I cannot understand why I cannot stop because I love them." The group responded, in unison, "We love you, Mack." Then, Josh told Mack: "I was once married too, and I loved my wife. She's a wonderful woman and we had a son. I love them both. I thought once I married her all those temptations would disappear, but they just kept coming back and our marriage broke up. After, I found Exodus, and I learned how I became gay. I was repeatedly molested by an older cousin when I was eleven and twelve, and I did not have a relationship with my father, so I didn't know how to have a normal relationship with a male. I just wanted a connection. It is only through my relationship with God, the

Father, that I am learning how to relate normally to other men. I wish I could have learned before I lost my wife, but maybe God was using that break up to push me to get help."

In this exchange, we see an older member, Josh, sharing a life experience similar to Mack's current struggle, revealing that he discovered his homosexual desires were the result of sexual abuse and an absent father. The implication here is that Josh believed he developed a sexual attraction to men because he craved same-sex "connection" in the absence of his father, and that this desire had become twisted and sexualized through the sexual abuse he suffered. While Josh did not explicitly indicate that these same reasons account for Mack's sexual struggle, it is clear that Mack might try to resolve his problem by searching for the causes of his homosexual desire in his past. Josh also advised Mack to do this searching now or risk losing what he holds so dear—his wife and children. In this way, Josh's shared experiences provided both incentive and a kind of narrative template that Mack could use to search his biography, locate similar events, and plug them into this explanatory frame. Josh had shown him what biographical events to look for and how they might fit together to explain the origin of his struggle.

In general, Expell members first learned this psychological explanation, whether from one another, from the study guide, from testimonials, or from some combination of these, and then were encouraged to fit this explanation to their own lives. Routinely, men were urged by the leader to "pray for God to show them what happened in their own lives to create their homosexual desires." As the men explored their biographies, they fit their experiences to this explanatory model, deflecting blame and learning to see themselves in a better light. Andy's account, presented below, is typical of how the men fit this model to their lives and used it to make sense of their past struggles. Andy believed that his homosexuality originated in the dynamics of a dysfunctional family. His siblings were troubled: his brother was an alcoholic; two sisters engaged in unspecified "addictive behaviors," while another was "rebelling against God." For Andy, *their* troubles were evidence that *his* struggle was also rooted in an improper upbringing. In the following fieldnote excerpt, Andy describes the origins of his homosexuality:

After we finished the opening prayer, Ed asked us if "God had revealed the damaged areas of our souls" to any of us. No one moved or spoke for a time. Then Ed reminded us that we need to be "transparent," that we should not be ashamed by what has happened to us. Finally, Andy spoke up, explaining, "[My father] is passive; he is non-assertive; he is indirect. He does not, never has been able to, speak out of a place of honesty about who he is and what he believes. He's never asked himself, that I can tell. He avoids asking hard questions about who he is and just, just, I just think my father's in hiding from himself. He just doesn't confront the hard things in life; he avoids them. My stepmother is colossally self-centered and self-righteous, just extremely, extremely so. She's very powerful, very manipulative, very cruel. She really was the power in the family and my dad was just sort of in orbit around her. It was a very, very unhealthy situation. There were clear signs I was in, I had serious emotional problems from a very early age, but my family never dealt with it, except to—my stepmother warned me very hostilely about masturbating, which I did all the time, from the time I was five on, which I now have read is a sign of emotional difficulty."

Andy used this explanation to frame an account of his sexual struggle as emerging from his failure to bond with his father. He described his family as fitting what ex-gays would call a "classic case," a power imbalance between a passive father and a domineering mother. Looking back, Andy felt he did not have a strong same-sex role model. He also now defined his masturbation and homosexuality as linked to the emotional difficulties in his family, thereby understanding his homosexuality as "sexualized emotional needs." In similar ways, other members of Expell commonly sought to explain their homosexuality as arising from the failures and sins of others.

Both Accept and Expell constructed new theological frameworks, recombining aspects of existing religious and secular cultural resources to reorder understanding and to fit new and positive meanings to their respective experiences. These new theologies not only enabled the men to perceive that their prior struggles were caused by others' sinful behavior, but also recast their quest for self-understanding and fulfillment as religious work. The focus on the self thus did not feel self-centered but rather seemed an effort to act in accord with a higher calling. The construction of these revised theological frameworks provided the men with the ideological tools to understand themselves and their situations positively in the present and to perceive themselves as *better* Christians than those who condemned them. As we will see, however, having the means—a new version of theology—to remodel how one understands himself is necessary but insufficient for the task at hand. Remodeling the self requires more than just a good cognitive blueprint; it requires careful execution and attention to detail. In this case, getting the details right meant getting the feeling right.

Feeling Right: (Re)learning to Feel like a Good Christian

So far, we have seen how the men learned their respective group's revised version of theology, as well as how the group tried to help them adapt this theology to their own situations and understanding of events. Of course, knowing how to do something and doing it are very different things—a fact the men quickly discovered as they grappled with fitting the group's theology to their own lives. Thinking about themselves differently was challenging, and it required practice, persistence, and a willingness to endure the uncomfortable feelings that arose in the process. The men in both groups went through this struggle. They intellectually revised what it meant to be a good Christian, but still had to learn how to feel like a good Christian and to manage all of the negative emotions that arose during the learning process. In the following sections, I show how the men learned to feel "right" and how the groups aided them.

The men found that their changing definitions of what it meant to be a good Christian prescribed not only new ways of thinking and behaving but also new "feeling rules" (Hochschild 1979). For instance, Accept defined a good Christian as someone who upheld their inclusivity principle, or the belief and practice that everyone was included equally in God's love. By implication, good Christians should engage only in inclusive and compassionate practices. As a result, they should feel unconditional love for others and an appreciation of diversity. Expell defined good Christians as those who forgave the sins against them and who struggled righteously against their homosexuality. Consequently, good Christians should feel forgiveness, remorse for their homosexual sin, and dedication to their ongoing struggle. If they could not generate the feelings appropriate to their new definitions of good Christian, the men's changed behaviors would feel contrived and hollow, eventually undermining their healing and their commitment to the group. So, for the men to successfully become the good Christians prescribed by their newly adopted theologies, they had to learn and adhere to these new feeling rules.

Because the men focused their attention most heavily on what they thought and did, altering the way they felt was perhaps the most difficult part of their transformation to a gay Christian or an ex-gay Christian. To help the men get the feeling right, Accept and Expell literally had to teach the men how and what to feel. Robert Benford, in his work on social movements, explains that this kind of emotional control in groups is exerted, in part, by "teaching people how they should feel in a given situation of a certain type—when to evoke and when to suppress particular feelings" (2002, 65). By working with individuals to construct shared feelings appropriate to the group, groups can solidify their membership and present a unified meaning and purpose. Wrong or inappropriate feelings can threaten individual transformation and create discord and/or doubt within the group. Controlling emotions is therefore an important component of individual change and group success.

Accept and Expell members implicitly recognized the importance of proper feeling to individual transformation and often monitored one another's emotions, particularly those of newer members who were most likely to experience "wrong" feelings. When a member experienced and expressed inappropriate emotion, group members rallied to sanction this feeling, showing its "wrongness" by linking it to sinful thought or behavior. Next, members modeled the appropriate feeling, showing the wayward member how to restructure emotions more positively. These strategies are evident in the following fieldnote excerpt in which Accept members discuss the concept of wickedness:

> *Chris:* The wicked are those who are unhappy; they hate
> themselves and so are mean to others.
>
> *Danny:* I used to be wicked, so lonely, hurt, and angry that
> I could only make myself feel better by hurting others.
>
> *Alex:* Many bring themselves up by pulling others down.
>
> *Scott:* (new member) Like racists so filled with hate, and the
> Christian Right—they do so many mean things. . . . I
> hope I see them going down as I am ascending to the
> gates of heaven.
>
> *Mark:* I don't. I hope I can hold hands with them as we
> enter. . . . Scott, we do not know how God will judge
> and we cannot do so. I just want them to know I am

> worthy too. I want to see my old pastor, who de-
> nounced me, in heaven so that he knows I made it too.
>
> *Chris:* The point is that they should acknowledge us as
> worthy, good Christians, not to bring them down—
> that's wicked.
>
> *Scott:* I know; it's just hard sometimes.
>
> *Mark:* It's hard because the wicked have hurt you, but to
> become wicked yourself is even worse because it is
> against God's will. Acting out of love is hard, but it
> will become easier as you let go of all that anger.
>
> *Scott:* Yeah. [*pause*] Okay, I can see what you mean. If I feel
> like them, it's easy to act like them. I guess I should
> focus on the good feelings and act from them instead.

Here, the group defined wickedness as being judgmental, like the Christian Right. When Scott, a relatively new member (approximately four months at this time), became angry and said he hoped to see these wicked people descending to hell on his way to heaven, he was expressing feelings inconsistent with Accept's inclusive ideology. Group members then policed him, explaining why his desire to see these wicked people go to hell was to act like them—judgmental and sinful. Instead, they urged him to "act from love" and modeled ways of feeling that were more consistent with a good Christian identity. In this way, the group collectively established and enforced a feeling rule, the observance of which was defined as evidence of being a good Christian. The men's emotion work, or their efforts to change how they felt (Hochschild 1979, 1983; Erickson 1997), was simultaneously work that enabled them to see themselves as good Christians. New feelings— anger transformed into love—were created and then defined as evidence of being the good Christians the men sought to be.

Expell also used sanctioning and modeling as emotion management strategies when group members experienced feelings that contradicted Expell's theology. Several men, for instance, experienced a "fall," or homosexual encounter, while I was attending the group. Often, the men experienced these incidents as evidence that they were failures, that they were weak, unworthy, and sinful. Most importantly, these encounters made them doubt their ability to successfully resist temptation; they felt doomed to struggle and fail. So, when such falls occurred, Expell had to work hard to show members how to transform these feelings of defeat into renewed hope and pride in continued resistance, feelings that would strengthen commitment to the healing process and the group. For the group to employ helpful emotion management strategies, a "fallen" Expell member first had to provide the details of his encounter and repent. At that point, the group could rally, physically and emotionally, around the fallen, teaching him how to turn his shame into more appropriate emotion. One of the activities used to reconstruct emotional experience is captured in the following fieldnote excerpt:

> We gathered in a circle around Josh, who was sitting in the middle staring at the ground. We joined hands and the leader prayed, asking God to forgive and strengthen Josh. Then, Josh (crying) told us the details of his homosexual encounter. . . . When he finished his story, he said, "I am so ashamed, just very, very ashamed. I was doing so well, praying when I felt tempted, focusing on Jesus. But when I wrecked the car and couldn't work, I had too much time, got depressed, drank, and found this man. I couldn't stop myself. I let everyone down, God too, and I just don't think I can start all over. I must be sickening." Then, the leader walked to him, put a hand on his head, and prayed for Josh's forgiveness, strength, and conviction. Each group member did the same in turn. When we finished, we sat on the floor very close to Josh.
>
> The leader told him, "You must stop punishing yourself now. You have repented; God has forgiven you. We are all sinners, we all stumble, but the truly righteous, the truly faithful, get back up on the side of God. Feeling shame is normal because it lets you know you sinned, so be grateful for the feeling. Then, don't give in, push away from it. Rejoice in your continued resistance in spite of Satan's attempts to draw you in. You are a child of God." Josh was quiet and then prayed, asking God for "forgiveness and the strength to resist Satan and to do [God's] will" and assuring God that though he may "fall from the path of righteousness [he] would struggle to find the way back."

Josh's sense of shame and defeat, if continued, would have undermined both his ability to adhere to the codes of action and feeling prescribed by Expell's definition of a good Christian ("I don't know if I can start all over") and his commitment to the group. To mitigate

Josh's shame, the leader first sanctioned Josh, explaining that, while shame was a useful first response, Josh could not wallow in it because doing so would be giving in to Satan, a sinful act. Next, the leader modeled an appropriate response for Josh and the other members, showing them how to reinterpret a fall or, indeed, any other behavior they considered sinful, so that it became evidence of continued resistance—an opportunity to reject Satan and accept God, an occasion to rejoice—rather than a failure. In this way, Josh's fall became an example of how to resist and struggle righteously as a good Christian.

Married members of Expell learned similar emotion management strategies, but they also had to contend with the feelings surrounding their roles as husbands and household leaders. For these men, such falls were doubly stigmatizing; they not only had failed to resist temptation as Josh had, but also had failed as spiritual heads of their families and broken their marital vows. In such cases, the men had to cope with their shame in relation to God and the group as well as the hurt and disappointment of their wives. Without controlling and transforming these negative emotions, the men were likely to doubt their ability to resist sexual temptation and to have more difficulty in their marriages, a relationship that provided a critical incentive for the men to continue to work to transform themselves.

To enable these men to cope with such situations, the Expell leader and group members showed fallen married members how to reframe this experience not only as an opportunity for continued resistance but also as a chance to build a stronger marriage. At one group meeting, for instance, Ed, a recently married member who usually attended meetings with his wife, confessed that he had been fired from his job that week because he had been looking at homosexual pornography on the computer at work. Ed explained his experience this way during a group meeting: "I just had to look. In the back of my mind, I thought about my vows to God and to Julia [his wife], but it didn't stop me. I am so weak, so pathetic. God has blessed me with great gifts, and yet I fail so much. When I was fired, I knew I'd have to tell everyone. I am so sorry, so, so much ashamed. Why can't I stop? I don't want to fail God or Julia. I want to be a real Christian man who lives as God wants and acts as a real Christian leader in our home. I thought, for a second or two, about driving my car into a pole on the way home, but that would be yet another sin. Sin seems to be piling up so fast that I can't see a way to get out from under it." The group prayed over Ed, asking God to give him strength to do his will. Then one group member reminded Ed that "there is nothing too big for God." The group leader agreed, explaining:

> God has shown you a way out. He has shown you the areas of yourself that need healing and provided a way to work on them. Your shame is a guide to what you should do and evidence of your desire to resist such sexual feelings. Now, push aside your shame and rejoice because your Father has removed the temptation of the computer and made you be honest with your wife. He has joined you with a good Christian woman who will help you resist sin and become whole. God is guiding you towards building that relationship and becoming the man He wants you to be. And here you are, with her, working to resist such temptations, showing your commitment to healing. God gives us what we need as long as we choose the path of righteousness.

Just as with Josh, the group diminished Ed's sense of shame, failure, and hopelessness ("I can't see a way to get out from under it [sin]") by reframing the event as evidence of Ed's will to change and of God's hand in his life. By removing temptations (lack of computer access because he was fired), God was perceived as providing Ed with an opportunity to resist his desires more successfully. Further, Ed was encouraged to see this situation an additional opportunity to build the right relationship with his wife, who God had given him to help with his healing process. In this way, the group showed Ed how to reinterpret his fall as evidence of his continued resistance and of God's help. His actions, as long as he "chooses the path of righteousness," reveal not dismal failure but a commitment to becoming the man God intended and to his marriage. This struggle marked him as a good Christian.

The importance of these emotion management strategies to the men's successful transformation to either a gay or ex-gay Christian is illustrated most powerfully, perhaps, by cases where transformation failed. In these instances, we see that ineffective emotion management impaired the individual's capacity for personal change and weakened his connection to the group. For example, a man who had been an Accept member for less than a year was having trouble replacing his anger at those who had cast him out of his old church with the forgiveness and love prescribed by Accept. When he expressed this anger at group meetings, members corrected him and tried to model how to feel love instead of anger in much the same way they did in the discussion of wickedness above. Initially, he responded by asserting his right to be angry. Eventually, though, he gave up explaining his anger and simply listened to the group's discussion, agreed with their points, and announced his intention to pray and try to forgive—until the next time. After a meeting that contained such an incident, I asked him about how he felt when his anger came up at a meeting. He replied: "I just can't do what they want me to do. I'm not Jesus, and I can't forget what they [leaders of his old church] did to me. I know I should and I know the group is right, but I am not that good. I wish I could just talk about the anger, get it out, you know? But every time, they tell me to just let it go. It makes me feel separate and different— like I'm not as good as them—so I just don't talk about it much anymore." This man's inability to comply completely with Accept's feeling rules undermined his ability to see himself as a good Christian and his connection to the group. While his thinking was compatible ("I know they are right"), he could not muster the appropriate feeling and therefore did not feel at home in the group. While he attended meetings regularly, he continued to struggle on the periphery of the group.

Sometimes both groups' emotion management strategies failed entirely, making individual healing impossible and actually pushing members away. We see this failure most vividly in Expell, perhaps because continued homosexual activity carried greater personal shame than did an Accept member's continued anger at those who rejected him. This heightened sense of shame made it harder for Expell members to admit their temptations and failings publicly in group meetings, and they were therefore less willing to subject themselves to the group's emotion management. This dynamic may account for Expell's relatively high turnover rate. While there was a core group of about twelve long-term members when I joined the group, at least seven more men attended a few times and then dropped out. I interviewed two of these men and had informal conversations with two more, but I was unable to contact the other three men. Their reasons for dropping out varied—from not being "ready" to having too much to do at work— but all four men described being put off by the negative feelings Expell meetings generated for them. As relatively new members in the early stages of struggling to resist their homosexual desires, these men worried that they would either have to confess transgressions or lie about them. One dropout explained his feelings this way: "I just don't want to announce my failures all the time. I'll tell God, I'll pray, I'll try to resist, but I am too private a person to withstand having to tell the group. I get more embarrassed than I already am." Another dropout said that he lied about his behavior just to avoid telling anyone in the group, so he "felt like the group was making [his] situation worse. [He] had become a homosexual *and* a liar." For these men, the emotion management strategies that were supposed to help them transform negative emotions backfired—actually highlighting and heightening them. Under these conditions, the men could not stay committed to the healing process or the group and dropped out.

When these emotion management strategies were successful, they enabled Accept and Expell to teach group members how to manage the negative emotions that arose during the healing process and to transform them into emotions appropriate to group definitions of a good Christian. In doing so, the groups enabled the men to feel right, and the men could then use these appropriate feelings to signify and confirm their new gay or ex-gay Christian identities. Further, these positive feelings were rewarding for the men, particularly in light of the shame and alienation of their recent struggles, and they took the emergence of good feeling as proof that Accept and Expell were effective and legitimate groups, worthy of their support and participation. They were on their way to becoming committed group members.

Becoming Committed Group Members

The men's successful transformation to gay or ex-gay Christians required still more than adopting the respective group's revised theology and learning to feel the way a good Christian should feel according to that theology. The men's changes in thought, behavior, and feeling could not be very rewarding, nor could they last very long, in the absence of a like-minded community. For the men to solidify and sustain their new identities, they also had to feel like they belonged in their respective groups. Creating this sense of belonging meant forging connections to the group and building collective identity, or "the shared definition of a group that derives from members' common interests, experiences, and solidarity" (Taylor and Whittier 1995, 172). The men formed this solidarity through the *expression* of shared emotions. The idea here is that when a group member expressed emotions that other group members had also experienced, then they could recognize their own feelings mirrored in another's expression (Melucci 1988, 343). This recognition drew the men together, creating a sense of belonging and we-ness; "we" being the people who feel similarly. The construction of a we who feel this way necessarily implies the construction of a "they" who feel differently. In this sense, the expression of shared emotions helped to draw boundaries between a group and others, marking who belongs and who does not (Taylor and Whittier 1992).

In Accept and Expell, collective identity was, in part, facilitated as new members learned and adopted each group's altered theologies and interpretations and learned appropriate feelings, but it was also built and maintained through the expression of shared emotions. Specifically, group members firmed up collective identity when they utilized two different forms of emotional expression: (1) oppositional—those that helped draw boundaries between an "us" and a "them," solidifying resistance to opposing groups—and (2) supportive—those that shored up ideological and emotional connections between the individual member and the group. For gay Christians, oppositional emotion usually took the form of generating righteous anger and dismay at the conservative Christians who continued to denounce homosexuality and exclude homosexuals from the ranks of the saved. During the Baptist boycott of Disney, for instance, many Accept members, particularly long-term members, voiced their outrage at Baptist efforts to exclude them, commenting on the Baptists' fear of their children being in the same place as "big, bad, infectious gays." As one member said, in a tight, sarcastic voice, "The *good* Baptists are panicked that their pristine kids might actually visit a place where a *gay* man might have once been." Another responded, "Yeah, we turn the magical kingdom into the kingdom of black magic. They condemn us, throw us out, and somehow we're the bad people. I say they need to spend more time actually reading the Bible." During this exchange, the men shared their outrage at being excluded, using sarcasm to mark the boundaries between themselves (as unjustly persecuted) and the misguided (and not so nice) other. In their shared expression of anger, they created a shared definition of situation and self.

For newer Accept members, the open expression of this outrage resonated with their own anger, an anger that they had been afraid to express either because they doubted others felt the same way or because they were worried such condemnation was deserved. Hearing this anger expressed was an enormous relief. During an interview, a new member told me: "I knew I had found a home when I listened to Jamie and Scott bitch about the Disney boycott. They said everything I felt but was too afraid to say to anyone, sometimes even myself. It was so freeing to hear their anger, to hear someone say, well, say the Baptists are wrong." For this man, recognizing similar emotions in others created positive feelings—a sense of belonging, of being right, and of being good—that bolstered collective identity and fueled his commitment to Accept.

Ex-gay Christians used oppositional emotions in precisely the same ways, expressing anger and fear with regard to gays and other Christians who felt homosexuality was a sin worse than any other. Sometimes this anger arose when the men discussed how gays thought they were "in denial about their sexuality," or when they described how other Christians spoke of homosexuality as an especially bad sin. During an Expell group meeting, for example, one member spoke about his feelings toward churches that treated homosexuals as worse sinners that other people: "It makes me so mad, the way they treat people who struggle with homosexuality. It's like we're lepers and must be sent away, but the adulterer, the drunk, the liar, they can stay?" In the conversation that followed, the men echoed this anger and discussed how desperately Christians needed to recognize that sexual sin is just sin like any other. After this meeting, as we walked to our cars, one man commented that he thought the meeting was "really good, because we could share each other's anger and really feel like brothers in Christ as we let it go." Here again, we see not only how shared emotional expression created shared definitions of the situation and self, thereby enhancing collective identity, but also how such sharing made the men feel like they *belonged* to a group of good people who really (and uniquely) understood the situation. Such feelings were rewards for doing the identity work necessary to fashion a Christian identity that was aligned with Expell's theology.

Likewise, supportive emotions generated a sense of we-ness when speakers recounted their own stories about being gay and Christian. These accounts were usually very evocative, inducing emotional resonance in listeners. For example, the following fieldnote excerpt, in which Accept members have just finished singing the hymn "Just as I Am," reveals how the expression of supportive emotions also drew the men together. Many of the men were visibly moved by the song; some were in tears, others could not look up, and some were murmuring, "Thank you, Jesus." Their conversation went like this:

> *Chris:* It is so incredible, so amazing, that hymn. All we have
> to do is reach out our hands to Jesus and he is always

        there, whether we are gay, straight, or whatever. It
        overwhelms me, that kind of love.

Mark: I know. Jesus stood beside me when I came out. He
        never let me feel like a total outcast, though everyone
        else, even my family, tried to make me feel that way.

Terry: "Just as I Am" always makes me think of the biblical
        story where people are about to stone the woman for
        adultery. Then Jesus comes and says, "Let he who is
        without sin cast the first stone." Then the woman
        opens her eyes and all the people are gone. Jesus says,
        "And neither do I condemn thee." I remember this
        story whenever anyone tries to make me feel like I am
        not among the saved, and I remember Jesus and love. It
        helps a lot.

Tyler: Yeah, people need to learn that Jesus is about accept-
        ing, not rejecting. So much suffering would disappear. I
        felt so bad for so long, and it was so hard. Then, the
        sheer joy of finally really hearing and believing the
        words in this hymn, a hymn I knew my whole life
        [*shakes head*]. It was wonderful to finally let go all the
        negative stuff I'd learned and know I am loved.

As the men shared their reactions (verbal and nonverbal) to this hymn, they acknowledged the fear, anxiety, and sadness they felt prior to be-lieving they were loved "just as they are" (i.e., gay). The men thus came to recognize themselves in each other because "people like us feel a certain way." This emotional solidarity was the foundation of their collective identity.

    In the same ways, Expell members shared what they referred to as "testimonies" that described their transformation from homosexual sinner to ex-gay (moral) Christian. Typically, these testimonies were given at the end of group meetings. Because of their length, I include only an outline of the testimonies here: A group member would stand up and share his story of his childhood, his sinful behavior, his in-troduction to the group and discovery that his homosexuality was a result of psychic or physical abuse, and his progress since he put his faith in God's healing power (cf. Ponticelli 1999). In the course of the testimony, the speaker often described his feelings of fear and shame at his initial behavior, his anger at those who caused his homosexuality, and his joy and relief at learning about and pursuing a cure. Speakers sometimes cried or raised their voices in anger. Such displays and the content of the talk visibly moved the audience. Group members in the audience often nodded agreement during such talks or broke out in tears or prayer, often clenching and unclenching their fists or opening their palms up to God. They told similar stories and expressed resonant emotions in response to such testimonies. At the end of one testimony, for example, one member said, "Brother, you and I have been down the same road, always looking around, scared someone would find out." During an interview, a relatively new member (five months) explained how hearing these testimonies had helped him feel like part of the group: "When I heard their testimonies, I knew God had brought me to the right place because I knew all of it, except the parts where I felt better. I knew it before they even said it—not the details, but the feelings." Here again, emotional expression allowed for mutual recognition, fostering collective identity and the positive feelings of belonging. Such positive feelings confirmed the men's choice of group; they were where they were supposed to be.

Using these kinds of emotional and ideological strategies, the men were able to transform their uncertainties about what it meant to be a Christian who experienced homosexual desire into a spiritual understanding of what it meant to be gay and Christian and a felt sense that they were where they belonged. This transformation resulted from two key and overlapping processes. First, the men learned, through interaction in their respective group, how to fill newly constructed interpretive spaces with a revised version of theology that accommodated their sexuality or sexual struggle. This revised theology freed the men to construct positive and moral definitions of themselves, opening the possibility of thinking, acting, and feeling differently. While learning this revised theology posed relatively little difficulty for the men, adapting the theology to their lives often generated difficult and contrary emotions which, if allowed to continue, could jeopardize the men's efforts to become gay or ex-gay Christians. As a result, the men also had to engage in a process of emotion management that mitigated these negative feelings, taught them to feel positively about their situations and selves, and established a sense of collective identity. In this case, emotion work fueled the process of ideological change and was synonymous with the men's identity work. Both of these processes—ideological maneuvering and emotion work—were critical to the men's transformation; theological revision allowed for the creation of new meanings, and emotion management enabled the construction of good

feelings around these meanings. These feelings legitimated new meanings and served as rewards for doing the hard work of redefining situation and self. Such rewards did much to ensure that the men would
stay committed to both their own healing and the group.

As we have seen, whether new group members could successfully
negotiate the adaptation of a revised theology to their lives and commit to their respective group depended, to a considerable extent, on
the kind of interactions group leaders (and often established group
members) were able to generate in weekly meetings. Group leaders had
to facilitate interactions that not only conveyed new meanings but also
literally showed the men how to feel in ways that supported and legitimated their new self-understandings. In doing so, leaders functioned
as sources of religious authority, pointing out the "truth" of God's Word,
and as therapists who worked to help the men heal their damaged psy-
ches. In this dual capacity, leaders merged religion, a traditional source
of moral authority, with the new "therapeutic gospel," in which salvation is connected to good feeling and self-esteem (Moskowitz 2001,
1–9). As a result of this merger, "proper" feelings became linked with
divine expectations, making particular self-feelings serve as evidence
of moral and religious righteousness. Healing the self was now religious work.

More broadly, this merger has implications for understanding the
role of religious authority in a therapeutic culture. Whereas some scholars (Nolan 1998; Rieff 1966) have posited that religious authority is
being eroded and the power of religious leaders and doctrine is being
usurped, to a large extent, by psychological experts, this study suggests that religious belief and a therapeutic ethos are not necessarily
conflicting or competing. Instead, as is evident in Accept and Expell,
the religious and the therapeutic can become intertwined and mutually reinforcing. In this case, the therapeutic became invested with the
sacred, and religious righteousness was linked to subjectivity and the
therapeutic process. The language of therapy—of damaged selves that
need healing—complemented religious explanations of homosexuality and of the men as victims of human sin. In this instance, then, a
therapeutic approach was adapted as an important part of the explanation of and solution to the men's struggles, but it did not supersede
or replace religious belief. Instead, as we will see in the next chapter,
the men had to ensure their new beliefs were in accord with God's
Word before they could feel themselves to be authentic gay or ex-gay
Christians.

7 | Authenticity and the Good Christian

Presentations of this research have often evoked questions from audience members about the men's motive and intent for doing the kind of transformative work described in the last few chapters. I have often been asked if these men are not just fooling themselves and making the Bible say what they want it to so they can feel less guilty about their homosexuality. Those who ask these sorts of questions seem troubled by the men's revised theology because it does not match their version of Christianity. The answer to these skeptics' question is yes and no. By choosing (or being pushed) to step outside conservative evangelical Protestantism and joining a group that endorsed an alternative theological view, the men were choosing a theology that was more affirming of their sexuality or their sexual struggle. But the men's goal was never to make the Bible condone their sexuality (Accept), to excuse or lessen the sin of homosexuality (Expell), or to change any aspect of Scripture. Indeed, for these men, biblical truth was the most important thing in their lives, and it guided how they lived. So, their quest was not to "make the Bible say what they wanted it to" but rather to figure out what their homosexuality meant within a Christian context.

That what the men now perceived of as the truth about homosexuality differed from other Christian interpretations is not surprising or unique, nor is it strange that other believers think one or both groups are wrong. There are multiple and diverse scriptural interpretations across and even within denominations, and these varied interpretations have been the source of much denominational debate and hostility. Most recently, for example, this hostility was visible in the uproar over whether Gene Robinson, an openly gay man, could become an ordained bishop in the Episcopalian Church. In another example of denominational split over this issue, the authors of the 1991 Methodist "Report of the Committee to Study Homosexuality" could not decisively offer a position on homosexuality and instead drafted two competing additions to their Social Principles to give to the General Council of Ministries. The first argued there was no "satisfactory basis" to "maintain the condemnation of all homosexual practice," while the second asserted there was no "satisfactory basis" to "alter [the] previously held position that we do not condone the practice of homosexuality" (Yamasaki et al. 1991, 28–29). To date, no changes have been made, and the issue is unresolved in the Methodist Church. Further, believers on all sides of the issue feel that they (and others like them) are the ones who have gotten it right.

Like other Christians, the men in this study earnestly debated the meaning of homosexuality, trying to discern divine truth. To write off their attempts to reconcile their sexuality and their faith as self-serving manipulation of the Bible would be a grave misrepresentation of the men's intentions and efforts. In fact, as we have seen, the men's most pressing and central concern was that they live their lives in accord with biblical directives. It was for this reason that the groups had to link each step of the process of transformation to God's Word to persuade the men to proceed. Before the men would give up their adherence to existing interpretations of homosexuality, the groups had to show them that existing interpretation was flawed by human bias— and therefore was not God's Word. Similarly, each new theological revision offered within either group had to be connected to and consistent with biblical tenets before the men would consider it as a legitimate guide for structuring their lives. Now, in order to take the final step in their transformation, to authenticate their new identities of gay or ex-gay Christian, the men likewise had to first ensure the religious validity of these identity meanings.

As the men in both groups moved closer to becoming established group members—that is, they knew group theology, used it to structure their actions and feelings, and felt connected to the group—they repeatedly told me that they had to "make sure they were right with God" before they committed entirely to the group. For these men, being "right with God" had two components. First, they had to be sure that group theology stemmed directly from God's Word. Second, they had to know that they were doing it right; that is, they had to have proof that they were now behaving and feeling the way they should as good Christians. It was only through fulfilling these two requirements that the men could wholeheartedly embrace their new identities. In this chapter, we see how the men validate and authenticate their new theology and their new selves, paying close attention to how the men made sure they got the theology right. In what follows, I show how the men authenticated their redefined selves and thereby became full-fledged gay or ex-gay Christians. To do so, we first look at how group theology was shifted back into the sacred realm and thereby became legitimate as divine mandate. Then, we examine how the men learned to use their emotions as evidence that they were living out this mandate as God's will for their lives.

Making New Meanings Sacred

At this point, the men had acquired and created all of the ideological and symbolic resources necessary to remake themselves into moral and good Christians; they had a revised and affirming theology, new rhetorical and emotional strategies, and a community to support them. However, as we saw in the preceding two chapters, the men were only able to create these resources by maneuvering key pieces of theology from the divine to the secular realm so that they could redefine meaning without challenging the integrity of the Bible. While these new meanings and revised theologies helped the men construct new understandings of their situations and selves, they had yet to be cemented as valid interpretations of God's Word. For these new theologies to guide how the men lived in a way that felt legitimate and right with God, they had to be shifted back into the sacred realm, explicitly reconnected to Scripture, and infused with divine authority. The importance of connecting revised theology to Scripture cannot be overstated because it is only through this connection that new meanings become legitimate and the men's new beliefs and feelings can be validated. Kathleen Boone captures the essence of this relationship between human experience and Scripture: "The 'final authority' of Christ is equated to the authority of scripture. . . . [I]t is clear that whatever subjective impressions or emotions one may experience in this encounter [personal experience with Christ] must be validated by linking them in some way to the biblical text—which, unlike human experience, is always inerrant" (1989, 33). Because the men perceived that human experience could be misleading, they were hesitant to rely only on their own thoughts and feelings to gauge what was right. As a result, their experiences were judged reliable only after they were validated through association with the Bible. It was for this reason that Bible study was the centerpiece of Accept and Expell meetings; the men had to prove the legitimacy of their revised theology by making explicit links to the Bible and, to use Mol's (1976) term, "sacralizing" the new meanings constructed in the human realm.

To re-anchor their revised theologies in the divine realm, Accept and Expell members had to do the work necessary to ground them in the Bible. They did so in the context of group meetings through a discussion of biblical passages that were interpreted to align goodness (e.g., moral Christian behavior) with inclusive love or righteous struggle, respectively, and to define evil (e.g., immoral Christian behavior) as exclusion or failure to resist. Through these discussions, each group linked its revised theological beliefs to direct orders from God, making them valid biblical mandates—truth not of the men's making—and shifting them back into the divine realm, where they were protected by the weight of divine authority. Doing so legitimated the men's own experiences within the group. The following two examples, drawn from fieldnotes, show how the men typically shifted their new theologies back into the divine sphere and then used them to validate revised understandings of past and present experiences.

For Accept to shift their theology of inclusivity into the divine realm successfully, they had to focus on Scripture that emphasized the connection between Christ's teachings and acting compassionately and lovingly toward all people. During the time I attended Accept, many Bible study lessons focused on this connection, but the example I offer below was particularly persuasive to the men because it was among those passages in which Jesus specifically equates loving and following him with caring for the needs of others. In this lesson, group members examined the following conversation between Jesus and his disciple Peter in John 21:15–25:

When they had finished eating, Jesus said to Simon Peter, "Simon, son of John, do you truly love me more than these?"
"Yes, Lord," he said, "you know that I love you."

Jesus said, "Feed my lambs."

Again Jesus said, "Simon, son of John, do you truly love me?"

He answered, "Yes, Lord, you know that I love you."

Jesus said, "Take care of my sheep."

The third time he said to him, "Simon, son of John, do you love me?"

Peter was hurt because Jesus asked him the third time, "Do you love me?" He said, "Lord, you know all things; you know that I love you."

Jesus said, "Feed my sheep. I tell you the truth, when you were younger you dressed yourself and went where you wanted; but when you are old you will stretch out your hands, and someone else will dress you and lead you where you do not want to go." Jesus said this to indicate the kind of death by which Peter would glorify God. Then he said to him, "Follow me!"

After these verses were read aloud, the men began to discuss them by focusing on what they considered to be the two key questions evoked by the passage: Why does Christ ask Peter "Do you love me?" three times? and What does feed my sheep/lambs (i.e., flock) mean?

One member initially suggested that Christ asked whether Peter loved him three times because Peter had denied him three times. In this way, he argued, Christ was asking Peter to remedy this denial. While some members agreed with this answer, others were quite wary of it because they thought it implied that Christ was punishing Peter rather than offering him unconditional love and guidance—something Christ would not do. If Christ's purpose was to punish Peter, why would he also ask Peter to care for his followers at the same time? Instead, these members asserted that Christ's repetitive question, answer, and command pattern was a way of teaching Peter and asking for unwavering love. As one member put it, "This passage teaches us that Christ wants us to love him at the very deepest level, and he is very specific about what that love means we are called to do. When we love him, we are called to 'take care of his sheep,' or his flock of believers." All of the members agreed that "feeding sheep" referred to loving and tending to others and felt that Christ was teaching us that if we love him, then we will show that love by doing his work—loving and caring for people.

One of the few women in the group, Mary, spoke up at this point, explaining that she had once "been fed" by group members and that it had changed her life. A few months ago she had lost her job and had no home computer to use to develop a resume. She was deeply worried about finding work quickly because she had little money saved. Jamie offered to type her resume on his home computer, and they scheduled a time to do so. Shortly before they were to meet, Jamie's mother passed away, and he had to leave for the funeral. Instead of just calling her and rescheduling, Jamie, recognizing her desperation for a job, called Danny to arrange for her to do her resume at his house. Then he called her and told her what had happened and that she could meet Danny at the same time to do her resume. After this conversation, she explained: "I just broke down in tears because someone valued me so much that he would help me even in the face of his own suffering and pain at the loss of his mother. His 'feeding' me in this way made me feel that this is truly what Christians should do, and I have been trying to 'feed' others the same way. Now, after studying this passage, I know that this feeling stems from Jesus' command for us to live out this kind of love." When Mary finished speaking, Brandon responded by saying, "Amen sister! Christ tells us plainly that if we love him, then we show this love by outreach to others. And he does not specify who is worthy of such care. All of his sheep require care, and that is what I intend to do." This outburst was followed by a ripple of "Amens" and "Hallelujahs" around the room. It had been confirmed; love and inclusion were commands from Christ.

This example illustrates how the group commonly worked to imbue their theology of inclusion with divinity and to elevate it to divine order. By interpreting the question, answer, and command pattern of Christ's discourse with Peter as a way of *teaching* his followers, the group interpreted the lesson as a direct order from Christ. Once this theology had been successfully shifted into the sacred, group members could then use it to validate their belief and feeling that inclusion was the Christian course of action. We see this validation, for example, when Mary links her feeling "that this [caring for all others] is truly what Christians should do" to "Jesus' command for us to live out this kind of love." Here, a belief or feeling about what is right becomes right, becomes certain truth, when it is connected to the divine. Drawing on this and similar Bible study lessons, group members came to believe their new theology did reflect God's will and thus could wholly embrace and use it as a trustworthy guide for their lives.

Expell members validated their revised theology in precisely the same way. While they could not explicitly link their psychological explanation to Scripture because the Bible says little about psychological trauma or unmet emotional needs, they did connect the struggle to be righteous to God's Word. Given that the men believed that God condemned homosexuality, they linked their struggle against it to a divine command to fight hard against temptation and sinfulness. This command was again legitimated as divine truth through association with the Bible and Jesus's example and could thus be used to justify the men's experiences as they struggled with their homosexuality.

As within Accept, Expell members collaborated during group meetings to establish and solidify the links between their beliefs and the divine. At meetings, members were prompted to discuss the difficulties of their struggle and their particular temptations so that the group could keep the members accountable and give encouragement. As they did so, the group continually worked to forge a link between the members' struggle to overcome homosexuality and directives from God to resist temptation and pursue a righteous path. For instance, the group's study guide, *Sexual Healing*, refers to this pursuit as a form of "spiritual warfare," warning, "We must always remember that we have been born into a battle—the battle of evil against good (Satan against God), and that as members of Christ's body, the Church, we will suffer wounds from the battle. Jesus was very clear on that point. He said that we will have tribulation in this world, but that we share the ultimate victory with Him. . . . 'If you should suffer for the sake of righteousness, you are blessed' (1 Peter 3:14)" (Foster 1995a, 239).

In this excerpt, the author first makes the point that suffering and hurt are inevitable parts of the "battle" between good and evil and that the reward for remaining faithful through the struggle is the "ultimate victory." This idea is then connected to the biblical verse in 1 Peter, thereby validating its content and transforming it into divine directive. The link between suffering to be righteous and being like Jesus is clear and powerful, and the legitimacy of these ideas is forged in their scriptural grounding. In this way, the men could liken their pain and continued fight to resist sexual temptation to Jesus's own struggle and could validate their revised theology as the sacred rules for living their lives. In the fieldnote excerpt that follows, we see how the group typically showed the men how to use this link and validate their revised theology.

At the beginning of one meeting, Jeremy asked if he could share what was going on in his life because he was having "a very hard time" and needed the group to keep him "accountable." Group members gave him their attention and listened carefully as he explained his struggle. Fairly recently (he is never clear about the time frame), Jeremy broke up with his partner and left San Francisco to move into a nearby Christian home whose owners rented rooms to sexual strugglers to help them "walk out of the lifestyle." He had been "progressing in [his] healing" and had not felt the need to "act out" until recently. This desire, he said, was triggered by a message he received a few nights ago. That night, upon his return to the Christian home, residents told him his ex-boyfriend had called him five times. These calls frightened him because it meant his ex-boyfriend had tracked him down and might show up one day. He explained that he was afraid both for his physical well-being, because his boyfriend had been abusive, and for his emotional and spiritual well-being because he really missed him. If he spoke to or saw him, Jeremy feared he "would do something stupid." Though he had resolved not to answer the phone, Jeremy believed his ex-boyfriend might just show up, and he would be "weakened" in his spiritual struggle and overwhelmed by temptation. Jeremy appeared to be truly frightened by this prospect; he was shaking and pale, continuously wringing his hands. Yet he assured us he had come too far and was not "going to give in to evil," and he asked for us to pray for him that he would be given the strength to resist.

The group leader assured him we would pray for him and told him: "Remember you are in the palm of God's hand. While God can cover you up so that nothing can get to you, every now and then he is going to open his hand up and show you to the rest of the world. You will be open to worldly things, but you are still in the palm of God's hand and nothing can snatch you out." Brian broke into the conversation here: "Yeah, imagine God is showing you to Satan and saying, 'Ha, ha, look what I've got and you can't have him back.'" Another member told Jeremy that God expects us to struggle but also promises to give us the strength to overcome evil. She asked us to read Psalm 34:17–22 aloud together: "The righteous cry out, and the LORD hears them; he delivers them from all their troubles. The LORD is close to the brokenhearted and saves those who are crushed in spirit. A righteous man may have many troubles, but the LORD delivers him from them all; he protects all his bones, not one of them will be broken. Evil will slay the wicked; the foes of the righteous will be condemned. The LORD redeems his servants; no one will be condemned who takes refuge in him." When the group finished reading this passage, there was a heavy quietness in the room for several moments until Brian spoke: "God allows us to be tested, even broken or crushed in spirit, but as long as we call out to him in our struggle, we are protected." Josh agreed, adding, "We know we will face trouble, the evil one will tempt us, but the Bible tells us as long as we struggle for righteousness, we will be in our Savior's hands." Some members responded with "amens," while others nodded.

All of the advice, support, and encouragement that followed Jeremy's plea for help reiterated the idea that struggle was inevitable. However, the group highlighted one important aspect of struggle, turning to Psalm 34:17–22, to remind Jeremy that God knows of his struggle and promises to reward him as long as he chooses to be righteous and to act in accord with God's Word. As one married Expell member explained it, "I know God will allow me to struggle—even Jesus did—and to be tested, even to stumble and fall, but Jesus tells me that as long as I reach out to him, he will protect me and take me to the victory. I truly believe, like God says in Genesis, that he gave me Abby [his wife] as a helpmate in this struggle. He works through her to give me strength. When we pray together in his presence, I know we push evil away." This man connected his suffering to Jesus's example, his wife to the "helpmate" created in Genesis, and his salvation to resisting temptation. His difficulties and their solutions thus became interpreted through links to biblical examples, making them valid and authoritative in his life. In much the same way, all of the men in Expell came to link their suffering and struggle to Jesus's or biblical example and to perceive it as a test of righteousness, one, as explained in the Bible, that could lead them to redemption.

By linking the struggle for righteousness to divine imperative and example, Expell shifted its revised theology back into the sacred realm, investing it with great authority and importance. This shift enabled group members to confirm their notion that struggle per se was worthy and necessary, that doing so was the Christian course of action, and that it would give them divine protection. This link made the struggle of becoming and being an ex-gay Christian more than just a transformation or healing of self; it became, through association with the Bible, an act of conforming to God's will. In this way, struggling to be righteous became moral Christian behavior.

Authenticating the New Christian Self

While shifting their revised theologies into the sacred realm enabled Accept and Expell members to be certain about what thoughts, feelings, and behaviors constituted a good Christian identity, the actual shift did little to help them evaluate their progress as either a gay Christian or an ex-gay Christian who lived out this theology. Their revised theologies, now divinely inspired, called for new ways of being and doing, and the men sought evidence that they had authentically transformed themselves to correspond to these new prescriptions. How could they be sure they were the good Christians mandated by their revised theologies?

Answering this question first requires an understanding of the concept of authenticity. Sociologist Rebecca Erickson has persuasively argued that authenticity is a "self-referential" concept and should "be regarded as the extent to which one fulfills the expectations or commitments one has for self" (1995, 131). These self-expectations and commitments establish criterion for evaluating one's performances, and feelings of authenticity (or inauthenticity) are generated through a comparison of one's actions and emotions to these criteria. Performances that closely match these standards create a sense of being authentically who one wishes to be. The men in this study, of course, desired to be good Christians, as defined by Accept and Expell, who acted and felt in particular ways. However, because the men also perceived that God had created, and wanted them to live in accord with, their true selves, it was critically important to the men that these proper actions and feelings emerge spontaneously. The men perceived that if they were authentic, that is, if they "believed in their hearts" the group's theology and were living from their God-given selves, then right and good feelings would spring forth without hesitation or manipulation.

By contrast, inauthenticity was marked by inappropriate feelings or staged performances. In addition, the men knew, from their own biographies as gay men who had staged heterosexual identities, that performance could be faked and therefore was not enough to signify a real transformation. As a result, they relied on the experience of spontaneous "right" feeling as a barometer of authenticity. An Accept member explained the importance of emotional experience this way: "Sometimes people do and say all the right things; they *talk* love and *pretend* acceptance, but they are still angry or hurt and don't feel it. Being a good Christian means changing in your heart; you have to feel it." This man's distrust of behavior and his emphasis on feeling shows why and how emotional experience was used as a standard to assess authenticity.

For these reasons, the men relied heavily on feelings as evidence of authentic transformation to a gay or ex-gay Christian. Evaluating feelings as evidence of an authentically changed self, however, was not a skill that just came naturally to the men. Instead, just as the men had had to be taught the groups' revised theologies and how to apply them to their lives, the groups had to show the men how to use their emotions as proof of their success. To do so, group leaders and established members showed newer members first how to note and monitor their emotions, enabling the men to compare their actual feelings to expectations of how a good Christian should feel. Because Accept's and Expell's definitions of a good Christian were explicitly linked to feeling rules, the men could use their level of adherence to these rules to chart their individual progress. The closer their actual feelings matched expectations, the more authentic and successful they judged their transformations. In addition to assessing authenticity by how closely feelings matched expectations, the men also learned how to evaluate their level of authenticity by gauging how naturally (e.g., spontaneously and effortlessly) they experienced the proper emotion. If the right emotions emerged without thought or work, then the men perceived them to be evidence of real change in themselves. In these ways, the men learned to use emotional experience as a yardstick to measure their relative authenticity.

For these men, then, spontaneous right feeling "proved" a successful transformation to either a gay Christian or an ex-gay Christian. Ironically, though, the feelings that the men used as markers of authenticity—those that arose *naturally*—had to be *learned*. This paradox, that the men had to learn how to feel if they were to experience their true selves (Erickson 1997, 6), was invisible to the men, and they instead perceived that the changes in how they felt resulted from healing and thereby getting closer to being the person God intended. Initially, though, group members had to be shown how to do this kind of interpretive work. The following fieldnote excerpt, in which an Accept member described an incident with his neighbor, is representative of how such interpretation was taught:

Scott: We were cleaning up our yards [after a bad storm], and we got to talking. After a while, he [the neighbor] asked me if I was still going to that church. I asked him which one, and he said, "The purple church with all the fags in it." I started to think, "What an asshole," but then I felt sorry for him, sorry he was filled with such vileness. I just told him that colors and labels meant little to God but what was in our hearts meant a great deal and went inside.

Mark: God must have felt great joy at what was in *your heart.*

Scott: What do you mean?

Mark: Don't you see? Instead of anger at his mean comments to you, you thought about him and felt compassion for him because he lives with such bad feelings. Feeling compassion instead of anger allowed you to teach him an important lesson about love. You truly did Jesus' work.

In this exchange, Mark directed Scott's attention to the feelings that were generated during the incident and showed him how to evaluate his feelings, using them as indicators about himself. By telling Scott he had done "Jesus' work," Mark also reinforced group notions about how a good Christian is supposed to feel. While Scott initially judged his neighbor ("What an asshole"), he immediately, and without calculation, altered this feeling to sympathy. Because this alteration was a seemingly natural impulse, it could be interpreted as a sign of successful transformation. Mark passed his test.

These kinds of instructive interactions showed group members how to scan their feelings for evidence of authentic change in themselves. As they learned to do so, they began to highlight and intensely value the emotions indicative of change. This emphasis took attention away from members' experiences of lingering struggle or contrary emotions and placed it solidly on what they were doing right, enabling the men to note progress even while still struggling. We see this focus on right feelings in the following two interview excerpts with Expell members. Both excerpts focus on the men's changed reactions to struggling to resist temptations with either pornography or other men:

You can't get away from it on the Internet. Things God meant for good become corrupt and distorted, and we don't know what is beautiful anymore. It [porn] is like a deadly mushroom; it looks pretty, and you eat it and it kills you. Now that I have a close relationship with God, I can see the impurities of these things. The closer you get to God and his purity, the more his light shines on your life, and you want to discard the baggage. Before I didn't, but now God's light shows me what is not clean, and I *want* to throw it away. The mushroom is still pretty, and sometimes I want to eat it, but then I see its ugliness and want to get rid of it. That's what's important—I *want* to be rid of it and I resist it.

It used to be I'd see a good-looking man and feel drawn to him. It was exciting even though I felt guilty. I'd have fantasies about the sex. Then, I'd go home and dread making love with my wife. She's a wonderful, loving Christian woman, but the sex part was so difficult for me. It felt forced, wrong somehow. Now, I see an attractive man, and sometimes I notice, but I turn my head without even thinking about it. As I build my walk with God, I am learning to turn away from what is unhealthy. I desire to turn away because I know it is wrong, and I want to turn towards my wife. She is God's gift to me, and I deeply want to honor that.

Clearly, both men have learned to use their emotional experiences to assess their progress as ex-gay Christians, citing changed reactions to pornography (e.g., pretty to ugly, desirable to repulsive) or to other men (e.g., from fantasizing to turning away) as evidence. Further, even though both were sometimes still tempted, noting the "prettiness" of the mushroom or the attractiveness of a man, neither man highlighted this persistent sexual desire—a focus that could undermine the sense that they were authentically transformed ex-gay Christians. Instead, the men fixed their attention on the positive desire to be "rid of," "resist," and "turn away from" the pull of pornography and other men. This kind of desire was proof of progress and authentic change.

After the men in both groups learned how to highlight and interpret their emotions as evidence of a changed self, they were able to successfully use this evidence to confirm who they perceived themselves to be. Feeling a certain way (spontaneously) meant that they had achieved being a certain someone. That the men used this connection between feeling and being to authenticate their new identities is evident in the following two interview excerpts, in which each man used his feelings to support a view of himself as a good Christian according to group definition:

> When I first heard the Baptists were boycotting Disney, I admit I thought for a moment that they didn't deserve heaven. But then I felt sorry for them and deeply sad that they were so hateful, and I really desired for them to know how good it is to love and accept our differences. I now feel love for everyone because that's what God tells us and that is what Christianity is really about. (Accept member)

> I used to feel so badly about myself when I had homosexual desires, like I was no good at all. I no longer have to fight off those bad feelings because I know now that what is important is not that I have these feelings but that I resist them and try to follow God's will. Being a Christian does not mean we won't be tempted but that we will resist temptations. (Expell member)

In these excerpts, feeling is synonymous with being. Both men described how feeling love (Accept) or pride in their efforts to resist (Expell) qualified them as Christians. The doubts the men once experienced about themselves as good Christians were thus diminished or alleviated because the men learned to invoke their refashioned (but seemingly spontaneous) feelings as evidence of being good Christians. This authentication was like a final stamp bearing the label gay Christian or ex-gay Christian, and the men perceived that their transformations were complete. This is not to say that they believed that their struggle was over or that they would not slide into old habits, but the men now saw themselves in a positive light. The unworthy and stained had been transformed into the moral and good.

This transformation had tremendous consequences for the men's lives, at least in the short term. (Given the duration of my study, I cannot assess long-term consequences.) Where they had once been stigmatized and shamed, they now felt like worthy, good people. Where they had once been alienated and outcast, they were now surrounded by a supportive community of like-minded Christians. Where some had once believed they were condemned to hell, they now trusted in their salvation. These new self-understandings are evident in the following interview excerpts in which the men described how they now saw themselves:

> I felt good about myself because I finally knew, and no one will ever tell me different, that I am a child of God, worthy for good and happy things to happen to me because of God's plan for me. (gay Christian)

> Before I thought there was nothing right in me; I thought everything was bad because of what other Christians said, [but] there really is a higher truth, a higher reality—I'm a good Christian. God created me as a person of worth and value. (ex-gay Christian)

As these excerpts suggest, the transformation process that the men underwent enabled them to feel like worthwhile and deserving people through the construction of new meanings, new identity options, and new ways of being, doing, and feeling as a Christian.

The collective work of these groups also helped to expand culture by creating new cultural niches in which people who were, until relatively recently, kept silent and invisible could now openly discuss issues of homosexuality and faith and have a voice in the larger religious and cultural debate. Importantly, these cultural niches were linked to divine authority through association with the Bible, making them legitimate and protected spaces from which the men, and others like them, could fend off criticism from homophobic antagonists. The presence of this protection, or layer of insulation, is evident in the men's above references to "God's plan" and a "higher truth," indicating that the men felt their new beliefs, way of living, and self-meanings were grounded in God's truth, making them impervious to mere human assault (e.g., "no one will ever tell me different"). In this way, the men's newly minted positive self-images were insulated from human critics, and they had a secure theological vantage point from which to question the righteousness of their conservative Christian counterparts who clung to exclusionary practices or belittled their struggle.

The Immediate Consequences of Change in the Men's Lives

Such changes obviously had profound psychological implications for the men, ranging from higher self-esteem to lifted depression to, in some instances, quelled suicidal impulses. As a result, many men felt that they could perform better at work and that they were able to develop stronger and more satisfying personal relationships. As their shame lifted, they felt that they could be more open and honest with family members and/or friends. Doing so allowed them to create relationships in which they felt known and valued. So, too, were the men able to create intimate relationships that were more meaningful and durable, though the form of intimate relationship varied depending on whether the men were gay or ex-gay Christians.

Becoming gay or ex-gay Christians also changed the men's sexual behaviors, making them less vulnerable to sexually transmitted diseases. Most of the men, when they had felt ashamed of who they were, had tried to hide their homosexuality. For men in both groups, this desire to keep their homosexuality invisible prompted them to engage in risky sexual behaviors, such as anonymous sex with multiple partners. Now, many of the gay Christians sought long-term, monogamous relationships. For ex-gay Christians, their transformation helped them to curtail, and sometimes to cease, risky sexual behaviors, at least for a certain period of time. Some of the men who were married now found that they could tell their wives about their sexual behavior. As one man put it, "For the first time, I felt like I wanted to be honest with my wife about the sex." This new openness offered some women the chance to take protective measures. This shift in sexual behavior greatly diminished the risk of those involved being infected with a sexually transmitted disease.

As a group, however, gay Christians tended to benefit more fully from their transformations than did ex-gay Christians. Gay Christians had gone through a process of accepting their homosexuality and were, for the most part, comfortable with it in the context of their faith and able to pursue the lives they wanted. For ex-gay Christians, the road was much tougher because making a successful transformation to an ex-gay Christian was not the same thing as successfully changing one's sexuality. Becoming an Expell member meant that the men learned *how* to struggle against sexual temptations and to *value* that struggle; it did not necessarily mean that the men were able to alter their sexuality. In essence, while being an ex-gay Christian could (and sometimes did) mean that an individual had successfully developed heterosexual desires, it often meant that an individual was embroiled in a struggle against homosexuality that could, and perhaps was even likely to, fail.

Examining what it means to alter one's sexuality provides some insight into how and why Expell members were often caught in a cycle of constant struggle—trying to change, failing, and starting over. To begin, consider the distinction between sexual behavior—sex acts, seduction displays, and courtship rituals—and sexual desire, or what people want to do (Schwartz and Rutter 2000, 2). Obviously, it is easier to modify behaviors than desires (Haldeman 1994; Spitzer 2001a, 2003). Exodus leaders are well aware of this difference. Bob Davies, who was the North American executive director of Exodus from 1985 to 2001, notes that changing sexual behavior is "one of the easiest steps to attain," but that it "resolves little" (2001b, 13). Instead, he asserts that the "deepest possible sense of freedom" from homosexuality comes from changing "thoughts and sexual attractions" (2001b, 14). For the members of Expell, then, a successful change in sexuality had to include alterations in both sexual behavior and desire.

So while Expell members could become successful ex-gay Christians in the sense that they were committed to the struggle to change their sexual desires, their ability to change their sexuality was less successful and more turbulent than Accept members' attempts to reconcile their homosexuality with their faith. While Accept members, with one exception, experienced positive, significant changes in their lives, only five Expell members reported that they, at this point in their lives, had experienced a significant change in sexuality (e.g., felt more heterosexual than homosexual desires over an extended period of time). For these five men, this change did not mean that they no longer felt homosexual urges, but rather that these urges were fewer and less intense, making it easier for the men to resist them. Their heterosexual desires also became more pronounced. One man was able to save a faltering marriage and develop a satisfying sex life with his wife, while two others were able to marry and reported being happy, even though one of these men still consistently viewed homosexual pornography. One of these men described this change: "On a sexual desire scale from one to ten, with ten being the most desire, I used to be an eight to nine for homosexual desire and one to two for heterosexual. Now, I've flip-flopped. Sometimes, I am still tempted, but not powerfully or for long." Some level of sexual change was thus possible for some of the men.

The rest of the men did not experience this kind of change in their sexuality. Six men altered their behavior but reported little change in sexual desire. For these men, changing their behavior was rewarding because they felt less sinful, but they often became frustrated and depressed over their lack of progress. Four other men dropped out of the group because they had not experienced change and continued participation made them feel worse.

The outcomes for individuals within Expell are consistent with those found in larger studies of sexual change. Robert Spitzer, a noted Columbia University psychiatrist who was instrumental in getting homosexuality removed from the American Psychiatric Association's list of mental disorders in 1973, recently conducted a study that examined the success of sexual change, mostly within ex-gay ministries and related therapy groups. His sample was composed of 200 self-selected individuals, 143 men and 57 women, who were predominately homosexual before they began some form of sexual reorientation therapy, either within Exodus or from therapists, and had achieved a change from homosexual to heterosexual attraction that had lasted at least five years (Spitzer 2003). This sample thus only included people who believed they had been "successful" in changing their sexuality (74 other people who volunteered were excluded from the study for a variety of reasons (e.g., they had a change in behavior but not desire, were not predominately homosexual, etc.). Of this select group, Spitzer concluded that 11 percent of the men and 37 percent of the women had achieved "complete change" (2003, 410), but that 66 percent of the men and 44 percent of the women had "satisfied the criteria for good heterosexual functioning" (411). Spitzer concluded that some people can make significant changes in sexual orientation, while others can only change behavior and/or sexual identity (2003, 415). While significant sexual change is possible, and those who achieve it find it to be very beneficial, Spitzer remarked, in an editorial for the *Wall Street Journal,* that "complete change was uncommon," and he "suspected that the vast majority of gay people would be unable to substantially alter a very firmly established homosexual orientation" (2001b). Further, when I asked Bob Davies, the recent North American executive director of Exodus, about the success rate in Exodus, he responded with anecdotal evidence, explaining that a "long-time counselor with Exodus estimated that a third of his clients had significant changes in their sexuality, another third had little change, and a third gave up and/or returned to active homosexuality" (2001a). At present, the only conclusion possible is that some people can achieve some level of change sometimes. Clearly, more research is required if we are to understand fully how often sexual transformation is possible, the extent of such transformation (behavior versus desire), and what the benefits and risks of such therapeutic processes are for individuals.

Given the relatively small number of people able to make significant changes or complete transformations in their sexuality, being a member of an Exodus ministry like Expell can backfire for individuals who do not experience change, making membership, at best, frustrating and, at worst, emotionally debilitating. It is true that some members benefit tremendously from ministry participation and that some, even those who change only behavior, are more satisfied with a single, mostly celibate life than they were as acting homosexuals. For others, though, failing to experience change can be devastating. Exodus ministries assert that change is possible *if* an individual wants to badly enough and desires to live in obedience to God's Word. Failure to change can then become an individual failing; the individual did not desire to change/follow God enough. Some people, as in the case of three men in this study, pray for years for a change that does not come. They become frustrated and wonder, as one man put it, "why God had not healed [them]. What was wrong?" Others may come to believe that their lack of progress stems from their unworthiness or lack of true desire. In such cases, members may feel like "double failures," sinful homosexuals and Christians too weak in their faith to elicit healing from God. Failure to be healed becomes their failure as Christians. Only one of the men in this study had this experience while I was attending the group, but he reported that it made him "so depressed that [he] did not want to live."

For married men, a lack of progress was even more threatening. Like most Christians, the men viewed marriage as an idealized form of intimate relationship, one that is sanctioned by God. Making little progress toward heterosexuality over a long period of time, something the men attributed to their own failings, often put their marriages on shaky ground and risked the blessing granted from God. These men loved their wives and children (if they had them) and felt great pressure to change to keep their families intact. Further, the consequences of any "fall" or "acting out" of homosexual behavior were greater for married men. In their case, a homosexual encounter was not only the sin of homosexuality but also the sin of adultery. At times, they were not truthful with their wives, adding the sin of lying to their list. Some of these men became stuck in a cycle of trying very hard, making some progress, backsliding into some form of homosexual behavior, feeling great shame, asking forgiveness from their wives and God, and resolving to try even harder. Over time, this cycle was exhausting and incredibly frustrating. Yet, because of their intense desires to be good Christians and stay married, few of the men gave up. They kept trying, ever vigilant and ever prayerful, sometimes making progress and sometimes failing. Amazingly, as we will see in the next chapter, their wives took this journey with them.

The Wives
of Ex-gay
Christian Men

In 1998, Lisa's friend Dan invited her to a birthday party so that he could introduce her to his friend Steve. She liked Steve from the start, and they began dating in spite of rumors that he and Dan were involved. Lisa saw these rumors as people buying into stereotypes of men who had some feminine attributes, and she paid no attention to them. After all, Dan was married with a child, and Steve had children from a previous marriage. Her relationship with Steve blossomed quickly. He was everything she was looking for: a friend who was fun and loving, a man who wanted to be an involved father, and a devoted Christian who taught Sunday school. The only troubling aspect of their relationship, according to Lisa, was that Steve did not seem to desire her sexually. She assumed his restraint was the result of a decision to save sex for wedlock. Less than a year after they met, Lisa and Steve were married.

In many ways, their marriage was fine, but Steve remained sexually apathetic, making Lisa feel like something was wrong with her. Further, Steve and Dan's friendship was worrisome. They spent a lot of time together, occasionally going out to clubs until late and often fighting bitterly. Lisa's friends and parents became concerned, and she had fights with them about Steve, always defending him. When Lisa confronted Steve about his behavior, he blamed her for their difficulties, telling her he would go to marriage counseling only after she went to therapy and made progress on her problems. Eventually, Dan's wife discovered the affair he was having with Steve. It was the pastor of their church who, along with Dan, finally convinced Steve that he had to tell Lisa the truth. Lisa remembers exactly how she felt when Steve told her he was gay and having an affair with Dan: "The night he told me, I could have thrown up all over him. It was awful. I was so mad; I had been ugly to my friends and lost my relationship with my parents because I believed him. I had just really trusted. I remember feeling lost because my marriage wasn't what I thought it was. It was such a betrayal. It's so hard when you find out. You get these images in your head of them together. This image would go through my mind, and I would think, ugh. It just made me sick."

Like Lisa, Susan noticed some "clues" early in her relationship with Leon, such as "his slightly feminine mannerisms," but she dismissed them because he "had dated lots of girls." They had grown up in the same town and started dating in high school. Leon was "very considerate, polite, and kind, a very gentle person." They fell in love quickly and were married in 1964 at age twenty. Because Leon was in the military, the couple had to endure long physical separations during the first fourteen years of their marriage, and Susan concentrated on the task of raising their children. Life went on, as Susan said, with just the "normal struggles" of a military family.

It was not long after Leon began living at home permanently that Susan began to notice little things that gave her cause for alarm. For instance, Leon began keeping a spare shirt in his car. When Susan asked him what it was for, he told her he did not like stopping at the grocery store in his uniform. Wearing his uniform in public had never been a problem before, and Susan reasoned that he might be stopping other places where he would not want to be identified as military personnel. Such incidents gave Susan nagging suspicions, but when she questioned Leon about his activities and whether he had same-sex attractions, he repeatedly told her she was a "pervert." Susan began to pray for God to either take away her "perverse imagination or expose [Leon]." Finally, in 1995, Leon was arrested for soliciting sex from a male police officer. At first, he lied to Susan, telling her a story about picking up a hitchhiker involved in a drug deal and being arrested because police assumed he was part of the deal. A few days later, however, he began to tell her the whole truth about his arrest and the large numbers of men who had been his sexual partners over the last three decades. Susan vividly recalled how she felt at that moment: "I hit him. I think I started by pounding on his chest, and I was yelling, 'How could you do this to me?' I was so angry, so betrayed at his unfaithfulness. I never even had a serious relationship with anyone else in the world, and I find out he had been with, literally, hundreds of men. Men—he wanted men. I could not believe it. . . . I was also grateful he was being honest with me for the first time. I mean, when you have these suspicions for over thirty years and all of a sudden you find out you weren't crazy, you didn't have a perverse imagination, it was kind of a relief in a lot of ways."

Both Lisa and Susan were devastated when they found out about their husbands' same-sex proclivities and infidelities. They had married men they loved and trusted. When this trust was broken, they responded with the anger and pain that most people experience when a partner is unfaithful. But their situations were different in one important way: these women discovered not only that their husbands were cheating but that they desired men. This same-sex desire was incredibly threatening to the women because they took it to mean that they could not satisfy their husbands' sexual desires. Further, rather than simply breaking marital trust through infidelities, these men's activities added another layer of betrayal. They were not the kind of people (e.g., heterosexual) that they had implicitly claimed to be when they were married, a fundamental deception.

The above interview excerpts reveal Lisa's and Susan's responses to these deceptions. Their sense of betrayal, hurt, revulsion, and rage still permeated the language each used to recount their moments of discovery. They were not unique. Every woman in this study who discovered her husband's homosexuality after marriage shared these same vivid and powerful feelings. As each woman told her story, I was struck by the intensity of these feelings—but not surprised. It was easy to anticipate and understand the women's reactions to such a painful discovery. What I had more trouble understanding, however, was why these women chose to stay in their marriages and how they worked through such feelings to be able to do so.

Some people might see these women as the proverbial doormats, too weak willed and dependent to walk away from marriages based on false pretenses. Others might see these women as role models who epitomize what it means to be committed to a relationship and who take "for better or worse" seriously. As we will see, however, these women defy such easy categorization. Neither willing hostages nor heroines, these women simultaneously conformed to their roles as good Christian wives and innovatively reshaped these roles into opportunities to exert some control and agency over their situations. In doing so, these women made staying in troubled marriages at least somewhat satisfying for themselves and played an integral part in keeping their husbands in heterosexual relationships while their husbands attempted to live heterosexual lives. This chapter focuses on how these women coped with the challenges to their marriages and examines the consequences of the women's decisions to stay married. To begin, I explore these women's marriages before and just after the discovery of their husbands' homosexuality, concentrating on how it made them feel about themselves and what they did about it. Next, I focus on what happened when the wives joined a support group, examining how these groups helped the women to stay in difficult marriages. Finally, I analyze the impact of support group participation on the wives' lives and the larger social order.

Finding Out: Uncertain Desires and Super Sleuths

One late afternoon, before I had conducted any interviews with these women, I was sitting in my office talking about this study with a friend. When I explained that many of these women married men they did not know were gay, she interrupted, saying, "No way. Those women had to know. They may not have wanted to admit it, but they knew. You don't live with someone and not pick up on that sort of thing." I disagreed. It seemed entirely plausible that these men could express themselves in ways that created, for others, the impression that they were heterosexual (Goffman 1959). In fact, in an ethnographic study of men who had anonymous homosexual encounters in public restrooms, Humphreys found that many men (over 54 percent of the sample) were married and that their wives knew nothing about their homosexual activity (1970, 105). Further, scholars agree that one of the primary facets of gender socialization for men is that they learn to express their masculinity through heterosexual displays (Connell 1987; Segal 1994; Messner 2001). In this sense, most men have had extensive training and practice in the presentation of themselves as ardent heterosexuals. Whether men actually feel heterosexual desire or not, most know how to act to stage a convincing heterosexual performance (Connell 1992).

As sociologists Brissett and Edgley point out, "It makes no necessary difference in the last analysis whether an individual wishes to be deceitful or honest. . . . [T]he meaning of his enterprise will be established in the expressive/impressive dimension of his behavior" (1990, 7). In other words, how people are understood by others is not a function of who they are "inside," or even whether they seek to reveal or conceal themselves. Instead, people derive meanings about an individual based on the impressions they get from another person's behavior, language, and appearance (Stone 1981). For these reasons, I had no trouble believing these women did not detect their husbands' homosexuality. My friend argued that it was awfully hard to so carefully control the information you convey to another person when you are with that individual constantly. In a marriage, she asserted, there had to be mixed messages.

When I had completed the interviews, I discovered that my friend and I were both right, though to varying degrees. Each woman in this study found out about her husband's homosexuality in one of two ways: either she learned about her husband's homosexuality after they had been married for a period of time, ranging anywhere from just one year to over thirty, or, in a few cases, the man told her about his "homosexual problem" before they were married. Of the fifteen wives I interviewed, twelve found out after marriage. In most (seven) of these cases, husbands either were forced to confess under the weight of damning evidence or were caught outright in compromising situations. Only one man told his wife of his struggle uncoerced, approximately two years into their marriage, though he presented it as a past struggle rather than a present concern—a lie she would soon discover. In four other cases, husbands told their wives because they wanted to leave them and pursue relationships with their male lovers.

None of these women knew, prior to finding explicit evidence or being told, that her husband was gay, though some women sensed something was not quite right in their relationship. Of these twelve wives, seven never detected anything odd about their marriage until just before or upon their discoveries about their husbands. From their perspective, they had had successful and satisfying marriages. This satisfaction was evident during interviews when I asked whether they had any clues about their husbands' sexuality prior to finding out. One woman responded: "It [his homosexuality] wasn't visible at all. Because of the way he acted, nobody would have suspected this at all. This man was so macho and it was, well, you would just never in a million years think anything like that. There was no way. He was so good to me, just so loving and caring, and we had a great sex life. I was his world. He just did everything for me, spoiled me rotten. And so I just couldn't imagine there would be anything else but that. We were in nirvana. We were in a wonderful place." Another woman commented: "When people ask me, 'Well, didn't you know?' I get irritated and I'm like, 'No, I had no clue.' We were close, emotionally and physically, and I thought we were really happy." Obviously, these women had no hints about their husbands' closeted sexual desires and were happily married; all seven women noted fulfilling sex lives, emotional intimacy, and shared happiness. The idea that their husbands had same-sex desires was unimaginable. These men had managed such convincing heterosexual performances that their wives not only never questioned their sexuality but also felt completely secure in their marriages.

Not all of these twelve women felt that their marriages were on such solid ground. Five sensed something was wrong with or missing from their marriages, though pinpointing the source of the trouble was difficult. Lisa and Ellie noted that their husbands did not seem to desire them sexually. As Lisa said, their "sex life just wasn't there like it should have been," though they were physically affectionate. This sexual disinterest sent up a red flag for these women, but they could not figure out what it meant. Four noted that their husbands became very angry with them quickly about little, silly things and tended to blame them for anything that went wrong. In retrospect, the women perceived that this anger may have been the result of their husbands' sexual struggle, but at the time they did not understand it and were deeply hurt by such reactions.

Four of these women also recalled having the sense that there was an unknown barrier in their relationship or that something was being held over them. One woman's words best captured the sense these women shared: "We had a pretty good marriage, but it wasn't long after we were married that I felt like there was a ghost. That's the only way I know to describe it. Just something hovering over us. I could never identify it." These women knew only that something was wrong but were unable to discern what it was. Sexual apathy, irrational anger, and a vague "ghostly" sense do not logically or easily lead to the conclusion "well, he must be gay," so these women were stuck in a pattern of trying to piece together what was wrong in their marriages. In this sense, my friend's assessment of the situation was correct; in these marriages, husbands were giving mixed messages and wives were aware of problems, but none of these wives was able to link marital trouble to her husband's sexuality until, as one woman put it, "all hell broke loose."

Three of these fifteen women knew about their husbands' homosexual struggle before marriage. This might seem like an odd starting point for a marriage, but these women either believed the men's sexual struggle was under control and/or were in love and decided to help the men overcome this problem. Carla, for instance, met her husband, Bill, when she attended a lecture at her church given by an Exodus representative. Bill was introduced as the leader of a new Bible study for those struggling with homosexuality. Carla felt drawn to him and attended the Bible study. Soon, they started dating, and, as early as their first date, Carla knew she wanted to marry him. When I asked if she had been concerned about his sexual preferences, Carla said: "No, I knew all about his background and stuff. I was worried about what my family and friends were going to say, but it was never a question for me. I remember, clear as day, God saying, 'This [marriage and ministry work] is what I have been preparing you for.' I knew he had struggled with this [homosexuality], but he was out of it and had been for about four years." Carla was convinced Bill's struggle was over and that God was calling her to help him run his ministry.

Unlike Carla, Hannah did not know about Harry's same-sex attraction until they had been dating for over two years. By that time, she "had grown to utterly just love him to death" and knew he loved her. She was puzzled, though, because Harry did not make sexual advances or seem to desire her passionately. Finally, she just asked him if he struggled with homosexuality. She remembered the conversation that followed: "I was the first person he'd ever told. He told me he did not want to live the other lifestyle, that he was not going to make that choice, and that he wanted to fight this because he wanted to be like the average person and everything. He wanted to be with me. I knew he meant it, so I said, 'Okay, let's fight it together.'" In this instance, Hannah decided to stay with Harry because they wanted a life together, and she perceived he was committed to working through his struggle. Simply, her love for Harry made her willing to undertake the struggle with him.

Knowing about their husbands' struggles prior to marriage did not insulate these women from the pain of discovering later infidelities or from the difficulties of the struggle itself. It just made them less surprising. For each of the women in this study, regardless of when she learned of her husband's homosexuality, discovering his struggle initiated a long journey for her as she tried to come to terms with her marital situation. While many of the wives did contemplate leaving their husbands at some point, few made serious moves in that direction.[1] All of the women described their decisions to stay as at least partially faith based, asserting that God had brought them together with their husbands and that they had to honor the vows they made before God. These reactions were normal within the context of conservative Christianity. In a study that examines feminine power within fundamentalism, Brenda Brasher (1998, 152) points out that "the tie between earthly marriage and God's order create strong taboos around divorce," making divorce a stigmatized option. Nancy Ammerman, a prominent sociologist of religion, asserts that "the message of the church is that the Bible binds couples together for life, no matter how bad the marriage may seem" (1987, 144). These women, too, as one woman explained, saw divorce as an "ugly option," one they would use only as a last resort.

In addition, many women wanted to stay because they loved their husbands and had built families with them. As one woman explained, "We loved one another. We were committed to one another. I knew that. Our kids were teens and pre-teens, and I just could not imagine life without him." Other women were stay-at-home mothers and were worried about making it on their own psychologically and economically. One woman, who was in her fifties, explained that she had been a stay-at-home mom whose "identity was tied into her husband," and she did not feel she could start another life. Shame, and the worry they would have to tell others about the issue if they left, also compelled them to stay. As another wife told me, "I didn't want to go out on my own because I wasn't sure what I could do and I didn't want our families to find out about the situation. There's a lot of shame." Because of their religious beliefs, love for their husbands, fear of being on their own, and sense of shame about the situation, these women decided to stay in their marriage and "work through it."

To figure out how to work through the problems, though, the women first had to make sense of what was happening. After the initial shock of discovery passed and the women had determined they were going to stay in their marriages, they were left with three pressing questions that they had to answer before they could work to resolve the issue: What is wrong with me? What is he really doing? and Why is this happening?

Unworthy Wives

Most of the women who discovered their husbands' homosexual infidelities after they were married experienced feelings of rejection. But instead of solely blaming the men for their betrayals and shortcomings as husbands, these women turned inward and struggled to figure out what they had done or had not done, how they might have caused their husbands to stray from the marriage. For ten of these twelve women, this discovery created doubts about their femininity and their worth as wives, at least temporarily. Each of them asked some form of the question, "What is wrong with me, as a woman, that would contribute to my husband's desire to have sex with men?" Though they recognized that relationships were not simple matters of attraction, this question reveals that they did, at least to some extent, buy into the familiar cultural prescription for how women can supposedly attract and keep men: If a woman is pretty, thin, and well-dressed; if she is pleasant and submissive; and if she is a good cook, housekeeper, and mother, then she is likely not only to be desirable to a man but also to keep him satisfied (cf. Bartky 1998).

This prescription is also present in the lore of conservative Christianity. As Bartkowski notes in his study of gender negotiation in evangelical families, women are encouraged to closely monitor "their own bodily and sexual practices in order to appease their man's virtually boundless desire" or risk extramarital affairs (2001, 41). Women are urged to tame the male, containing his sexual energy so he acts morally. To do so, women attempt to approximate ideals of feminine beauty and behavior, often "competing" to be the objects of male attention. These women felt compelled to wonder what they had done to change the rules of the game. One woman expressed her confusion this way: "I just didn't understand why I wasn't good enough. I worked out hard, was very toned, and I tried to be a good wife. I would never just go screaming at him and get in a hollering match." This woman perceived she should be ahead in the competition—she took care of herself, looked good, and was nice—so she could not figure out why her husband was not satisfied with her. She, like many of the wives, reasoned that there must be something lacking in her, as a feminine person, if the prescription was not working as it should.

Because the women felt they had to compete for their husbands' affections, they responded to the idea that their husbands desired men in one of two ways. First, a few women (three) were relieved that there was not another *woman* because they felt less likely to be replaced. One woman explained her relief, saying: "Thank goodness it's not another woman. At least it is not another woman I have to worry about. I still really questioned myself and felt inadequate, but a man was less threatening to me because a man could not do what I do in the family." Here, this woman perceived that she did not have to compete for her husband with men. While he may desire men physically, only a woman is able to fulfill the role of wife and mother. Her relief that he is attracted to men and not other women stems from her belief that women offer men something other men fundamentally cannot—a family and traditional home life. In this sense, these women felt they remained number one in their category of competition, a slot potentially threatened only by other women.

The majority of the women, however, found their husbands' desires for men far worse than an attraction to another woman because they felt excluded from the competition. While these women shared the idea that there were two categories of competition, other women and men, they, unlike the women above, were distressed that their husbands desired men because they perceived they had no way to "fight back" or re-win their husbands. The wives' frustration and sense of futility are expressed clearly in the following interview excerpts:

> When I found out about the homosexual struggle, I was like, "There's no way for me to compete." I think I would know how to fight another woman for his affections but how in the world would I fight another man? I don't have the body parts.

> I was never insecure in my femininity until this stuff happened. Then, it's like, 'Wait a minute. . . . He's married to me, he's attracted to men, and what does that make me?' I think part of it, what our culture says to us, is that if your husband is in an affair with another woman, there's a chance you could get him back. All you'd have to do is look prettier, lose another ten pounds, be nicer, or whatever. You know what to do basically. You know intuitively what another woman is like. You don't specifically know that person but you know other women. But when it comes to trying to get your place back from another man, it's a whole different ballgame because you don't intuitively have that knowledge.

These excerpts reveal the women's perception that they had been thrown into an entirely new and foreign "ballgame," one that they lacked both the equipment and the knowledge to play competitively. Their husbands' same-sex desires were intensely threatening because the women were forced to watch from the sidelines and felt unable to intervene effectively to change the outcome of this game. Neither the women who approached their husbands' same-sex desire as a relief nor those who found it especially threatening believed that they could compete for their husbands' attention. They were stuck.

Detective Work

Before most wives could decide how to handle their marital plight, they had to know more about what was happening and why. To put it mildly, these women no longer trusted their husbands. Most were uncertain as to whether they now knew the whole truth and whether their husbands were still acting on their homosexual desires. They felt compelled to find out what, exactly, was going on, hoping that they might be able to control or change the situation once they understood it. Since they did not trust their husbands to tell them the truth, the women became detectives, investigating their husbands' lives with astonishing rigor. Many of the women felt uncomfortable "spying" on their husbands, often commenting that they "were not proud of what they did" and that it made them feel "sort of sleazy" and "deceptive." They felt compelled, however, to find out what was happening in their husbands' lives. Many wives became adept at tracking computer use, checking e-mails when they could, and figuring out how to discern which Internet sites and chat rooms their husbands had visited. Some also began keeping a strict inventory of their husbands' personal possessions, noting when any were missing or in odd places. One wife, for instance, was alarmed by a missing manicure set, while another was upset when she found a missing shirt stuffed under boxes in the trunk of the car.

The women further began monitoring the men's activities: they phoned them often at work, went along on trips, visits with friends, or errands whenever possible, and sometimes spied on them. One woman even hired a private detective to find out what her husband did on alleged business trips. One wife's description of her activities captures the thoroughness with which these women pursued their detective work: "I went looking for everything I could find. I mean copies, e-mails; I was prepared. . . . I went through his briefcase when he was out. I would look at his pay stubs because one of the things it said on there was how many hours leave he had earned during that pay period, how many hours he had used up until now and what he had left, and some of his activities (sexual encounters) were during the workday. There were a couple of times that I would call him at the office and the call was transferred to his cell phone." Often, this extensive detective work did uncover more lies and deception, but such discoveries only made the women more vigilant, more intent on controlling what was happening. This form of detective work never helped them understand the situation better. Instead, they only became more confused, asking "*Why* would my husband do this to me?"

In an effort to understand what was happening in their marriages, the women engaged in another, and from their perspective more useful, form of detective work. They began to try to find out all they could about homosexuality. Because of their conservative Christian backgrounds, they distrusted secular sources of information and turned instead to friends who were good Christians, to religious leaders, and to religious books and Web sites. Because this information was linked to Christianity, the women believed it trustworthy and granted it legitimacy, using it to begin to shape their understanding of homosexuality.

Through one or more of these sources, the women learned about Exodus and its theory of homosexuality as a psychological disorder caused by childhood trauma. Excited by what they were learning and its potential to help them understand what was happening in their marriages, the women began to make connections between the childhood scenarios that, according to Exodus, cause homosexuality and their husbands' biographies. The following two interview excerpts illustrate the women's excitement as they began to make sense of their husbands' activities:

> When I finally told my best friend—she's a strong Christian woman too—we talked for an hour. Then, about thirty minutes later, she called me back and told me to get on the Internet and look at Exodus International. It was a homosexual recovery program with like a 75 percent success rate. I started reading the testimonies, and I was just in awe. The classic situation fit Tom's family exactly. His father was an alcoholic who was emotionally distant and abusive, so he never had a father figure. It began to make sense.

> I wanted information, so I started searching the Internet, and I went to Exodus and Regeneration. I couldn't believe it. I just started reading the personal stories, the testimonies, and it all started to come together. Steve had been sexually abused when he was twelve and never received any counseling. He was

rejected by a father and two mothers. . . . I mean, he has all
the classic issues. Everything I read is—it's all him.

For these women, Exodus and similar sources provided a way for them
to understand their husbands' behavior. Previously uninterpreted biographical details now became important clues offering insight into
present life situations. By comparing Exodus's "classic scenario" to
events in their husbands' lives, the wives constructed what they believed was the cause of the men's homosexuality.

This new understanding was a great relief to the women in many
ways. It helped them make sense of the events that had transpired in
their marriages, but more importantly it let the wives "off the hook"
and gave them hope for the future. Exodus's explanation of homosexuality made it clear that the women were not the source of the problem. One woman best expressed the wives' relief when she commented:
"I didn't realize at first that this [homosexuality] wasn't something that
had just started. . . . It was a relief that this was not my fault. These
things were set in motion long before I knew him. Neither during the
time period I knew or was married to him did I contribute to his homosexual behavior or temptations." This kind of realization allowed
the women to resist the imposition of blame for their situations and,
perhaps more importantly, to reject common cultural (and religious
subcultural) notions that women are responsible for controlling men's
sexual behavior. Exodus's theory of homosexuality clearly showed the
wives that their husbands' sexual aberrations were not linked to their
feminine performances. In this way, learning this new explanation alleviated the wives' fear that they were failures as women.

This explanation also enabled some of the women to make what
they felt was an important distinction between the men's physical desires and emotional attachments. As they embraced Exodus's theory
of homosexuality as a psychological disorder, about half of the wives
began to conceive of the men's sexual urges as a symptom of a problem that did not necessarily threaten their marriages. By splitting the
physical and emotional, these women could perceive that, while their
husbands wanted to have sex with men, their emotional commitment
and loyalty were to their wives. One woman described her husband's
problem in terms of a split personality. One persona, the fake one,
picked up men and smoked, "almost as if he were someone else," while
the real person loved his wife and valued his marriage. Another woman
explained that because her husband did not have "real lovers," but

only anonymous liaisons, she knew she was "more important" to him. His "sickness" played out sexually, and his affairs were "more of a physical thing than an emotional thing."

This splitting made it easier for the women to understand how they had been so deceived: their husbands did love them and were emotionally loyal, but their illness caused them to act out homosexually. While such activities were still hurtful, the women were comforted by the idea that their husbands loved them first and foremost. As one woman put it, "I felt like I could breathe again when I knew he still loved me, that he had never been in love with anyone else. He's even told his male partners how much he loves me. He just has this problem because he grew up in an abusive family." From this perspective, the problem is not in the marriage or emotional commitment, but rather is entirely a manifestation of the men's childhood traumas. In these ways, learning Exodus's explanation for homosexuality diminished the women's sense of rejection, both as women and wives, making it easier for them to begin to forgive their husbands and work to stay in their marriages.

Further, Exodus's explanation created for the wives great hope that their marriages could be restored. Not only did their husbands still love them and act out only because they suffered from a psychological illness, but Exodus also asserted that homosexuality could be cured through redemptive prayer, by healing the damage caused by traumatic events in childhood. To fix their marriages, then, the women had to see to it that their husbands were "fixed." There were many testimonies available, from ex-gay Christian men and their wives, that the women took as proof that cures were possible.

Inspired by their new understandings and hopes, the women began to focus their energies on helping their husbands overcome homosexuality. They did research and found books for their husbands to read and local ex-gay groups for them to attend. They policed their activities, trying to censor materials and avoid situations that might be tempting for the men. They encouraged prayer, found and marked appropriate biblical passages for their husbands, and sought help for their husbands from a variety of religious people. Most significantly, they tried to reduce the stresses in their husband's lives, believing that stress might trigger an incident of "acting out."

In trying to reduce stress in their husbands' lives, many of the women assumed additional responsibilities for managing domestic and financial matters. They also tried not to "burden" their husbands with their own feelings about what was going on. "If I would have told him how hard this was for me," one woman explained, "then he would have to deal with my feelings too, and that would be too much. It could cause him to act out. He's got to get a bunch of his stuff fixed before he can reach out fully to me, and I need to help him do that. I have to be very patient. That is what a good wife does for her husband." The quest to fix their husbands, and their husbands' thoughts and feelings, became the wives' primary focus. To be good wives, their own needs had to be pushed aside, at least for the moment.

This strategy might, perhaps, have helped the situation and been tolerable to the women if the men's struggles had been reasonably short, if they had continually made progress, or if all the men had been equally committed to the process. Few situations worked this way, though, and the women's intense focus on their husbands became a source of great frustration and despair. For these women, fixing their marriages meant fixing their husbands, which meant subjugating their needs to help them. As little progress was made over long periods of time, the wives did not know what to do except to try harder, making this issue loom larger and larger in their lives. One woman, who is married to an ex-gay and leads a support group for wives, explained this cycle this way: "If you leave a group of wives together in the same room, they will talk about their husbands' needs for two to three hours. . . . The dynamics of the situation are the same. The wife, the scenes, over and over again are 'I don't know who I am anymore. This thing has consumed our lives. I don't know what I want. I don't know what I need. I don't know what to do or how to handle this anymore.' So they try harder to be good wives, do more for their husbands, and end up in the same place." At this point, the women felt like their lives had been overtaken by their husbands' struggles. The long-term focus on his needs made her feel lost, and the lack of steady progress was disheartening. This stagnation, particularly in light of the sacrifices they made and the burdens they bore, became tough to take, and many women began to feel stuck once again. If good wives help their husbands, and all that work was not paying off, then what else could they possibly do?

Godly Submission and Resolution

It was at this point, when the women were feeling frustrated, alone, and discouraged, that many found and began attending a support group for wives. Though a few women had discovered support groups earlier, most women did not know they existed until they stumbled across them while researching homosexuality and ex-gay ministries. A few had a support group associated with their church. About two-thirds of the women were able to physically attend support groups, while the other third could not find a group close enough to their homes to attend and instead participated in an Internet support group. Some women were involved in both kinds of groups. Regardless of how the women found a group or which they attended, these groups provided a supportive, like-minded community for the women and were instrumental in helping them deal more effectively with their marital situations. Through their participation in support groups, the women learned to refocus their energies and redirect their goals in ways that felt more satisfying. If not for these groups, fewer of the women would have stayed in what were draining and difficult marriages.

Giving up Control to Get It

Joining a support group helped these women both cope with and navigate through their very difficult marital situations in many ways. The support groups offered the women a "safe" place in which they could talk freely, often for the first time since they discovered their husbands' homosexual affairs, about their fears, anxieties, and dilemmas. Surrounded by others with similar problems and beliefs, the women felt less isolated and odd. "You don't know there are others like you, who are in love with a struggler," one woman explained, "until you walk into that room and see those people. No one publicizes it. So you finally see you are not so alone. You pray together. There is someone you trust that you can call when it gets really hard. It has been such a relief."

The support groups also provided a space in which the women's needs mattered most. In this space, the wives were expected to treat *their* feelings and problems as the focal point, thus taking advantage of the opportunity to discuss how they experienced their husbands' deceptions and struggles. Through conversations with long-time group members, newcomers also learned practical information about how to protect themselves. Often, the women learned about the very real danger of contracting sexually transmitted diseases from their husbands. They were warned to practice safe sex and told the details of getting tested for various diseases. Some women learned to protect themselves financially, in case of divorce, by gathering information about their husbands' infidelities and by setting aside what some called "squirrel money" to be used in an emergency. In short, these groups gave them both information and emotional support.

The support groups, however, did more than offer practical advice and an emotional outlet. By far, the most important aspect of the women's participation in these support groups was that they learned to approach the problem of their husbands' sexual behavior in a different way, one that enabled them both to feel like good Christian wives and to break out of the cycle of trying to control the men's lives at their own expense. The approach they learned was strikingly simple: Submit yourself to God's will. As conservative Christians, many women already believed that they were to submit to male headship, via their husbands and God. However, submitting to their husbands was problematic because they were behaving sinfully. Yet, if the women did not submit to masculine authority, then they were not behaving as they should. The support groups provided an answer to this dilemma; the wives should circumvent their "sick" husbands and submit to God, the preeminent masculine authority. They began to perceive that they had not truly been relying on God for help. While they had been praying, they were also trying to manage and control their situations on their own rather than "giving them up to God." Their mistake, as they saw it, was in not trusting God entirely.

Submitting to God meant giving up trying to control how their husbands lived, trusting God to protect and provide for them, and focusing on building a relationship with God. The importance of making this shift in focus—from their husbands to God—was particularly evident in an interview with a woman who was married to a "struggler" and led a support group. When I asked her what major changes the women had to make when they joined the group, she told me that they had to learn how to really "submit to God." I asked what that meant and she responded: "To become their own person again . . . they need to be focusing on what God wants them to do in the relationship. They are not the cause of what their husbands [are] doing. They are not the cure, and *they basically have no control, so it's time to give it up.* I don't say it like that in the group; I try to be nice and tactful, but those are the things [necessary changes]. Once you've figured out that you have no control and you need to lean on God and to trust Him, then you need to figure out what God wants you to do in the relationship and your life. This is not your whole life. This issue of sexual addiction is not your whole life, which it can become" [emphasis added]. This leader voiced the belief that all the women in this study eventually shared: they could regain control of their lives only by giving it up and relying on God to give them directions. Building a relationship with God, rather than with their husbands, became the new focal point of the women's lives. Their task was now to ensure that their husbands' sexual struggles did not overwhelm them and become all consuming.

This shift in focus did not imply that the women were no longer bound to nurture their husbands and work on their marriages; indeed, the motto of one support group was "Love your husband, but trust God." In an Exodus booklet for wives of strugglers, Nancy Brown, a struggler's wife and support group leader, described how women should handle this situation: "Do not feel that you will be able to 'fix' your husband if he will let you. It's not possible. Now you must trust God to give you the desires of your heart. In the same way, do not allow the devil to quench your love for your husband by backing away because he doesn't understand your loving concern" (2000, 13). The key to resolving their situations, it seemed, was to strike a balance between submitting to God entirely and continuing to love and support their husbands. Achieving this balance meant that the women would no longer try to figure out how to fix their husbands and would trust God to do so. Their task was to build a close relationship with God so that they could discern and employ his will, nurturing their husbands as God directed. As Brown reminded the wives, they were "very important to God's plan for the universe" and a "key, essential element next to God himself in helping [their] husbands to overcome homosexuality" (2000, 10). All the women really had to do now was practice submission to God.

As with conservative Christians generally, the women in this study had varied ideas about submission to authority.[2] Some perceived that God had established a clear hierarchy—God, men, women, and children—in the Bible. Men were familial leaders, responsible for their family's well-being, who were expected to exercise a compassionate authority that simultaneously served the family's best interests and accorded with biblical principles. A wife might offer input in decision making but must ultimately submit to her husband's decisions and, regardless of whether she agrees with him, implement his solutions. About half of the wives held this conceptualization of submission. One woman best explained this shared notion when she said that being a Christian wife required "recognizing that my husband is the head of our family and ultimately . . . he respects my input, but ultimately he makes the decisions. If I've given my input and he chooses something else, then I'm called by God to submit because he's my authority basically."

By contrast, eight of the wives professed a belief in mutual submission, an equal male and female obligation to submit themselves to God and to one another, pushing individual concerns and desires aside for the common good of the marriage. For them, decisions should be made jointly through discussion and compromise. These women often cited biblical verses about the importance of "submitting to one another" and lamenting pastor's tendencies to "preach on submission but leave out these biblical verses."

Regardless of their position on submission within a marriage, the women agreed that good Christians must submit themselves to God. Further, the idea that they could, through submission, allow God to work through them to fix their marriages was quite appealing because it offered a solution and allowed them to feel better about themselves. Where they had once felt unworthy as women/wives because of their husbands' sexual activities, and uncomfortable with their own sneaky detective work, they now had a way to feel like good Christian women teamed up with God to help their husbands. Saving their marriages, as we will see, became more than personal desire; it became serious religious work.

At first glance, it seemed that these women pursued the religious work of submitting to God's will by completely redirecting their energies toward building a close relationship with God and becoming much more passive in their marriages. As the wives came to realize they could not control what their husbands did, they increasingly turned to God. The passive language they used to describe this realization and change of focus marked a decided shift from their zealous detective work and efforts to fix their husbands to a willingness to accept whatever God brought into their lives. The following interview excerpts illustrate both this shift and how the women experienced submission:

> What I've recognized now and what I see in a whole new light is that God is not going to give me more than I can bear. He's going to provide me with a way through this [marital situation], and so I must pray, pray, and pray harder. . . . [P]art of what God wants me to know is that my first love needs to be

him, and I need to let him wrap me up in his love. I don't think I've ever really done that. That's why I've felt so unworthy. First, I need to allow God to love me that way, and then that gives me the strength to help Steve and be patient and do what God tells me I need to do. . . . God loves me and will not leave or forsake me. Knowing has released me, and I think God is preparing me for something, maybe a ministry.

The main thing I had to change was coming to God in a relationship—not as one-sided. . . . I've gotten to the point where I'm letting go of control, where I just come to listen to him more and know him more. What he has to say is not always what I have to say, but I've learned to go to him with everything. I've totally let go and let him take care of it [marriage]. I feel freed from the worry. It's like, "Whatever Lord. I'm just waiting on you." I know God loves me and is going to use me to do something.

You get to this place in your life where you are so confident of God's love and interaction in your life that it's like you are floating. It's like the things around you don't touch you inside. When I learned to trust God, I developed a sense of patience, well-being, and peace. I knew God would tell me what to do, and, as long I listened, I could bear it all. It was through his strength that I could help my husband.

In these excerpts, we see that the women perceived that they were no longer actively trying to control what happened in their husbands' lives and had begun to submit entirely to God. For them, regaining a sense of control over their lives could be accomplished only by giving it up to God. Once they trusted completely in God, the women believed that God would work, both through them and on his own, to heal their husbands and fix their marriages. Further, through their reliance on God's love, they would have the strength to persist and aid their husbands. The passive terms that the women used to describe their submission, words like "waiting" and "patience," suggested that the women simply had to surrender control of their lives to God and sit back and see what happened next. This sense is misleading. Surrendering paradoxically meant giving up control of their lives and exerting enough control and discipline to resist the temptation to try to fix their husbands and, instead, "going to God with everything." It turned out that submitting to God required stringent control.

While this kind of control took discipline and effort, it was far more rewarding to the women than struggling to control what their husbands did or did not do, an activity that often yielded frustration. For most of these women, their attempts to "control" their husbands worked sporadically, if at all. Wives would perceive that their husbands were making progress, only to have them "slip up" again. Only a few women (three) trusted that their husbands' struggles were won; that is, they would not act out again. Given this frustration, most wives found that the act of submission was empowering in several ways. First, the women's descriptions of their experience of submission as being "released" and "freed," or like "floating," indicate that they felt relieved of a tremendous obligation—the obligation to get their family back in order. What happened now was up to God; the women would work as faithful helpers, but they were no longer responsible for the master plan. Second, submission was also a transformative act. Whereas the women had once felt rejected by their husbands and unworthy as Christian wives because they could not contain their husbands' sinful sexuality, they now felt loved by God, the ultimate masculine figure, and believed they were a critical component of God's work. Their notions that God "had a plan" for them and would "use" them to do divine work made their actions important. They were a vehicle for God's work, a belief that provided a source of self-esteem (God works through me so I must be valuable) and a sense of empowerment (I can do what I need to do because God gives me strength).

This belief further transformed the wives' experiences of their familial struggles from a stigmatizing situation to an opportunity to be godly. Interactions that once seemed threatening and evoked shame now became chances to do sacred work. "As awful as it has been to go through this," one woman explained, "I now know it is not my fault or me and that God is using me. That makes it much better. I've had to learn to sacrifice in my dealing with this with Ed, but the sacrifices are for God, for my family, so they don't feel bad. They feel good, sort of like I'm praying." Submission elevated sacrifice into a form of worship, changing potentially demeaning activities into sacred opportunities. In these ways, submission not only seemed to offer the women a resolution, but also enabled them to feel like worthy Christian wives, empowered by God to do serious religious work.

Submission as a Power Tool?

The idea that devout Christian women, like those in this study, experience submission as empowering is not novel or contested. Christian commentators have long touted the powers of submission. In one of the most widely read texts, *You Can Be the Wife of a Happy Husband,* author Darien Cooper writes: "Resist the temptations to interfere with his leadership because you feel his [husband's] decisions or actions are too forceful, harsh, or wrong. Don't argue your point or try to manipulate him. . . . Interestingly, as you follow, your husband will lead; but if you become aggressive, he may regress. You nag, and he will rebel. If you desire to please him, he will want to please you" (1974, 78–79). The key to a happy marriage and a husband who strives to meet his wife's needs is, according to Cooper, to submit.

Researchers have also found that women, much like those in this study, often find this submissive strategy rewarding. Griffith's (1997) study of evangelical women, for example, reveals that women can experience submission, an act usually associated with forfeiting personal agency and contributing to a sense of inferiority, to be empowering, freeing and transforming. Like the wives of sexual strugglers, the women in Griffith's study believed that total submission to God yielded big rewards in the form of healing emotional wounds and lessening familial difficulties. Seen in this way, Griffith concludes that "the doctrine of submission becomes a means of asserting power over bad situations, including circumstances over which one may otherwise have no control" (1997, 179). Submission becomes particularly important as a resource for creating a sense of power when women face life conditions they cannot control or alter in other ways. The wives in this study turned to submission after they had tried, and failed, to fix their husbands, and by extension their marriages, in other ways. All they had left as a resource was their adherence to religious doctrine, which promised them results if they followed God's directive.

Submission, as it is explained by Christian authors and practiced by the women in this study and others (Ammerman 1987; Stacey 1990; Pevey, Williams, and Ellison 1996; Griffith 1997), is simultaneously an act of acquiescence and coercion. While most of the coercion is passive—that is, women are encouraged to surrender control in order to push powerful masculine others (God and husbands) to protect and provide for them—the doctrine of submission also contains a potential "loophole" through which women may more aggressively pursue their interests. This loophole is the idea that women, those who have submitted, can use biblical mandates overtly to push their husbands toward proper Christian behavior.

In their study of female submission in a Southern Baptist women's Bible class, Pevey, Williams, and Ellison note the possibility that "women may gain power by reminding their husbands and children of the directives of a powerful masculine God" (1996, 188). Ironically, by fulfilling her feminine obligation to submit to God, a woman can make use of God's masculine authority to trump her husband's authority and try to convince him to behave differently. In other words, while the women may have felt empowered because they perceived they were now teamed up with God, they actually created some real influence over their husbands' activities by putting God to work for them in ways that they felt advanced their own interests.

In some ways, this strategy was relatively successful. As we will see, this strategy did not help the men change per se, but it did help the wives convince their husbands that they had to keep trying. When their marriages reached crisis points, in which the men were about to leave, the wives invoked God's Word to keep the men in their marriages and to keep them trying to live heterosexual lives. The risk in this more aggressive strategy, of course, is that in "going over her husband's head to the top" a woman may weaken her position as a good (i.e., submissive) wife and may end up undermining her relationship with her husband, making matters worse. Given this risk, why and when would women employ this strategy in their marriages?

For the most part, the wives in this study were submissive, giving control up to God and being patient while their husbands were healed. When asked directly about their actions, they always described them as entirely submissive: "I'm just waiting on God." Yet, in practice, some of the wives' accounts of interactions with their husbands revealed a more overt and aggressive approach to influencing their husbands' behavior. Seven wives, at some point in their marital struggle, invoked divine authority to sway their husbands. In four of these instances, the women were willing to draw on God's masculine authority only when they were at a critical point in their marriages, usually when there was a strong indication their husband might leave. (These were the only women whose husbands had seriously contemplated leaving their marriages at the time of this study.) How they invoked God's authority seemed to depend on whether they had children who were still dependent on them.

The two wives without dependent children drew on biblical injunctions against homosexuality and adultery to try to convince their husbands to stay. Beth's story of what she calls "the crisis point" in her marriage provides a good example of how these two women wielded God's masculine authority when necessary. Beth explained that in 1997 and '98 her husband, Phillip, was involved with a male lover, and the relationship had become serious. In spite of Phillip's declaration that he wanted to stay married, Beth saw that he was becoming as committed to this man as "he had once been committed to her," and she feared he would leave. He "started to call himself gay" and to "believe all the lies of pro-gay theology that you could be gay and Christian." Beth would not accept this label. As she said, "If God was not going to call him gay, I sure wasn't going to call him gay." Her refusal angered Phillip, and they had heated discussions about what the Bible said about homosexuality. Then, one day at work, Beth felt something was wrong and called Phillip at home. There was no answer. She called his cell phone and, when he answered, she discovered he had left her to be with his male lover. She remembered asking him to come home because he was going against God. She told him that, while he could argue whatever he wanted about homosexuality, there was "nothing, and I mean nothing, in the Bible that made adultery okay. Adultery is sin and God hates it. You cannot do this." Phillip came home, as Beth said, because "nothing could relieve him from the guilt of adultery." In this instance, Beth invoked God's authority to persuade Phillip that he had to come home. In a critical moment, she pushed aside patience and ideas about following her husband's lead, bringing in the heavy artillery to tip negotiations in her favor.

The two wives who had dependent children drew on biblical passages about the husband/father role in the family to influence their husbands' actions. For example, when Holly's husband, Roger, told her he wanted to end their marriage to pursue a relationship with a male lover, she immediately brought up their son, who was then a senior in high school. She reminded Roger of his "vow before God and his God-given obligation to serve his family" and of "how hard it would be on [their son] to do this to him now." Roger acceded, and they began to go to Christian counseling together. But at the end of their son's first year in college, they replayed this scene, with Holly again trying to persuade Roger to stay by invoking God's directives for husbands and fathers. We see here how some wives actively invoked divine authority, using God's mandated form for and obligation to the family to push their husbands back into line.

The other three wives who employed these more aggressive tactics did so only when their husbands stubbornly clung to habits that the women perceived as impeding their healing and chances for marital success. Ellie's account of her struggle with her husband about his computer use best exemplifies how these women occasionally used divine authority to manipulate their husbands. Ellie remembered what happened one night when she went into the computer room and saw a dialogue on the computer screen that ended with the question, "Would you have sex with me?" She told her husband, "I think you need to get off of that." According to Ellie, he got very defensive and told her she "didn't need to worry about it" and that he "wasn't doing anything." After a while of going back and forth about it with little progress, Ellie explained that she "really started to put the guilt trip on him," telling him that he knew "what he was doing was wrong in God's eyes. It wasn't right; it was sinful." She added that "whenever he did things like this and I showed him how wrong it was to God, he would listen to me most of the time." Notice here that Ellie's husband does not heed her opinion when she tells him what she thinks. It is only when she points out that God does not want him to do such things that he listens. Ellie was aware of how powerful God's Words were to her husband, invoking them when her pleas failed to alter his behavior.

In these critical moments, we see how the wives were momentarily able to usurp divine masculine power, the same power that could subject them to their husband's authority, and use it as a tool to assert their will. The wives drew on this power sparingly, willing to use it only in dire circumstances when their husbands were about to leave the marriage or to disrupt behavior profoundly detrimental to the marriage. Their reluctance to wield such power may stem from biblical beliefs about how wives should relate to husbands and/or may reflect conservative Christian consensus that too much aggression by wives can undercut the relationship and, as Cooper warned, cause husbands to "regress" (1974, 79). When it was used, though, this strategy provided a wife with a significant power tool, one that at least allowed her to be heard, regardless of whether her husband stayed in the marriage. This loophole in submission doctrine gave the women a sense of agency; when it really mattered, they could seriously influence their husbands, albeit through and because of their shared belief in the masculine authority of God.

In many ways, the women's experience of submission was very rewarding. When the wives submitted to their husbands and God, they felt liberated, at least to some degree, from the weight of their husbands' struggle and the anxieties it caused. Submitting also transformed them into worthy Christian wives, redefining shaming incidents into sacred work. Through submission, wives could further grasp some vestige of masculine authority. The end result was that submission felt like an act of empowerment, not oppression. These experiences not only were real, but also had positive consequences for many of the women. Using submissive strategies, the women reaped psychological benefits, replacing their feelings of rejection, shame, and failure as women and wives with feelings of worthiness, agency, and value. In some cases, when the women subverted the power dynamics of traditional gender relations and used the authority of a masculine God to exert some control over their husbands' behavior, submission allowed women to achieve their goal of preserving a marriage. Submission should thus not be equated with a willingness to be exploited and subjugated. Nonetheless, these women's experiences must still be understood as part of a larger cultural system of male privilege, one that works so successfully because it makes conforming feel freeing and being subjugated feel like empowerment.

There is little doubt that the wives' activities, while experienced as liberating and empowering, also helped to reproduce the larger religious and social systems that subordinate women. By their participation and compliance, the women perpetuated a system that gives men voice and power and limits women to subtle influence. But these women were not isolated cases. Women who feel good and powerful only as they approach cultural ideals of feminine beauty and behavior similarly participate in the reproduction of this oppressive social system and find it rewarding. Gender socialization teaches us that the way to feel good about ourselves as women is to meet male needs and expectations. Our worth as women is then evaluated, by others and ourselves, by how well we accomplish this feat. Doing femininity well feels great—rewarding and empowering—yet such good feelings can be derived from compliance with a system of male advantage. For the system to work, women must participate in it, and they sometimes do so willingly and with conviction because it can feel good to do so (or holds the promise of good feeling) and can offer material advantages.

Philosopher Sandra Bartky calls these good feelings "repressive satisfactions" because they result from the fulfillment of individual needs established in the interest of the dominant group and "whose possession and satisfaction benefit not the subject who has them but a social order whose interest lies in domination" (1990, 42). For the women in this study, and for devout Christians more generally, the pull of this system is perhaps magnified because it is legitimated by an all-powerful masculine God. These women were neither selfless heroines sacrificing all for the good of others, nor willing hostages to men working to fulfill only male needs. Instead, these women tried to make good lives for themselves by creatively reconfiguring the few tools they had, within a system that afforded them little opportunity, in ways that allowed them to advance their interests. That they aided in the reproduction of an oppressive gender system does not discredit their ingenuity and their acts of resistance, but should instead show us the very real difficulties subordinates face when they try to live comfortably within oppressive social structures.

Finally, it is important to note that the wives' willingness to aid their husbands and stay in difficult marriages was essential to their husbands' success in continuing to struggle against homosexuality and, by extension, to Exodus's success as a transformation ministry. Married men who struggled with homosexuality were often torn between their love for their wives/families and their sexual desires. They were motivated to fight those sexual desires, in part, because they believed homosexuality was biblically condemned—but also because they *wanted* to be with their wives and live godly lives in heterosexual marriage. If wives left when they discovered their husbands' sexual proclivities and betrayals, then a significant piece of what compelled the men to struggle against homosexuality would be gone. The stigma of marital failure, amplified within conservative Christianity, would then heap further shame on the men, making their sexual struggle more difficult. It is likely that, in the absence of a supportive wife and a marriage, quite a few more men would walk out of Exodus. In this sense, Exodus has a real interest in helping wives cope with their husbands' struggle so that they stay in marriages. This is not to say that Exodus representatives consciously manipulate wives to further their agendas; the people I met in the course of this study were earnest in their desire to help others. If their goal, however, is to advance God's heterosexual order for humankind (husband/leader, wife/obedient helper), then wives must play their part. The support groups are designed to help them to do so, to keep them from straying too far from the existing gender order.

9 | Conclusion

The Parameters of Change

I followed the now familiar hallway into the living room and hugged group members in greeting. It was my last Accept meeting. We stood in small groups, talking and joking with an easy camaraderie born of intimacy and practice. There was nothing different about this meeting, except that I was having trouble concentrating on what was happening. My attention kept drifting from what group members were saying to the contours of their faces. I knew their stories. I had them written down in neatly catalogued fieldnotes and interview transcripts. But on that last day it felt more important to remember the faces that went with those stories.

The leader's announcement that it was time for prayer and prayer requests (when individuals asked the group to pray for them with regard to a particular problem or concern) drew my focus back to what was going on. Prayer was the most serious part of the Bible study because it was in prayer that members felt closest to God and most certain of God's love and guidance. The atmosphere of the room always changed at prayer time; the men's expressions softened as they turned from discussion to prayer, and their voices took on a greater reverence. The prayer requests at my last meeting were typical—to bring an ill friend to health, to help find a job, to show a mother that her son is not going to hell because he is gay, to pray for a person at church, and to lead a friend struggling with his homosexuality to the truth of God's love. After these requests were made, we joined hands as we sat in the circle. The two people who sat on either side of the empty chair (the symbolic chair reserved for the member yet to find the group) touched the seat, as if to include those who had yet to make their way to the group. We bowed our heads, and the leader began to pray:

> Dear Heavenly Parent, you have heard our voices, and you see the hearts of your children who sit before you. We ask you to forgive our sins and give us the strength to respond to evil and hardship with Christ-like love. We ask that you heal the wounds of ourselves, our brothers, and our sisters and fill them with your truth and your love. Show Vince (the friend) and Denise (the mother) how you love and accept your gay children, to ease their struggles. Guide Derek to the job that will be rewarding and fulfilling for him. Bring healing and comfort to Mandy as she fights her illness. Give her and her family and friends the strength to know and accept your will for her life. Thank you for the fellowship and love we have shared in this room tonight and for all the healing you have brought in our lives. We pray others will open their minds to your truth and stop hurting your gay children. We pray you will walk beside those in this room who struggle in their lives and heal all their spoken and unspoken hurts and needs. Thank you for your love, strength, guidance, and many blessings. In Jesus' name we pray. Amen.

As we said "Amen," we squeezed the hands we were holding for a long moment, a gesture of solidarity that implied that we were somehow shaking hands on an agreement just made. Then we looked up.

———

I was nervous as I drove to my last Expell meeting. I'd been worrying for weeks about how to thank the group for allowing me to participate and about how to say good-bye. They had been so slow to let me attend their group and slow to accept me. Their trust had to be meticulously earned. Now that I had it and was part of the group, leaving felt like I was abandoning or betraying them. I wondered how I could convey my gratitude for their help and my empathy for their struggles. When I figured out the answer, I got nervous because I knew the best way to communicate these things to them was to express my feelings through prayer. As in Accept, prayer was the most earnest part of Expell meetings, the time when members asked for God's forgiveness and guidance, working to build the right spiritual relationship to rid themselves of homosexuality. Because I did not share members' religious beliefs, I had avoided praying aloud in their prayer semicircle as much as possible because it had felt inappropriate for me to participate this way. Now that it felt right to speak during prayer, I was not sure I knew how.

It was time. We were standing in the prayer semicircle, and someone put a CD of worship songs in the CD player. The CD began, and the group sang, their eyes closed, arms outstretched, and palms open to the heavens. Some swayed with the rhythm, entirely caught within the song. Others were completely still, yet had a kind of intensity that displayed, perhaps, an even greater fervor. When it ended, we stood quietly for a moment, then we held hands, and Tim nodded to me as he said, "Let us pray." I began: "Dear God, thank you for allowing me to be part of this group, for all the kindnesses offered to me, and for all the guidance as I've tried to learn. I am grateful for such gifts. I ask that you watch over the people here, easing their struggle and healing them so they can be the people they strive to be. Amen." Another group member began: "Dear Lord, thank you for bringing Michelle to us, so that she can leave here to tell others about our group, others who need to receive your healing and those who need to understand that churches need to help sexual strugglers, not cast them out. Amen." Then, Tim began to pray, a slightly shorter version of the typical closing prayer:

> Dear Heavenly Father, we stand before you in awe for you are a truly awesome, awesome God. Father, we love you and are so thankful for our many blessings. We thank you for forgiving our sins, for the healing you bring into our lives, and for the strength you give us to fight temptations. We ask that you work in our lives, helping us to live in relationship with you and healing our many wounds. Thank you, Jesus. It is only with your strength that we can do anything. Father, help us to know your will for our lives. Help us be obedient. We pray that other sexual strugglers will come to know the truth of your Word and be healed. Fill us with your love. In Jesus' name, amen.

The group responded with "Amen" and "Thank you, Jesus," squeezed one another's hands for a long moment, and slowly moved out of the circle.

———

What I remember most vividly about praying in these two groups was the squeezing gesture that concluded their prayers. This gesture seemed a kind of hand shake, a way of bonding each group together and symbolizing their agreement about overall group goals and the strategy for attaining them. Because this gesture followed prayer, it also solidified each group's pact with God; members promised earnestly to seek God's truth and will (as defined by the respective group) in exchange for God's help. For group members, ending each meeting by renewing such promises strengthened their resolve to continue with the "healing process."

Group prayers, however, were not simply designed to help the individual members who were in attendance. One of the hopes voiced in prayer, and mutually agreed on through this squeezing gesture, was that group ideology would spread and help to change how all homosexuals are treated in our society. This hope was fostered by the groups' recognition that, in order to diminish the stigma surrounding homosexuality and promote better treatment of gay people, changes were necessary within Christianity and society. We see this recognition in Accept's prayer that "others will open their minds to your [God's] truth and stop hurting your gay children" and Expell's prayer that churches "will help sexual strugglers, not cast them out." Though social change was not the primary concern for either group, both wanted to influence how dominant Christianity and culture perceived homosexuality and reacted to homosexuals.

These groups, in conjunction with MCC and Exodus, have been successful in exerting this influence. The ideological work of these groups has left an enduring cultural imprint, one that has indelibly altered the meaning of homosexuality within Christianity, though perhaps not necessarily in the ways the groups intended. This chapter explores this influence, analyzing the social consequences and significance of these groups. More specifically, this chapter examines the relationship of these marginalized groups to dominant culture by evaluating the larger societal impact of the groups' newly constructed cultural spaces.

Pioneering Cultural Space

The men and women in this study were remarkable—and ordinary. Each faced daunting challenges and obstacles with great creativity and determination, working courageously to reconcile faith, sexuality, and family. Yet these extraordinary tasks were done in pursuit of goals most people share: to fashion lives that feel moral and worthy, to live with integrity, and to build satisfying relationships with important others. While their struggles, whether with their own sexuality or their spouse's sexuality, were experienced as individual crises that carried stigma and tremendous risk, they did not result primarily from what these individuals did or failed to do. Instead, these crises emerged within a social order that connects morality and the appropriate structuring of gender, intimate relationships, and family only to heterosexuality. To be gay in this social order (or married to a gay person) not only calls into question one's abilities and right to participate in the fundamental relationships upon which we construct our lives and culture, but also questions the very nature and goodness of one's self. Participants in this study were responding to these challenges.

As we have seen, how participants responded to such challenges was also significantly constrained by these social conditions and group members' own belief structures. All of the men and women in this study were initially committed to some, relatively similar, form of conservative Christian doctrine, and their understandings of themselves and their world were too intricately interwoven with this doctrine for them to discard it or even challenge the validity of its central tenets. As a result, they had to work within the ideological boundaries of their belief system, the same system that legitimated their oppression, to solve the problems posed by their sexuality or their spouse's sexuality. To do so, group members worked innovatively to build an affirming subculture that circumvented dominant authority and challenged select pieces of conservative Christian doctrine, without threatening the integrity of the doctrine as a whole. As this analysis has shown, they accomplished this feat through a process of ideological maneuvering, shifting ideas creatively between the secular and divine realms, thereby allowing them to sidestep dominant power and make revisions, and yet to stay within the boundaries of a cherished belief system. At the same time, the groups had to make the hard work that this ideological transformation required emotionally rewarding, generating the feelings that induced and sustained participation. In short, these groups provided relatively safe spaces and common ground in which participants could develop, share, and celebrate an oppositional ideology, rhetoric, and feeling among themselves.

The importance of the construction of these cultural spaces to the process of social change cannot be overstated. It is within such spaces that subordinates can begin to develop the ideas, symbols, networks, and rhetorics that enable the formation of practices and discourses of resistance to dominant groups. Further, as James Scott has noted in *Domination and the Arts of Resistance,* "none of the practices and discourses of resistance can exist without tacit or acknowledged coordination and communication within the subordinate group. For that to occur, the subordinate group must carve out for itself social spaces insulated from control and surveillance from above," thereby allowing for the creation of an "offstage subculture" in which resistance can be formed and voiced (1990, 118). The construction of this kind of subcultural space is alone "an achievement of resistance" because it must be wrested from dominant culture and occupied by those who risk much by their attendance (Scott 1990, 119).

It was in this way that group members, while they were working to reconcile individual crises that originated in and were negotiated through a set of social arrangements, also helped to pioneer and sustain cultural change. Whereas less than thirty years ago Christians who experienced homosexual desire had only two options within their faith, to be ousted or to exist in hiding, these men and women, along with similar others, created new spaces or niches, in the form of congregations, ministries, and support groups within Christianity, in which gay and ex-gay people (and their families) could participate. These niches allowed members to redefine themselves as Christians in ways that accommodated their sexuality or sexual struggles. Such spaces enabled group members to resist the stigma imposed on them by dominant others, creating a sense that they had been liberated from their oppression. Within these spaces, group members also felt empowered, often for the first time since they recognized their homosexuality, to make choices to act in ways that cast them in a positive moral light. Clearly, the construction of these niches expanded culture and enabled members to resolve their dilemmas, transforming their fear and shame into righteousness. These groups have become progressively larger and more visible, insisting that mainstream Christianity and culture at least take notice. Gay Christian and ex-gay Christian have become viable identities that have a voice and a place, supported by groups and resources, within Christianity as a whole. In this way, these groups have inexorably expanded our cultural terrain, chiseling new identity niches out of old cultural materials to make room for new selves.

Yet, while these new niches reflected cultural change, eased individual suffering, and provided resources that were likely to be used later in further cultural alterations, they were also fraught with difficulty. These niches remained linked to dominant ideology and power, thereby constraining the degree to which cultural changes could be made and limiting the challenge that could be leveled against hegemonic notions of sexuality. At the same time that group members *felt* freed and empowered by ideological revisions, they were also *performing* activities that reasserted the superiority of traditional notions of gender, sexuality, and family. In doing so, they were reproducing, at least to some extent (more in Expell, less in Accept), the very secular ideologies and religious theologies that initially oppressed them. How was it possible that group members, in trying to resist oppression, actually recreated it and found the experience of doing so to be empowering?

Answering this question is important because it reveals how and why marginalized groups often recreate their own subordination, even as they work to resist oppression. Understanding this dynamic requires at least a brief examination of how elites often exert power. Such power is most successfully applied, according to sociologist Michael Schwalbe, through the creation of ideas and rules that subtly structure people's choices so that they are aligned with dominant agendas (1998, 165–169). If dominants were to use overt force or coercion to direct people's behavior, then they would likely face hostility and resistance (Scott 1990, 108–110). Instead, dominants use their influence (e.g., access to valuable resources like institutions, networks, etc.) to define only certain sets of beliefs and rules as legitimate, thereby ensuring that the only legitimate choices for acting will accord with their agendas (for more on how elites sustain their privilege, see Schwalbe et al. 2000). For the system to work, subordinates must cooperate, at least to some degree, and this cooperation is often elicited from a shared belief in the legitimacy of some aspects of dominant ideologies, making certain choices—those that move them toward accordance with dominant agendas—feel right and good. In this way, elite authority becomes largely invisible, concentrated in the structuring of choice, rather than in overtly pushing a particular course of action. Subordinates thus can feel as though they are empowered to devise and make choices on their own behalf, perhaps resisting in some ways and/or experiencing these choices as resistance, even while they are conforming (partially or entirely) to a dominant ideology that marginalizes them. As Schwalbe et al. (2000, 428) have noted, subordinate subcultures often "have a reproductive effect [on inequality] in part because they allow for psychic needs to be met, despite subordination."

It is because of this dominant sleight of hand that Audre Lorde has noted that marginalized groups are often caught in the dilemma of using the master's tools to dismantle the master's house, an activity that renders "only the most narrow perimeters of change possible and allowable" (1984, 111–112). If marginalized groups retain their beliefs in the legitimacy of dominant ideas, then they are apt to use these ideas as building blocks in their attempts to revise oppressive ideologies. Doing so might remodel outer appearance, but the fundamental dominant structure remains intact. Using the master's tools to facilitate social change is thus likely to result in the building not of a new house but of more comfortable servants' quarters, albeit with perhaps better amenities than previous structures.

The groups in this study were caught in precisely this situation, though certainly to varying degrees. As we have seen, all of the men and women in this study, as a matter of biographical circumstance, were committed to Christian doctrine and lived in accordance with this doctrine as a way of feeling like they were good people who did things right. When their or their spouse's homosexuality emerged, the disjuncture between what they believed and how they lived was intolerable. To resolve this tension in a way that felt right, participants had to stay within the dictates of Christianity, using these beliefs as resources to create solutions to their sexual and/or marital problems. The solutions they devised were experienced as liberating and empowering because they diminished the stigma imposed on the individual and offered courses of action. Expell members, for example, felt freed when they found that homosexuality was just ordinary sin and that their homosexuality resulted from others' sins against them, not from some inherent deficiency or innate evil as they had once believed. Thus freed, the men felt empowered to pursue the process that Expell promised would help them transform their homosexuality by healing what others had done to them. Accept members felt similarly emancipated when they discovered that loving, monogamous homosexuality was not a sin, a subversion of and resistance to conservative religious notions that homosexuals were damned. With this new interpretation, they felt empowered to endorse an inclusive theology that condemned those who judged others. In much the same way, wives felt as though they had been released from culpability for their husbands' actions when they learned that their husbands' homosexuality had nothing to do with them. Once they focused on submitting entirely to God, they were, as one woman put it, "teamed up" with God to fix their husbands and no longer had to worry about how to save their marriages. This switch gave the women a sense of control and power over their situations; by using God's will as a resource, they felt they could influence their husbands' behavior. The sense of liberation and empowerment experienced by group members, as we will see in the following section, was well earned and yet somewhat deceptive. While the groups did help individuals to feel (more or less) better, they also remained, to a greater or lesser degree, linked to oppressive gender and sexual hierarchies.

Modernizing Heterosexism

Group solutions to members' dilemmas, while helpful to some individuals, revised beliefs and subsequent behaviors in ways that sustained, at least partially, the dominant heterosexist ideologies that members struggled against initially. Further, each group's theological revisions and theories about homosexuality also could function to "modernize" heterosexism; that is, these revisions functioned in some ways to mask old prejudicial ideas with a new facade of therapeutic or social justice rhetoric, making them more palatable (and even moral) in contemporary society. In doing so, they sustained ideas about what constitutes appropriate sexual practices and, correspondingly, who is worthy and good and who is not. In this way, these groups helped to maintain the social inequalities surrounding sexuality.

Before examining how the groups modernized heterosexism, it is important to first explore what it means to do so. Heterosexism, of course, has a long history and went unquestioned until very recently. Prior to the social justice movements of the 1960s, most perceived homosexuality as wrong and homosexuals as bad. In fact, until 1973, the American Psychological Association had defined homosexuality as a psychological disorder. As a result of this kind of labeling, blatant discrimination (and sometimes violence) against homosexuals was commonplace with few social sanctions. For example, mainstream society openly "purged" homosexuals from jobs, the military, and the government, and police routinely raided gay bars or other social spots frequented by homosexuals (Marcus 2002, 21–22). Such activity reflected the antipathy toward homosexuality and the dominance of heterosexuality.

In the cultural aftermath of the civil rights movement, the women's movement, and gay liberation, however, these kinds of activities were called into question. Violence, blatant discriminatory acts, and exclusion, once ignored, if not endorsed, became less acceptable in mainstream society. Differences between groups are now supposed to be tolerated, and overt prejudice toward any group is now generally met with disapproval and social sanction. Tolerance and inclusiveness are required if one is to be what is commonly referred to as "politically correct." At the same time that people often now denounce discriminatory behavior, they also hold onto the ideas that make such behavior possible, such as labeling a group as "other" and somehow inferior. To be endorsed in the current cultural climate, these ideas must be woven into a cultural frame of inclusion, one that asserts dominant power more gently and subtly, with the appearance of tolerance. Dominant ideals, like the privileging of heterosexuality, have had to be repackaged to reflect this cultural shift.

To illustrate this kind of modernization, consider the recent case of the Promise Keepers, a Christian men's group designed to reassert traditional male authority in a culture changed by the feminist movements of the 1960s and '70s. Formed in 1990 as a response to feminist calls for equality in the home and workforce—calls that challenged masculine authority (Kimmel 1999, 1996, 309–314; Messner 2000, 24–26)—Promise Keepers could not simply declare that men should dominate women. Instead, Promise Keepers reconfigured the notion that men are supposed to be leaders in ways that addressed women's concerns about the role of men in families and society. The reason that men have not led engaged and responsible family lives, as women have urged them to do, according to Promise Keepers, has nothing to do with gender inequality but rather is the result of men not taking their leadership roles seriously enough. In fact, founder (and former college football coach) Bill McCartney organized these men's gatherings with the explicit purpose of "proclaim[ing] their love for God . . . reclaim[ing] their families for the kingdom . . . and stirring up men toward leadership, accountability, and spiritual revival" (McCartney 1990, 288). Promise Keepers encourages men to live Christian lives, which requires, among other things, that they are loving and providing husbands and fathers who fulfill a leadership position in the family (for a complete explanation of the "promises," see Bright et al. 1999; Abraham 1997). Put simply, men are divinely required to reclaim their leadership positions in the family but be nicer to their wives and children, leading sober, loyal, honest, and trustworthy family lives. In this way, Promise Keepers has reasserted traditional male dominance but has "put perhaps the most beneficent face possible on patriarchal authority" by taking into account some feminist criticisms of masculinity and encouraging men to act as more responsible and kind leaders (Stoltenberg 1999, 108).

In this way, Promise Keepers has embedded a call for the reassertion of male authority into an answer to contemporary critiques of masculinity, reasserting male privilege and superiority in the guise of calling for men to behave better as husbands and fathers—a call many people endorse. Promise Keepers agree with feminists that men should be more responsible in their family lives, but the problem is not that men wield more power than women; rather, the problem is that men have not done their Christian duty as head of the family. By integrating widely accepted criticisms of masculinity into its call for male leadership, Promise Keepers is able to make traditional patriarchy more appealing in a society less inclined to endorse overt male domination. In sum, Promise Keepers modernizes traditional male authority, repackaging sexism in a rhetoric of responsibility and care to make it more appealing in the current cultural environment.

In much the same way, Expell and the wives' groups have explicitly served this purpose with regard to heterosexism, while Accept's calls for inclusion are structured in ways that create the *potential* for heterosexism to be reasserted in the guise of tolerance. Through their revisions of conservative Christian theology, these groups, to varying degrees, have helped to market well-worn dominant sexual ideologies by repackaging them in kinder, gentler rhetoric and labels that have more appeal to a modern cultural audience. This repackaging, particularly because it is done in religious wrapping, cloaks the powerful coercion elites can muster, camouflaging reassertions of heterosexual privilege and superiority. It also makes it moral for people to act in ways that hurt and oppress others. What follows is an examination of how these groups function to modernize heterosexist ideologies and the likely larger societal consequences of doing so.

Expell

As a conservative Christian group whose purpose was to help members "cure" homosexuality, Expell obviously upheld heterosexuality as the ideal form of sexuality. In fact, Expell constructed an ideological trap for participants that had the potential to make homosexuality more stigmatizing and punishing than it was for members before they joined the group. While Expell never purported to challenge the dominant Christian idea that homosexuality is sin or the larger cultural notion that men should behave in certain (stereotypically masculine) ways, it did attempt to alter conservative Christian perceptions of homosexuality as especially damning and stigmatizing. Its solution, however, not only reiterated the expectation of traditional masculinity/heterosexuality, but also reasserted greater individual recrimination for failing to meet these expectations.

As we have seen, Expell held that God could cure homosexuality, through the establishment of a proper human-God relationship, *if* the afflicted truly desired to be healed. If all went well, Expell's resolution gave the men a second chance to act in accord with dominant rules, without enormous stigma and with the help of other believers. The ideological net was loosened—as long as the men went along with the program. If the men did not make progress (e.g., enact the "initiating" qualities of manhood, try hard enough to resist sexual "temptation"), then this lack of progress was taken as a sign that the men did not desire to be healed strongly enough, making them once again responsible for their sinful state. This time, there could be no doubt that the men's struggles were their own doing; they were seen as choosing a course of action defined as illegitimate and were again failed Christian men, only this time their failures were due to their own lack of faith and/or shortcomings. In this instance, failure to conform carried much heavier sanctions; not only were they again sinful, failed Christian men, but they were so by their own choice. We see here how coercion can get camouflaged as choice. Expell's genuine efforts to help those who struggled with their sexuality by lifting stigma and encouraging other Christians to offer aid actually forged an environment in which only those who made the right choice—to struggle and work toward dominant gender and sexual ideals—could sustain a moral redefinition of self.

The impact of Expell's theories about homosexuality was not limited to its members. These theories also helped to modernize heterosexism for the larger Christian community in much the same way that Promise Keepers modernized sexism.[1] Given the cultural shift toward tolerance, it was no longer entirely acceptable for Christians to kick homosexuals out of their churches. Expell, and Exodus more generally, provided Christians with a way to feel like they were acting in accord with the oft-cited mantra "hate the sin, love the sinner," enabling them to believe that they were behaving in loving, tolerant,

and supportive ways (Christ-like), even as they advocated discriminatory behavior. Expell's theology embedded the supremacy of traditional heterosexual notions of gender, sexuality, and family in
therapeutic rhetoric that posed Christian duty as an obligation to help
"victims," not damn them and cast them out. To make this shift, ex-
gay theories/theology, as we have seen, first transferred blame for any
sexual deviation from the individual to the sinful world. In doing so,
homosexuals came to be seen as victims of sin, not as inherently evil.
The role of the good Christian thus was to help heal homosexual victims, making Christians look like healers, not condemners, as they continued to assert the very same heterosexist dogma. At the same time,
the therapeutic discourse of healing the sick or disordered self as the
solution to the problem focused attention predominately on the individual, discouraging any examination of the social conditions that gave
rise to these difficulties.

In this way, ex-gay theology modernized heterosexism; that is, it
reasserted the primacy of heterosexuality, but it did so in such a way
that being heterosexist did not have to be construed as being exclusionary and condemning. In other words, ex-gay groups reconfigured heterosexism, keeping it intact and making its maintenance seem like the
characteristic helping behavior of therapeutic (self-help) groups. This
shift is apparent in the language used in Expell's and Exodus's vid-
eos, pamphlets, and study guides. Homosexuality is described in terms
of "brokenness," "sickness," and "neurosis," juxtaposed against the
"wholeness" and "health" of heterosexuality. This language presents
heterosexuality as the ideal and frames homosexuals as sick and in
need of help. Exodus's/Expell's work thus could be construed as helping people achieve wellness, rather than as heterosexist behavior. Expell
thereby reasserted heterosexual superiority, while framing its work as
Christian therapy for people who had been marginalized and hurt. By
wrapping traditional heterosexism in the therapeutic rhetoric of health
and spiritual well-being, Expell/Exodus made the endorsement of heterosexual privilege seem like helping behavior, not discrimination. As
did the Promise Keepers, Expell/Exodus found a way to reframe old
ideas to make them more acceptable to a modern audience.

The Wives

The wives' groups served as a complement to
Expell and Exodus, supporting the modernization of heterosexism. The
solutions that these groups devised to cope with the women's prob-

lems functioned to protect the gender order crucial to most conservative Christian conceptualizations of heterosexuality. When their husbands' homosexuality challenged the wives' notions of femininity and gender relations, threatening to undermine their commitment to their marriages and their support for the men, the support groups helped them to redefine this situation in ways that neutralized this threat, shifting the source of the problem to a psychological disorder. In this way, the support groups helped to limit what constituted the women's morally legitimate options for handling their marital situations, namely, to stay in their marriages and support their husbands. Because ex-gay theories presented homosexuals as in need of help, not damnation, as damaged but not innately bad, they tapped into the wives' traditionally feminine obligation to nurture and care for their husbands. Given this obligation, the wives could not justify leaving a wounded husband, whereas they may have been able to justify leaving an immoral, bad husband.

Further, by staying in their marriages and submitting to God, the ultimate Father and masculine figure in Christianity, as a way of nurturing their husbands, the wives retained their positions as feminine helpers to a masculine leader and recreated the "proper" gender order. In making this choice, the wives also sought to put husbands back into their rightful positions as family leaders. In other words, the wives' "borrowing" of God's masculine authority was not to elevate their own positions, though they sometimes used God's Word to advance their own causes, but rather was used to push wayward men back into the fold. While the women experienced this pushing as empowering because they held some sway over their husbands, their efforts reinforced the existing gender order and the primacy of heterosexuality.

The wives' cooperation illustrates how powerfully ex-gay theories of homosexuality and the modernization of heterosexism can impact how people think about homosexuality and respond to homosexuals. It diminished the women's anger, built sympathy, and created an obligation to help. Wives could thus feel virtuous for responding lovingly to a homosexual sinner, while, of course, reaffirming the view of homosexuality as a sin. They felt good about what they were doing, and what they were doing, in effect, was sustaining heterosexism.

Accept

At first, it seems absurd to say that Accept and MCC, which are gay affirming, might advance heterosexism in any way or reproduce oppressive power structures, even if inadvertently. The organization was developed specifically to help heal individual wounds inflicted by a homophobic society and to fight heterosexist attitudes in the church and society. As this study has shown, Accept/MCC did, in many ways, successfully create a revised theology that defends homosexuality. Their ideological revisions successfully challenged the unconditional condemnation of homosexuality within traditional, conservative Christianity, providing alternative biblical interpretations with vastly different consequences for Christians who are gay. Within this new religious space, gay and straight Christians should be equally valued, and the behavior that was deemed sinful was the judgment and condemnation of others. Certainly, this revised theology offers a different framework for morality and for structuring human relationships. In this sense, Accept and MCC have subverted heterosexist Christian doctrine and have made real progress toward the creation of a more hospitable cultural space for gay people.

Yet, to make this call for inclusion, Accept/MCC relied on the very power structures they attempted to subvert. Just as in Expell and the wives' support groups, Accept depended on the widespread power and authority granted to God's Word and Christian doctrine to legitimate its theological revisions. Indeed, members would consider this revised theology as a legitimate option only if Accept could show that it was consistent with *existing* theological interpretation. As a result, Accept's challenge to dominant ideas of homosexuality hinged on and reproduced the legitimacy of the same power structures that they worked so hard to undermine. This reliance may have limited the extent to which the group could challenge heterosexual hegemony.

Given this dependence on existing power structures, Accept/MCC constructed a theology that, at the very least, leaves open the possibility of reproducing the stigma attached to homosexuality and of reasserting the central and privileged position of heterosexuality in our society. This potential arises from the way group arguments were structured—a structure necessitated by the group's attempt to fit homosexuality into dominant Christian doctrine. As an examination of Accept has shown, pro-gay theology was used to build a defense of homosexuality, centered around the idea that God made people gay and loves them as they are. Because God made people gay, MCC contends, they have no choice in the matter and cannot alter their sexuality. This "no choice" position, proponents argue, makes homosexuals deserving of equal rights and inclusion in traditionally heterosexual social institutions such as the church and marriage.[2] This strategy mirrors social justice arguments for racial and gender equality that are predicated on the idea that innate differences are not grounds for discrimination.[3] Rather than asserting that people have the right to choose their sexuality without sanction, the strategy is defensive, making just treatment contingent on an apologetic "I can't help being this way" basis.

This strategy, as gender studies scholar Kathy Rudy points out, may "ultimately serve to marginalize" gay people (1997, 96). By equating the necessity of just treatment with the idea that gay people did not choose their sexuality,[4] and thus cannot help being gay, Accept/MCC implies that homosexuality is something one would avoid if possible, that it is not an acceptable choice, and that it is not as desirable as heterosexuality. Vera Whisman, in her compelling study of how gay men and lesbians experience their homosexuality (as chosen, born/determined, or some combination of the two), points out that the very question of whether homosexuality is chosen is "profoundly heterosexist" and suggests that a person would certainly change and be heterosexual if such were possible (1996, 6, 11–36). Thus, even though Accept/MCC members believe they are equal before God, their implicit assertion that gay people should have equal rights because it is not their fault that they are not heterosexual may be seen as reiterating the notion that heterosexuality is the ideal, the most desirable form of sexuality, the only form a person would choose if there were options.

While Accept and MCC have certainly enabled their members to see themselves as equally valued before God, they have also worked to construct a biblical mandate for social tolerance of homosexuality, one that simultaneously makes unjust treatment of homosexuals an affront to God and yet still may run the risk of upholding the larger cultural view of heterosexual superiority. Promoting tolerance, as Jakobsen and Pellegrini point out in *Love the Sin: Sexual Regulation and the Limits of Religious Tolerance,* is unlikely to be an effective way to level social hierarchies and advance freedom or justice. Instead, these authors assert that tolerance has precisely the opposite effect of reproducing social inequalities: "Tolerance establishes a hierarchical relation between a dominant center and its margins. Another way to put this is to say that tolerance sets up an us-them relation in which 'we' tolerate 'them.' . . . Being the object of tolerance does not represent full inclusion in American life, but rather a grudging form of acceptance in which the boundary between 'us' and 'them' remains clear, sometimes dangerously so. This boundary is also elevated to a mark of moral virtue. The tolerant are generous and open-minded even as they are exclusionary" (2003, 50, 52). Tolerance, though preferable to overt hostility, is thus not a successful way of encouraging equality. Instead, tolerance reassembles hierarchical relations by making it clear who and what must be "tolerated" by dominants. By grounding their demands for inclusion in arguments that might be heard as calls for social tolerance, Accept/MCC risks recreating the very hierarchies they sought to dismantle. If homosexuals become tolerated because they cannot help being gay, then heterosexism is in no way eroded. At best, the stigma attached to homosexuality is dulled, and homosexual people are worthy of only a gentler form of marginalization.

Further, as Jakobsen and Pelligrini also indicate, such tolerance can put a moral facade on discriminatory actions, obscuring exclusionary practices and enabling oppressors to feel virtuous. It is in this sense that Accept/MCC, like Expell and the wives' groups, may serve to modernize heterosexism. If the group's revised theology becomes read by dominants as, "We must tolerate homosexuals because they were born gay and cannot change," then the group has inadvertently recreated the supremacy of heterosexuality and cloaked its enactment and maintenance in the rhetoric of social justice. In this sense, Accept/MCC may have helped to construct a moral cover for heterosexism, thereby allowing people to feel good about their tolerance of homosexuals (or even to fight for equal rights for gays) while implicitly affirming the superiority of heterosexuality. In this way, even people who are gay affirming can fall into the trap of recreating heterosexual dominance.

So, while each of these groups brought about social changes, there was neither a radical overhaul of traditional ideas nor an overthrow of dominant authority. Given group members' commitment to traditional Christianity, the new cultural niches the groups constructed were made, at least in part, from dominant ideas/tools, and so resulted not in breaking free from oppression, but rather in the reconfiguration of ideological space so that it was more comfortable to inhabit even while it advanced some of the same ideas that had initially hurt group members. That this space was more comfortable was key in making the reproduction of dominant ideas and power largely invisible to group members.

Group solutions to individuals' dilemmas made members feel liberated from past oppression and empowered to choose to act in ways that allowed them to redefine themselves as moral and good Christians. This sense of power, however, was, to some degree, illusory; group solutions were inadvertently structured such that the only right choice, the only choice a moral Christian could make, was to act in ways that reconstructed dominant ideologies. Certainly, Expell and the wives' support groups were far more limiting than Accept, but none of the groups urged that people should have the right to choose their own sexuality. Participants (including group and ministry leaders) never noticed. So individual transformations worked, the groups were successful, and dominant ideologies, though altered to some degree (more in Accept, less in Expell and the wives' groups), remained intact.

Resurrecting Boundaries

If the men were able to resolve their dilemmas, feel better, build satisfying lives through group participation, and create viable spaces within Christianity for homosexuals, then does it matter that they also maintained, or risked maintaining, the cultural hegemony of heterosexuality? The short answer is yes. It matters because these groups help to shape larger societal views of gender and sexuality, views that, at present, contribute to the violence and discrimination that gay people face in our society. There are two obvious, yet important, characteristics of these groups, characteristics that suggest the implications of these groups' ideas to the larger culture. First, these groups are enmeshed in a larger cultural battle to determine who gets to define what constitutes appropriate sexuality. Second, these are religious groups, a characteristic that is significant because religion is, perhaps, the most powerful and persuasive moral arbiter in our society. As such, it is a key arena in the struggle over homosexuality and definitions of appropriate sexuality. For many, God's commands are uncontestable truth, reason enough to live one's life a certain way and to promote a particular social organization. For this reason, religious ideology is an incredibly important and influential resource to wield in controlling what forms of sexuality come to be seen as right or wrong and thus who is perceived as good or bad. Additionally, as we have seen throughout this study, religious ideologies are more insulated from criticism than are secular ones. Because they are anchored in the divine, religious ideologies are more impervious to human assault, making them quite difficult to challenge and change. Further, believers can be very hesitant to launch a challenge, as they perceive the consequences to defying divine authority to be nothing less than a threat to their eternal salvation. In sum, religious ideologies are a powerful force for prescribing morality.

The groups in this study were uniquely situated to launch a challenge to traditional religious ideology. No group working outside the boundaries of divine authority could successfully challenge these ideologies, at least not in the eyes of believers. This positioning gave the groups the opportunity to make significant changes in the meanings attached to homosexuality within religion, thereby redrawing moral boundaries. But their theological revisions and solutions to their dilemmas resulted, to some degree, in the reassertion of heterosexual ideals and the continued stigmatization of homosexuals, and so re-created, or risked re-creating, the moral imperative of heterosexuality within Christianity. It is this imperative that helps to structure and sustain the cultural prohibitions against homosexuality and that results in the denial of equal rights to gay people and, in extreme cases, violent acts against them. As Franklin concludes from her study of perpetrators of hate crimes against homosexuals, "antigay violence can be seen primarily as an extreme manifestation of pervasive cultural norms rather than as a manifestation of individual hatred" (1998, 20). Working from this conclusion, we can see that decisions to "love the sinner" or be nice to homosexuals because "they were born that way" may do little to improve how homosexuals are treated in our society. As long as cultural and moral norms uphold heterosexuality as the only appropriate form of sexuality, homosexuals will continue to be labeled as inferior and subjected to mistreatment. Though these groups were entirely genuine in their efforts to help gay people, and while they did resist the imposition of stigma by dominants and create more comfortable spaces for homosexuals within Christianity, no group entirely challenged these cultural norms.

Examining the processes by which these groups made ideological revisions, however, reveals much about the opportunities and constraints that marginalized groups face when they attempt social change. To begin to alter their social positions and create more comfortable social niches to inhabit, subordinates must find ways to lift the stigmatizing labels that dominants impose on them so that they have new cultural space in which to redefine themselves. We know, from existing studies of identity reconstruction in marginalized groups, that these groups create these new and more positive identity meanings by subverting the dominant ideologies that impose stigma (Francis 1997b; Karp 1992; Schwalbe and Mason-Schrock 1996; Mason-Schrock 1996;

Ponticelli 1999; Sandstrom 1996; Thumma 1991). What has been lacking in a sociological understanding of this process, however, is *how* marginalized groups can accomplish this feat, given that they are confronted with two large barriers. First, powerless people, by definition, lack the authority to challenge a dominant ideology. Second, marginalized groups, like most groups in society, often depend on these very ideologies for a sense of coherence and moral identity.

The present study shows us how Accept and Expell overcame these barriers by maneuvering around and within dominant ideologies to open the interpretive space within which a key piece of dominant truth could be deconstructed and suitably revised. Further ideological maneuvers enabled the groups to reattach these revisions to the overarching, legitimating framework, thereby allowing them to retain this framework as a source of stability. Through this maneuvering, the groups were also able to circumvent dominant authority and grasp the higher power of divine authority to reconstruct the meaning of homosexuality within a faith that they were unwilling to give up. In doing so, they resolved their individual dilemmas and created new cultural spaces within Christianity for those who faced similar struggles.

Given the power dynamics of their struggle, their revisions were necessarily selective, allowing the larger, legitimating structure of Christian ideology to remain intact. The groups' challenges thus left important pieces of the larger oppressive ideology in place. In fact, the result of their revisionist work was a kind of compromise: group ideologies provided explanations for the men's dilemmas that reduced the stigma of homosexuality, enabling them to feel like good Christians, but they also (more in Expell, less in Accept) reconstructed heterosexist ideas, allowing other people to feel moral in their practice. In the final analysis, we see that these groups created new rhetorics, images, ideas, and interpretations that enabled them to carve out more comfortable spaces within Christianity. The ideological changes these groups made may have been slight, insisting only on remodeling Christianity to allow a bit more space and tolerance for difference. Once made, though, such changes widen the pool of existing cultural resources that can be later used for further revision. The men and women in these groups courageously pioneered these changes, creating at least the possibilities for liberation yet to come.

Appendix

Data for this study were collected in two distinct phases. In the first phase, which took place between 1995 and 1997 as research for my dissertation, I collected ethnographic data on the two MCC Bible study groups, Homosexuality and the Bible and Accept, and on the Exodus ministry Expell. My purpose was to understand how the men experienced their struggle with homosexuality within the context of Christianity, as well as how they constructed such contradictory resolutions to this struggle. As I analyzed the data and began writing about it, I recognized how critical spousal support was to married men in Expell as they went through the process of trying to alter their sexuality. (By contrast, neither unmarried ex-gay Christian men nor gay Christian men cited intimate relationships as key sources of support as they worked to reconcile their sexuality and faith.) To gain more insight into this subset of married ex-gay Christian men, as well as to better understand the wives' role in this process and how they coped with it, I added a second phase of data collection. In 2001, I conducted an interview study with women who were, or who had been, married to ex-gay Christian men. Given the intensely personal and sensitive nature of this topic, both phases of data collection were, at times, trying and difficult. In what follows, I describe how data collection and analysis unfolded, what difficulties were encountered, and how they were handled.

PHASE I: ETHNOGRAPHIC STUDY
OF GAY AND EX-GAY CHRISTIAN MEN

Under the best of circumstances, gaining access to a group can be tricky because participants are often, and understandably, uneasy about a researcher attending their group with the express purpose of analyzing them. When the groups under investigation revolve around issues as politically charged and controversial as the relationship between homosexuality and Christianity, this discomfort is heightened considerably. So I was not surprised when both the pastor of the MCC church and the ex-gay leader were hesitant to allow me to attend these groups initially, though gaining access to MCC Bible study groups was, for reasons detailed below, much easier than it was to Expell ministry meetings.

The MCC Bible study groups I wanted to attend were affiliated with the only local MCC congregation in town. Most members openly attended church services, and the majority were "out of the closet" to friends, family and co-workers. As a result, anonymity was not a big issue to the men or to church leaders, and no one was particularly concerned that an outsider would learn the men's identities. Instead, when I asked for permission to attend the two Bible study groups, the pastor was worried about what I intended to do with the information I collected and voiced the concern that I might be "working for the condemners." In the conversation that followed, I explained I did not know what I would do with the information simply because I had no idea what I would discover. More importantly, I clarified my purpose; I was not interested in choosing "a side" in the debate but rather in understanding how these men experienced reconciling their faith and sexuality. Given these assurances, the pastor was quick to give me his blessing; he talked to group leaders on my behalf and arranged for me to attend these two groups.

By contrast, Expell, like all Exodus ministries, promised its members at least some degree of anonymity and worked to protect confidentiality. Few members were open about their sexual struggle in their everyday lives and therefore were very concerned that they might be discovered. Their confidence in the group thus depended on a certain level of secrecy. For this reason, the ex-gay group leader was much more reluctant to allow me to participate in ministry meetings. He and the church board that oversaw Expell feared that my presence would compromise members' confidentiality and inhibit group talk. Like the MCC pastor, these men were also worried about "whose side" I was on and what I would do with the information I gathered. These were substantial concerns, and I was worried that I would be denied access to the group, a denial that would seriously impede the study given that this ministry was the only one close enough to travel to on a weekly basis. I worked hard to ease these concerns, meeting repeatedly with the group leader, with board members, and with one of the pastors of the church that hosted the ministry. I reiterated that my purpose was to understand the experiences of people who struggled with homosexuality in a Christian context, explained the methodological procedures that would be undertaken to ensure participants' confidentiality, and answered questions about my own religious beliefs and background. After about five months of meetings and negotiations with group and church leaders, I was granted permission to attend ministry meetings.

My initial participation in all of the groups was awkward and uncomfortable, and I am sure that my presence stifled conversation at first. However, as I learned group practices and prayers, studied the Bible with them, participated in discussions about biblical passages, joked, made small talk, and shared my own experiences, I began to feel like, and be treated as, just another group member. I had more homework though. After each meeting, I recorded expansive fieldnotes on Bible study, conversations, and small group discussions. After the first month of fieldwork, I began coding my observations for emergent themes, paying close attention both to the process of reconciling homosexuality and Christianity and to the similarities and differences between the groups.

After a few months of fieldwork in each group, when the men had become comfortable with me, I began conducting interviews. Over the course of several months, I interviewed all of the men who attended the groups regularly, for a total of sixteen gay Christians and fourteen ex-gay Christians. (A few group members, particularly, though not exclusively, in Expell, dropped out of the group for one reason or another before I could interview them.) These interviews were semi-structured; that is, I established set topics to be covered in each interview but also allowed space in which the men could bring up issues pertinent to them. Interview topics included religious and family background, when and how they became aware of their homosexuality, life experience coping with their sexuality before joining a group, how they discovered a group, group experiences and life changes, as well as their current sexual and religious beliefs and practices. My interview strategy was to introduce each topic, allow the men to explain their experiences, and then probe for specific information and biographical stories.

Though these interview topics included highly personal and potentially embarrassing information, all of the men readily discussed these issues. Because I had spent months as a participant observing in each group before I interviewed any of the men, I was already familiar with their concerns and could frame non-threatening questions. Most importantly, we had established a rapport, and the men trusted and were comfortable talking with me. In this way, fieldwork really set the stage for successful interviews (cf. Schwalbe and Wolkomir 2001) by removing many of the barriers that can impede research on sensitive issues.

All interviews were tape-recorded and transcribed in full. Transcripts, like fieldnotes and notes on group literature, were analyzed inductively and coded for emerging themes and processes. As themes emerged, I wrote a series of analytic memos (Charmaz 1983) to make sense of the men's experiences, returning continually to the data to verify findings.

PHASE II: INTERVIEW STUDY OF WIVES OF EX-GAY CHRISTIAN MEN

As I completed analysis of the above ethnographic and interview data, it became apparent that the married men in Expell relied heavily on their wives for support as they went through the ministry process of trying to alter their sexuality. In fact, these men saw their wives as key motivators and one of the most important reasons for continuing on in the "healing process" when it got very difficult. For this subset of ex-gay Christian men, the process of transforming their sexuality was very much a "team" effort. I recognized that, to this point, I had only studied half of the team and that, if I was to understand how this subset of men worked to reconcile faith and sexuality fully, I would need to collect data on wives' experiences as well. I decided to interview wives to gain insights into how they perceived and coped with their husbands' struggle with sexuality. Collecting this data, however, proved far more difficult than I imagined.

Initially, I planned to interview the wives of married men in Expell, women I already knew, even though Expell did not have a formal Exodus support group for spouses during the time I attended. Since I had already interviewed the married men in Expell, I reasoned that interviewing these women would enable me to examine the experience of sexual struggle from both perspectives within a married couple. I also knew that there were not enough wives in the group to complete this study and planned to use a "snowball sampling" technique—that is, I would ask the wives in Expell to refer me to others in the same circumstance—to locate enough interviewees (Babbie 2004, 184). This initial plan failed pretty miserably.

I began this phase of data collection by contacting the Expell ministry leader; I explained what I wanted to do, described my goals, and reiterated assurances of confidentiality. He, however, expressed reservations about allowing me to talk with these women and asked to see a sample of the work I had done on the group. I sent him an article (Wolkomir 2001) and then got back in touch with him a few weeks later. I was, quite frankly, surprised by his reaction to the article. He was irritated and felt I had put the gay Christians in a more favorable light than the ex-gay Christians. He believed that I had named gay Christians more positively (Accept versus Expell) and that Expell members did not just reinterpret the truth of the Bible—it was there for all to see. I explained that the groups had been named for their purpose—either to teach members to accept homosexuality or to expel it from their lives—and that I was trying to show how two different groups revealed what they saw as biblical truths to their members, not argue anyone had it right. He remained pretty unconvinced, but we struck a deal. He would give group members my article, and then I could talk to them about it and see if the wives wanted to participate.

Because I had moved since completing my dissertation, I flew into town for this meeting, planning to talk to the group and hopefully do most of the interviews in about ten days. When I met with the group and the group leader, however, it was clear that I would not be able to interview anyone. The leader had given them my article, his opinion of it, and a strong recommendation that they not talk to me. The wives in the group decided to abide by his recommendation, and several contacted me later to apologize, explaining that disregarding the leader's suggestion might make group participation troubled. Given their husbands' precarious situations, they did not want to risk talking with me. I had to devise another strategy.

I turned to the Exodus Web site and got contact information for leaders of all the support groups for "spouses of sexual strugglers." I began by contacting those leaders within a reasonable driving distance, explaining the study and confidentiality procedures in detail, and asking if I could come to a group meeting to ask for volunteers. I got rejected no less than nine times. Frustrated, I sent e-mails to every leader on the list, omitting those I had already contacted, explaining the study and asking if I could attend a meeting to seek interviewees. Most leaders did not respond at all, three agreed to phone conversations, but none were willing to allow me to attend a group meeting. Finally, one leader, who ran an Internet support group for spouses of sexual strugglers, agreed to send a request for volunteers out to his listserv. In a few weeks, I received twenty-three responses from women who would consider participating. I talked to each of them by phone, and fifteen of the twenty-three agreed to be interviewed. About half of these women were clustered within a few states in the Deep South, and I planned a driving trip that would allow me to interview them and to talk with their support group leaders. The rest of the interviewees were scattered throughout the United States, including Michigan, Washington, California, Pennsylvania, Ohio, Florida, and Illinois. Because of time and funding constraints, I interviewed these women by telephone.

Like the interviews conducted with the men, these interviews were semi-structured, ensuring that the same topics would be covered but that the women could bring up information they felt was most salient to their situations. Interview topics included religious beliefs and background (particularly with regard to gender relationships), relationship/ marital history, when and how each woman discovered her husband's homosexuality, her initial feelings and reactions, her experiences in the support group, how she envisioned her role in helping her husband, the difficulties she faced, and how she coped with her marital situation. Given that I did not know these women, I anticipated difficulties getting the women to discuss some aspects of their marriages and the hardships they encountered, but these women were remarkably open. Prior to the formal interview, I gave each participant a chance to ask questions about me and the study, and many women asked why I cared about how they handled their marriages and about my religious beliefs. I explained my interest and my religious background and told them they did not have to answer any question they felt was too personal. This conversation seemed to put them at ease, and most were incredibly forthcoming.

The interviews ranged between one and a half to four hours, and all were tape recorded and transcribed in full. As with the other data for this study, I proceeded inductively, coding data for emergent themes and writing analytic memos that helped to make sense of the women's experiences, how they supported their husbands, and how they were able to redefine their marriages positively.

Given these methods of data collection, the small numbers of participants, and self-selection of participants, it clearly was not my intent to draw generalizable conclusions about gay and/or ex-gay Christian men, or their wives. Instead, this study was designed to discover the nuanced social-psychological interactions and processes, as well as the power dynamics embedded in such processes, that characterize how these group members cope with the conflicts between faith and sexuality. As such, the data does not enable predicted outcomes for gay or ex-gay Christian men (or for spouses of sexual strugglers) as a result of group participation, nor does it allow for general claims about how people who face similar situations will react. Instead, the data provide a lens through which to view, in great detail, how these groups negotiated this conflict and through which to examine the likely social consequences of such negotiations.

Notes

CHAPTER 5   CHALLENGING TRADITIONAL MEANINGS

1. I was never allowed to observe the private conversations that took place before the men came to an Expell meeting. My information about these conversations is derived entirely from interview data.

CHAPTER 8   THE WIVES OF EX-GAY CHRISTIAN MEN

1. Only one woman in this study was divorced, but her husband, in addition to his homosexual infidelities, stole money from her to fund his exploits.

2. Conservative Christian beliefs about gender and gendered relationships cannot simply be categorized as belief in a traditional family structure in which men are leaders/providers and women are helpers/caretakers (Stacey and Gerard 1990; Bartkowski 1997, 2001). Certainly, some conservative Christian commentators (Dobson 1991; Weber 1993) do see gender differences—men as rational and initiating and women as emotional and accepting—as divinely fixed, making men and women innately and irreversibly suited to a traditional patriarchal family structure. Others, however, contest such beliefs, asserting that men and women are quite alike and that all are required to exude the same Christian values (Scanzoni and Hardesty 1992; Gabriel 1993). While all Christians must submit to God, there is debate over whether women should submit to God *through* their husbands or *with* their husbands.

CHAPTER 9   CONCLUSION

1. Just as Promise Keepers emerged as a backlash to feminism, Exodus originated as part of a backlash against gay liberation. Exodus emerged approximately eight years after MCC (and the gay liberation movement) originated, at a time when gay rights activists had succeeded in making homosexuality increasingly visible and had gotten several pieces of gay rights legislation

passed. This success sparked an antigay backlash, which became well known, well organized, and widespread through Anita Bryant's 1977 successful campaign to repeal a recently established gay rights ordinance in Dade County, Florida (Marcus 2002, 188). Repeals of similar legislation in several other states followed, and the Religious Right was galvanized in their opposition to homosexuality. Exodus provided a counter-alternative to MCC's gay-affirming theology.

2. By exclusively calling for inclusion in heterosexual social institutions, rather than for the freedom of sexual choice, Accept/MCC advocated a single form of homosexuality, one that was patterned after the cultural ideal of heterosexual monogamy. As a result, the only way that homosexuality and homosexuals could be acceptable was to mimic heterosexual relationships. In this sense, Accept/MCC reproduced what Berlant and Warner refer to as "heteronormativity," or the assumption of heterosexuality as the "basic idiom of the personal and the social" (1998, 548).

3. MCC built its theology and support base in the late 1960s and 1970s in the midst of the civil rights and women's movements. The relative success of these movements built widespread consensus that people should not be denied rights because they were born with particular characteristics, helping to set historical (and legal) precedents for determining who gets equal rights and protections. These movements offered gay rights activists a template for lobbying, with some degree of success, for social change. MCC adopted this template.

4. In spite of its heterosexist underpinnings, this line of argument has been effective for the gay rights movement. In fact, the history of the gay rights movement reveals that it was only when the movement adopted this rhetoric and line of argument that they were able to make any progress in terms of shifting public awareness and attitudes. The earliest iterations of the gay rights movement directly criticized heterosexism, emphasizing an individual's freedom to sexual expression and explicitly rejecting marriage and monogamy as unjust heterosexual practices (Stacey 1998, 117). This initial approach overtly attacked heterosexist attitudes and highlighted an individual's right to choose sexuality, but it got little sympathy and did little to advance claims to equal rights. Only when the movement shifted to the "gay ethnicity" model, or the position that homosexuality was innate, did it begin to make legal and social progress toward increased tolerance and support for equal rights (Whisman 1996, 15–17). How much progress has been made is revealed in a 1998 report on public opinions surrounding homosexuality, prepared by Alan Yang, a political scientist at Columbia University, for the National Gay and Lesbian Task Force. This report shows marked increases in public support for equal rights in employment (from 56 percent in 1977 to 84 percent in 1997), for gays in the military (from 51 percent in 1977 to 66 percent in 1996), for same-sex marriage (from 27 percent in 1992 to 35 percent in 1997), and for gay adoptions (from 29 percent in 1992 to 40 percent in 1997). Correspondingly, there has also been a decrease in public disapproval of same-sex sexual relations from a high of 75 percent in 1987 to 56 percent in 1996.

References

About Exodus: Mission and Doctrinal Statement. Orlando, FL: Exodus International. http://exodus.to/about_exodus_mission.shtml (accessed July 2004).

Abraham, Ken. 1997. *Who Are the Promise Keepers? Understanding the Christian Men's Movement.* New York: Doubleday.

Adams, Jay. 1980. *Marriage, Divorce, and Remarriage in the Bible.* Grand Rapids, MI: Zondervan.

Ammerman, Nancy T. 1987. *Bible Believers: Fundamentalists in the Modern World.* New Brunswick, NJ: Rutgers University Press.

Babbie, Earl. 2004. *The Practice of Social Research.* 10th ed. Belmont, CA: Wadsworth/Thomson Learning.

Bankston, William, Craig Forsyth, and Hugh Floyd. 1981. Toward a General Model of the Process of Radical Conversion: An Interactionist Perspective on the Transformation of Self-Identity. *Qualitative Sociology* 4: 279–297.

Bartkowski, John P. 1997. Debating Patriarchy: Discursive Disputes over Spousal Authority among Evangelical Family Commentators. *Journal for the Scientific Study of Religion* 36: 393–410.

———. 2001. *Remaking the Godly Marriage: Gender Negotiation in Evangelical Families.* New Brunswick, NJ: Rutgers University Press.

Bartky, Sandra L. 1990. *Femininity and Domination: Studies in the Phenomenology of Oppression.* New York: Routledge, Chapman and Hall.

———. 1998. Foucault, Femininity, and the Modernization of Patriarchal Power. In *The Politics of Women's Bodies: Sexuality, Appearance, and Behavior,* ed. Rose Weitz, 25–45. Oxford: Oxford University Press.

Benford, Robert D. 2002. Controlling Narratives and Narratives as Control within Social Movements. In *Stories of Change: Narrative and Social Movements,* ed. Joseph E. Davis, 53–75. Albany: State University of New York Press.

Berger, Peter L. 1967. *The Sacred Canopy: Elements of a Sociological Theory of Religion.* New York: Anchor Books.

Bergner, Mario. 1995. *Setting Love in Order: Hope and Healing for the Homosexual.* Grand Rapids, MI: Baker Books.

Berlant, Lauren, and Michael Warner. 1998. Sex in Public. *Critical Inquiry* 24: 547–566.

Boone, Kathleen C. 1989. *The Bible Tells Them So: The Discourse of Protestant Fundamentalism*. Albany: State University of New York Press.

Boswell, John. 1980. *Christianity, Social Tolerance, and Homosexuality*. Chicago: University of Chicago Press.

Brasher, Brenda. 1998. *Godly Women: Fundamentalism and Female Power*. New Brunswick: Rutgers University Press.

Bright, Bill, Bill McCartney, Greg Laurie, and Jack Hayford. 1999. *Seven Promises of a Promise Keeper*. Nashville: Word Publishing.

Brissett, Dennis, and Charles Edgley. 1990. The Dramaturgical Perspective. In *Life as Theater: A Dramaturgical Source Book*, ed. Dennis Brissett and Charles Edgley, 1–23. New York: Aldine de Gruyter.

Brown, Nancy. 2000. *Marriage or Mirage? Practical Help for Women Whose Husbands Struggle with Homosexuality*. Resource booklet. Orlando, FL: Exodus International.

Chambers, Alan. 2002. *Exodus North America Update*. Orlando, FL: Exodus International.

Charmaz, Kathy. 1983. The Grounded Theory Method: An Explication and Interpretation. In *Contemporary Field Research: A Collection of Readings*, ed. Robert M. Emerson, 109–126. Prospect Heights: Waveland Press.

Cherry, Kitteredge. 1994. *Metropolitan Community Churches Today*. MCC pamphlet. Los Angeles: United Fellowship of Metropolitan Community Churches.

Coltrane, Scott. 1997. *Gender and Families*. Walnut Creek, CA: AltaMira Press.

Comstock, Gary D. 1996. *Unrepentant, Self-Affirming, Practicing: Lesbian/Bisexual/Gay People within Organized Religion*. New York: Continuum.

Connell, R. W. 1987. *Gender and Power: Society, the Person, and Sexual Politics*. Stanford: Stanford University Press.

———. 1992. A Very Straight Gay: Masculinity, Homosexual Experience, and the Dynamics of Gender. *American Sociological Review* 57: 735–751.

———. 1995. *Masculinities*. Berkeley: University of California Press.

Cooper, Darien. 1974. *You Can Be the Wife of a Happy Husband*. Wheaton, IL: Victor Books.

Dallas, Joe. 1996. *A Strong Delusion: Confronting the "Gay Christian" Movement*. Eugene, OR: Harvest House Publishers.

Davies, Bob. 1996. *History of Exodus International*. Resource booklet. Orlando, FL: Exodus International.

———. 2001a. Personal e-mail correspondence, July 19.

———. 2001b. *Portraits of Freedom: 14 People Who Came Out of Homosexuality*. Downers Grove, IL: InterVarsity Press.

Davies, Bob, and Lori Rentzel. 1993. *Coming Out of Homosexuality: New Freedom for Men and Women*. Downers Grove, IL: InterVarsity Press.

Denzin, Norman K. 1998. The Recovering Alcoholic Self. In *Inside Social Life: Readings on Sociological Psychology and Microsociology*, ed. Spencer Cahill, 34–43. Los Angeles: Roxbury Publishers.

Dobson, James. 1991. *Straight Talk: What Men Need to Know, What Women Should Understand*. Dallas, TX: Word.

Eastman, Donald. 1990. *Homosexuality: Not a Sin, Not a Sickness*. MCC pamphlet. Los Angeles: United Fellowship of Metropolitan Community Churches.

Edwards, George R. 1984. *Gay/Lesbian Liberation: A Biblical Perspective*. New York: Pilgrim Press.

Erickson, Rebecca. 1995. The Importance of Authenticity for Self and Society. *Symbolic Interaction* 18: 121–144.

———. 1997. Putting Emotions to Work (or, Coming to Terms with a Contradiction in Terms). In *Social Perspectives on Emotion*, ed. R. J. Erickson and B. Cuthbertson-Johnson, 71–101. Greenwich, CT: JAI.

Fine, Gary, and Kent Sandstrom. 1993. Ideology in Action: A Pragmatic Approach to a Contested Concept. *Sociological Theory* 11: 21–38.

Foster, David Kyle. 1995a. *Sexual Healing: God's Plan for the Sanctification of Broken Lives*. Study guide for ex-gay ministries. Nashville: Mastering Life Ministries.

———. 1995b. *Sexual Healing: God's Plan for the Sanctification of Broken Lives*. Video course for ex-gay ministries. Nashville: Mastering Life Ministries.

Fracher, Jeffrey, and Michael Kimmel. 1989. Hard Issues and Soft Spots: Counseling Men about Sexuality. In *Men's Lives*, ed. Michael Kimmel and Michael Messner, 365–374. 3rd ed. Repr. Boston: Allyn and Bacon, 1995.

Francis, Linda. 1994. Laughter, the Best Mediation: Humor as Emotion Management in Interaction. *Symbolic Interaction* 17: 147–163.

———. 1997a. Emotion, Coping, and Therapeutic Ideologies. In *Social Perspectives on Emotion*, ed. Rebecca Erickson and Beth Cuthbertson-Johnson, 71–101. Greenwich, CT: JAI Press.

———. 1997b. Ideology and Interpersonal Emotion Management: Redefining Identity in Two Support Groups. *Social Psychology Quarterly* 60: 153–171.

Franklin, Karen. 1998. Unassuming Motivations: Contextualizing the Narratives of Antigay Assailants. In *Stigma and Sexual Orientation: Understanding Prejudice against Lesbians, Gay Men, and Bisexuals*, ed. Gregory Herek, 1–23. Thousand Oaks, CA: Sage Publications.

Furedi, Frank. 2004. *Therapy Culture: Cultivating Vulnerability in an Uncertain Age*. New York: Routledge.

Gabriel, Ginger. 1993. *Being a Woman of God*. Nashville: Thomas Nelson.

Goffman, Erving. 1959. The Presentation of Self. In *Life as Theater: A Dramaturgical Source Book*, ed. Dennis Brissett and Charles Edgeley, 129–139. New York: Aldine de Gruyter, 1990.

Griffith, Marie R. 1997. *God's Daughters: Evangelical Women and the Power of Submission*. Berkeley: University of California Press.

Haldeman, Douglas C. 1994. The Practice and Ethics of Sexual Orientation Conversion Therapy. *Journal of Consulting and Clinical Psychology* 62: 221–227.

Hartman, Keith. 1996. *Congregations in Conflict: The Battle over Homosexuality*. New Brunswick, NJ: Rutgers University Press.

Hawkes, Brent. 1994. *The Bible and Homosexuality*. MCC video. Metropolitan Church of Toronto.

Herek, Gregory. 2000. Sexual Prejudice and Gender: Do Heterosexuals' Attitudes toward Lesbians and Gay Men Differ? *Journal of Social Issues* 56: 251–266.

Hill, Adrienne. 1998. *Married to a Gay Man: One Woman's Story of Marital Betrayal and the Lessons She Has Learned*. Resource booklet. Orlando, FL: Exodus International.

Hochschild, Arlie. 1979. Emotion Work, Feeling Rules, and Social Structure. *American Journal of Sociology* 85: 551–575.

———. 1983. *The Managed Heart: Commercialization of Human Feeling*. Berkeley: University of California Press.

How Did MCC Begin? 2002. Hollywood, CA: United Fellowship of Metropolitan Community Churches. http://www.mccchurch.org/mediaroom/35thAnniversary/indexpage.htm (accessed July 2004).

Humphreys, Laud. 1970. *Tearoom Trade: Impersonal Sex in Public Places.* Chicago: Aldine Publishing.

Hunter, James D. 1983. *American Evangelicalism: Conservative Religion and the Quandary of Modernity.* New Brunswick, NJ: Rutgers University Press.

Jakobsen, Janet, and Ann Pellegrini. 2003. *Love the Sin: Sexual Regulation and the Limits of Religious Tolerance.* New York: New York University Press.

Karp, David. 1992. Illness, Ambiguity, and the Search for Meaning: A Case Study of a Self-Help Group for Affective Disorders. *Journal of Contemporary Ethnography* 21: 139–170.

Kimmel, Michael. 1996. *Manhood in America: A Cultural History.* New York: Free Press.

———. 1999. Patriarchy's Second Coming as Masculine Renewal. In *Standing on the Promises: The Promise Keepers and the Revival of Manhood*, ed. Dane Claussen, 111–120. Cleveland: Pilgrim Press.

———. 2000. *The Gendered Society.* Repr. New York: Oxford University Press, 2004.

Lorber, Judith. 1994. *Paradoxes of Gender.* New Haven: Yale University Press.

Lorde, Audre. 1984. The Master's Tools Will Never Dismantle the Master's House. In *Sister Outsider: Essays and Speeches*, by Audre Lorde, 110–113. Trumansburg, NY: Crossing Press.

MacIntosh, H. 1994. Attitudes and Experiences of Psychoanalysts in Analyzing Homosexual Patients. *Journal of the American Psychoanalytic Association* 42: 1183–1207.

MacLeod, Jay. 1987. *Ain't No Makin' It: Leveled Aspirations in a Low Income Neighborhood.* Repr. Boulder, CO: Westview Press, 1995.

Mahaffy, Kimberly. 1996. Cognitive Dissonance and Its Resolution: A Study of Lesbian Christians. *Journal for the Scientific Study of Religion* 35: 392–402.

Marcus, Eric. 2002. *Making Gay History: The Half Century Fight for Lesbian and Gay Equal Rights.* New York: Perennial.

Marsden, George. 1991. *Understanding Fundamentalism and Evangelicalism.* Grand Rapids, MI: Eerdmans.

Mason-Schrock, Douglas. 1996. Transsexuals' Narrative Construction of the 'True Self.' *Social Psychology Quarterly* 59: 176–192.

McCartney, Bill. 1990. *From Ashes to Glory.* Nashville: Thomas Nelson Publishers.

McGuire, Meredith. 1992. *Religion: The Social Context.* Belmont, CA: Wadsworth.

McNeill, John. 1976. *The Church and the Homosexual.* 3rd ed. Repr. Boston: Beacon Press, 1988.

Melucci, Alberto. 1988. Getting Involved: Identity and Mobilization in Social Movements. In *International Social Movements Research*, ed. Bert Klandersman, H. Kriesi, and Sydney Tarrow, 329–348. Greenwich, CT: JAI Press.

Messner, Michael. 2000. *Politics of Masculinities: Men in Movements.* New York: AltaMira Press.

———. 2001. Becoming 100 Percent Straight. In *Men's Lives*, ed. Michael Kimmel and Michael Messner, 401–406. 5th ed. Needham Heights, MA: Allyn and Bacon.

Mission Statement of UFMCC. 2002. Hollywood, CA: United Fellowship of Metropolitan Community Churches. www.mcchurch.org/missionstatement. htm (accessed July 2004).

Mol, Hans. 1976. *Identity and the Sacred: A Sketch for a New Social Scientific Theory of Religion.* New York: Free Press.

Moskowitz, Eva. 2001. *In Therapy We Trust: America's Obsession with Self-Fulfillment.* Baltimore: Johns Hopkins University Press.

National Association of Evangelicals. 2000. A Christian Declaration on Marriage. Washington, DC: National Association of Evangelicals. http://www.nae.net/index.cfm?FUSEACTION=editor.page&pageID=47&IDCategory=9 (accessed July 2004).

Nepstad, Sharon. 1996. Popular Religion, Protest, and Revolt: The Emergence of Political Insurgency in Nicaraguan and Salvadoran Churches of the 1960s–80s. In *Disruptive Religion: The Force of Faith in Social Movement Activism*, ed. Christian Smith, 105–124. New York: Routledge.

Nolan, James. 1998. *The Therapeutic State: Justifying Government at Century's End.* New York: New York University Press.

———. 2002. Drug Court Stories: Transforming American Jurisprudence. In *Stories of Change: Narrative and Social Movements*, ed. Joseph Davis, 149–177. Albany: State University of New York.

Noll, Mark. 2001. *American Evangelical Christianity: An Introduction.* Malden, MA: Blackwell Publishers.

Nonn, Timothy. 2001. Hitting Bottom: Homelessness, Poverty, and Masculinity. In *Men's Lives*, ed. Michael Kimmel and Michael Messner, 242–251. Needham Heights, MA: Allyn and Bacon.

O'Neill. 1990. Founders of 'Ex-Gay' Ministries Come Out. *Outweek*, February 25.

One Nation under God. 1993. Video by Teodoro Maniaci and Francine M. Rzeznik. First Run Features.

Payne, Leanne. 1981. *The Broken Image: Restoring Personal Wholeness through Healing Prayer.* Repr. Grand Rapids, MI: Hamewith Books, 1996.

———. 1985. *Healing Homosexuality.* Grand Rapids, MI: Hamewith Books, 1996.

Perry, Troy. 1990. *Don't Be Afraid Anymore: The Story of Reverend Troy Perry and the Metropolitan Community Churches.* New York: St. Martin's Press.

Pevey, Carolyn, Christine Williams, and Christopher Ellison. 1996. Male God Imagery and Female Submission: Lessons from a Southern Baptist Ladies' Bible Class. *Qualitative Sociology* 19: 173–193.

Phelan, Shane. 2001. *Sexual Strangers: Gays, Lesbians, and Dilemmas of Citizenship.* Philadelphia: Temple University Press.

Piazza, Michael. 1994. *Holy Homosexuals: The Truth about Being Gay or Lesbian and Christian.* Dallas: Sources of Hope Publishing House.

Ponticelli, Christy. 1999. Crafting Stories of Sexual Identity Reconstruction. *Social Psychology Quarterly* 62: 157–172.

Rice, John Steadman. 1996. *A Disease of One's Own: Psychotherapy, Addiction, and the Emergence of Co-Dependency.* New Brunswick: Transaction Publishers.

———. 2002. "Getting Our Histories Straight": Culture, Narrative, and Identity in the Self-Help Movement. In *Stories of Change: Narrative and Social Movements*, ed. Joseph Davis, 79–99. Albany: State University of New York.

Reiff, Phillip. 1966. *The Triumph of the Therapeutic.* New York: Harper and Row.

Rodriguez, Eric, and Suzanne Ouellette. 2000. Gay and Lesbian Christians: Homosexual and Religious Identity Integration in the Members and Participants of a Gay Positive Church. *Journal for the Scientific Study of Religion* 39: 333–347.

Roof, Wade, and William McKinney. 1987. *American Mainline Religion: Its Changing Shape and Future.* New Brunswick, NJ: Rutgers University Press.

Rudy, Kathy. 1997. *Sex and the Church: Gender, Homosexuality, and the Transformation of Christian Ethics.* Boston: Beacon Press.

Sandstrom, Kent. 1996. Searching for Information, Understanding, and Self-Value: The Utilization of Peer Support Groups by Gay Men with HIV/AIDS. *Social Work in Healthcare* 23: 51–74.

Scanzoni, Letha Dawson, and Nancy Hardesty. 1992. *All We're Meant to Be: Biblical Feminism for Today.* 3rd ed. Grand Rapids, MI: William B. Eerdmans Publishing Co.

Scheub, Harold. 1998. *Story.* Madison: University of Wisconsin Press.

Schwalbe, Michael. 1998. *The Sociologically Examined Life.* 2nd ed. Repr. Mountain View, CA: Mayfield Publishers, 2001.

Schwalbe, Michael, Sandra Godwin, Daphne Holden, Douglas Schrock, Shealy Thompson, and Michelle Wolkomir. 2000. Generic Social Processes in the Reproduction of Inequality: An Interactionist Analysis. *Social Forces* 79: 419–452.

Schwalbe, Michael, and Douglas Mason-Schrock. 1996. Identity Work as Group Process. In *Advances in Group Processes,* ed. Barry Markovsky, Michael Lovaglia, and Robin Simon, 113–147. Vol. 13. Greenwich, CT.: JAI Press.

Schwalbe, Michael, and Michelle Wolkomir. 2001. Interviewing Men. In *Handbook for Interview Research*, ed. Jaber Gubrium and James Holstein, 203–220. Thousand Oaks, CA: Sage Publications.

Schwartz, Pepper, and Virginia Rutter. 2000. *The Gender of Sexuality.* Walnut Creek, CA: AltaMira Press.

Scott, James. 1990. *Domination and the Arts of Resistance: Hidden Transcripts.* New Haven: Yale University Press.

Scroggs, Robin. 1983. *The New Testament and Homosexuality.* Philadelphia: Fortress Press.

Segal, Lynne. 1990. *Slow Motion: Changing Masculinities, Changing Men.* New Brunswick, NJ: Rutgers University Press.

———. 1994. *Straight Sex: Rethinking the Politics of Pleasure.* Berkeley: University of California Press.

Smith, Christian. 1998. *American Evangelicalism: Embattled and Thriving.* Chicago: University of Chicago Press.

———. 2000. *Christian America: What Evangelicals Really Want.* Berkeley: University of California Press.

Spitzer, Robert L. 2001a. 200 Subjects Who Claim to Have Changed Their Sexual Orientation from Homosexual to Heterosexual. Paper presented at the American Psychiatric Association, New Orleans, LA, May 9.

———. 2001b. Psychiatry and Homosexuality. *Wall Street Journal*, May 23.

———. 2003. Can Some Gay Men and Lesbians Change Their Sexual Orientation? 200 Participants Reporting a Change from Homosexual to Heterosexual. *Archives of Sexual Behavior* 32: 403–417.

Stacey, Judith. 1990. *Brave New Families.* New York: Basic Books.

———. 1998. Gay and Lesbian Families: Queer Like Us. In *All Our Families: New Policies for a New Century*, ed. Mary Ann Mason, Arlene Skolnick, and Stephen Sugarman, 117–143. Oxford: Oxford University Press.

Stacey, Judith, and Susan Gerard. 1990. "We Are Not Doormats": The Influence of Feminism on Contemporary Evangelicals in the United States. In *Uncertain Terms: Negotiating Gender in American Culture*, ed. Faye Ginsberg and Anna L. Tsing, 98–117. Boston: Beacon Press.

Stoltenberg, John. 1999. Christianity, Feminism, and the Manhood Crisis. In *Standing on the Promises: The Promise Keepers and the Revival of Manhood*, ed. Dane Claussen, 89–108. Cleveland: Pilgrim Press.

Stone, Gregory P. 1981. Appearance and the Self: A Slightly Revised Version. In *Social Psychology through Symbolic Interaction*, ed. Gregory Stone and Harvey Farberman, 187–202. New York: John Wiley.

Taylor, Verta. 2000. Emotions and Identity in Women's Self-Help Movements. In *Self, Identity, and Social Movements*, ed. Sheldon Stryker, Timothy Owens, and Robert White, 271–299. Minneapolis: University of Minnesota Press.

Taylor, Verta, and Nancy Whittier. 1992. Collective Identity in Social Movement Communities: Lesbian Feminist Mobilization. In *Frontiers in Social Movement Theory*, ed. Aldon Morris and Carol McClung Mueller, 104–130. New Haven, CT: Yale University Press.

———. 1995. Analytical Approaches to Social Movement Culture: The Culture of the Women's Movement. In *Social Movements and Culture*, ed. Hank Johnston and Bert Klandermans, 163–187. Minneapolis: University of Minnesota Press.

Thumma, Scott. 1984. Straightening Identities: Evangelical Approaches to Homosexuality. Master's thesis, Candler School of Theology, Emory University, Atlanta, GA.

———. 1991. Negotiating a Religious Identity: The Case of the Gay Evangelical. *Sociological Analysis* 4: 333–347.

Travisano, Richard. 1981. Alternation and Conversion as Qualitatively Different Transformations. In *Social Psychology through Symbolic Interaction*, ed. Gregory Stone and Harvey Farberman, 237–248. New York: John Wiley and Sons.

Warner, Stephen. 1995. The Metropolitan Community Churches and the Gay Agenda: The Power of Pentecostalism and Essentialism. In *Religion and the Social Order: Sex, Lies, and Sanctity: Religion and Deviance in Contemporary North America*, ed. M. Neitz and M. Goldman, 81–107. Greenwich, CT: JAI Press.

Weber, Stu. 1993. *Tender Warrior: God's Intention for a Man*. Portland, OR: Multinomah.

Whisman, Vera. 1996. *Queer by Choice: Lesbians, Gay Men, and the Politics of Identity*. New York: Routledge.

White, Mel. 1994. *Stranger at the Gate: To Be Gay and Christian in America*. New York: Simon and Schuster.

Why Inclusive Language? 1995. Los Angeles: United Fellowship of Metropolitan Community Churches.

Wilcox, Melissa. 2001. Of Markets and Missions: The Early History of the Universal Fellowship of Metropolitan Community Churches. *Religion and American Culture* 11: 83–108.

———. 2003. *Coming Out in Christianity: Religion, Identity, and Community*. Bloomington: Indiana University Press.

Williams, Robert. 1992. *Just as I Am: A Practical Guide to Being Out, Proud, and Christian*. New York: Crown Publishers.

Wolkomir, Michelle. 2001. Wrestling with the Angels of Meaning: The Revisionist Ideological Work of Gay and Ex-Gay Christian Men. *Symbolic Interaction* 24: 407–424.

Yamamoto, Isamu. 1990. *The Crisis of Homosexuality*. Wheaton, IL: Victor Books.

Yamasaki, Nancy, et al. 1991. Report of the Committee to Study Homosexuality to the General Council on Ministries of the United Methodist Church. Study committee report. United Methodist Church.

Yang, Alan. 1998. *From Wrongs to Rights: Public Opinion on Gay and Lesbian Americans Moves towards Equality*. Washington, DC: Policy Institute for the National Gay and Lesbian Task Force.

Yip, Andrew. 1997. Attacking the Attacker: Gay Christians Talk Back. *British Journal of Sociology* 48: 113–127.

———. 2002. The Persistence of Faith among Nonheterosexual Christians: Evidence for the Neosecularization Thesis of Religious Transformation. *Journal for the Scientific Study of Religion* 41: 199–212.

Index

About the Author

Michelle Wolkomir is an assistant professor of sociology and codirector of the Gender Studies Program at Centenary College of Louisiana.